FINALS
Constitutional Law

CORE CONCEPTS AND KEY QUESTIONS

Robert Feinberg, Esq.
Editorial Consultant

Steven H. Palmer, Esq.

PUBLISHING

New York

This publication is designed to provide accurate and authoritative information in regard to the subject matter covered. It is sold with the understanding that the publisher is not engaged in rendering legal, accounting, or other professional service. If legal advice or other expert assistance is required, the services of a competent professional should be sought.

Series Editor: Lisa T. McElroy, Associate Professor, Drexel University College of Law
Editorial Director: Jennifer Farthing
Editor: Michael Sprague
Production Editor: Fred Urfer
Cover Designer: Carly Schnur

© 2007 by Kaplan, Inc.

Published by Kaplan Publishing, a division of Kaplan, Inc.
1 Liberty Plaza, 24th floor
New York, NY 10006

All rights reserved. The text of this publication, or any part thereof, may not be reproduced in any manner whatsoever without written permission from the publisher.

Printed in the United States of America

August 2007
10   9   8   7   6   5   4   3   2   1

ISBN13: 978-1-4277-9651-6

Kaplan Publishing books are available at special quantity discounts to use for sales promotions, employee premiums, or educational purposes. Please email our Special Sales Department to order or for more information at kaplanpublishing@kaplan.com, or write to Kaplan Publishing, 1 Liberty Plaza, 24th floor, New York, NY 10006.

INTRODUCTION	xii

I. THE NATURE OF JUDICIAL REVIEW — 1
  A. ORGANIZATION OF THE COURTS IN THE FEDERAL SYSTEM — 1
   1. Federal Court System
      a. Source of federal judicial power
      b. Scope of federal judicial power
      c. Limitation of the 11th Amendment on federal court jurisdiction
      d. Exceptions to the application of the 11th Amendment
         (1) Suits against state officials
         (2) Suits against state subdivisions
         (3) Distinction
         (4) Damages barred, not injunctions
         (5) Expansion of 11th Amendment immunity
         (6) Suits to recover under the ADA
         (7) State Consents
         (8) 11th Amendment today
  B. THE UNITED STATES SUPREME COURT — 3
   1. Jurisdiction of the Supreme Court
      a. Original jurisdiction
      b. Appellate jurisdiction
         (1) Power of judicial review
         (2) Statutory regulation of appellate jurisdiction
            (a) Appeal
            (b) Certiorari
   2. Limitations on Jurisdiction of Federal Courts
      a. Case or controversy requirements
         (1) No advisory opinions
         (2) Declaratory judgments
      b. Mootness
         (1) Collateral legal consequences
         (2) Where injury is capable of repetition
      c. Ripeness
         (1) Absence of real threat of harm
         (2) No claim of harm
      d. Abstention
         (1) Where state law is vague or ambiguous
         (2) Pending state criminal proceedings
         (3) Analogous pending state civil proceedings
      e. Standing
         (1) Injury in fact
         (2) Causation ("But For" test)
         (3) Specialized problems of standing
            (a) Taxpayer's standing
            (b) Third party standing — Raising the rights of others
               i. Where special relationship exists between the claimant and third party
               ii. Where third party is unable to bring suit on his (or her) own behalf
               iii. Associations
      f. Justiciability—Political Questions
      g. Adequate and independent state ground

Constitutional Law

II. SEPARATION OF POWERS — 8
A. THE POWERS OF CONGRESS — 8
1. Legislative Power — In General
   a. Express powers
   b. Implied powers
   c. Enabling clauses
2. Commerce Power
   a. Modern view
      (1) Limitations
   b. Regulation of local matters affecting commerce
   c. Racial segregation and discrimination
   d. Criminal statutes
   e. The 10th Amendment as a limitation on the commerce power
3. Taxing power
   a. Constitutional grant and limitation
      (1) Uniformity limitation
      (2) Direct tax limitation
      (3) Export tax limitation
   b. Use of taxing power for purposes of regulation
      (1) Doctrine of objective constitutionality
      (2) Modern trend
4. Spending power
   a. Modern view
   b. Use of spending power to regulate
   c. Spending power and election reform
5. War and Defense Powers
   a. Congressional provisions
   b. Scope of war power
   c. Military courts
      (1) Review by civilian courts
      (2) Jurisdiction
6. Investigatory Power
   a. Scope of investigatory power
   b. Enforcement of investigatory power
   c. Defenses available to a witness who refuses to answer questions before a congressional committee
7. Property Power
8. Power of Eminent Domain
   a. Limitation on power of eminent domain
9. Admiralty and Maritime Power
10. Bankruptcy Power
11. Postal Power
12. Copyright and Patent Power
13. Speech and Debate Clause
    a. Scope of immunity

B. EXECUTIVE POWER — 13
1. As Chief Executive
   a. Appointment power
   b. Removal power

- c. Obligation to report
  - (1) Veto power
  - (2) Override of veto
  - (3) No other legislative power
- d. Pardon power
  - (1) Caveat
- e. Executive privilege
2. As Commander-in-Chief
   - a. Military powers
   - b. Unsettled areas
3. International Affairs
   - a. Treaty power
     - (1) Self-executing treaties
     - (2) Not self-executing treaties
     - (3) Distinction
   - b. Executive agreements
     - (1) Ratification by Congress unnecessary

C. INTERBRANCH CHECKS UPON THE EXERCISE OF FEDERAL POWER — 16
1. Congressional limits on the executive
   - a. Impeachment power
   - b. Legislative veto
   - c. Investigatory power
   - d. Delegation to executive
   - e. Appropriations power
2. The President's power to veto or to withhold action under a statute
3. Judicial restraints upon President and Congress

III. THE RELATION OF THE NATION AND THE STATES IN THE FEDERAL SYSTEM — 17
A. NATURE AND SCOPE OF FEDERAL AND STATE POWERS — 17
1. In General
   - a. Exclusive federal powers
   - b. Exclusive state powers
   - c. Concurrent federal and state powers
   - d. No general police power
     - (1) General welfare clause
     - (2) Necessary and proper clause

B. INTERGOVERNMENTAL IMMUNITIES — 18
1. Immunity of federal government
   - a. In general
     - (1) Postal service
   - b. Taxation of the federal government by the state
     - (1) Tax on independent contractors
     - (2) State sales tax
     - (3) State property tax
     - (4) State income tax
   - c. Regulation of the federal government by the state
     - (1) State regulation of federal lands
2. Immunity of state government
   - a. Immunity against suits
     - (1) Suits by the federal government

Constitutional Law

    (2) Suits by a sister state
    (3) Suits by a private citizen
  b. Immunity against federal regulation
  c. Immunity against federal taxation

C. THE AUTHORITY RESERVED TO THE STATES — 20
  1. Source of power
    a. Constitutional limitations
  2. State regulation of interstate commerce
    a. Basic test
      (1) Discrimination
      (2) Nature of activity regulated
      (3) Balance of interests test
    b. Factors determining constitutionality of state regulation
      (1) Police power
      (2) Burden cannot outweigh state interest
      (3) Public health measures

D. RESERVED STATE POWER IN TAXATION — 21
  1. General Principles
    a. Nexus requirement
    b. Apportionment
    c. Discrimination
      (1) Privileges and immunities clause
    d. Relationship to services rendered
  2. Various types of state taxes
    a. Ad valorem property taxes
    b. Sales and use taxes
      (1) Sales tax
      (2) Use tax
    c. "Doing Business" taxes
    d. Net income taxes
    e. Flat license fee on "drummers"
    f. License tax on "peddlers"

E. NATIONAL POWER TO OVERRIDE STATE AUTHORITY — 23
  1. Supremacy clause
    a. Similarity between state and federal statutes
    b. Greater state protection permitted

IV. PROTECTION OF INDIVIDUAL RIGHTS — 24
  A. "STATE ACTION" AND THE ROLE OF THE FEDERAL JUDICIARY — 24
    1. 14th Amendment
      a. Application
      b. 13th Amendment
    2. State Action Requirement
      a. Where the private activity performs an exclusive public function
        (1) Company towns
        (2) Elections
      b. State involvement
        (1) No significant state involvement

V. DUE PROCESS AND THE INCORPORATION OF PORTIONS OF THE BILL OF RIGHTS   25
   A. INCORPORATION OF THE BILL OF RIGHTS   25
       1. 14th Amendment Privileges and Immunities Clause
          a. New revival
       2. 14th Amendment Due Process Clause
       3. Scope of the Due Process Clause
          a. Person
          b. Corporation
          c. Aliens
       4. Procedural due process
          a. Deprivation of liberty
             (1) Freedom from bodily restraints
             (2) Defamation by government
             (3) Physical punishment
             (4) Commitment to a mental institution
             (5) Injury to reputation
             (6) Competency to stand trial
          b. Property interests
             (1) Public education
             (2) Continued welfare benefits
             (3) Retention of driver's license
             (4) Public employment
             (5) Prejudgment garnishment
             (6) Distinguish
             (7) Forfeiture of property
             (8) Business licensing
          c. Type of process required
          d. Irrebuttable presumptions
             (1) Civil proceedings
             (2) Criminal cases
       5. Substantive due process
          a. Economic regulation
          b. Fundamental rights
             (1) Contraceptives
             (2) Abortion
                (a) Consent requirements
                (b) Public funding
                (c) Late-term abortion
             (3) Family relations
             (4) Private education
             (5) Marriage
             (6) Obscene material
             (7) The right to die
          c. Right to travel
             (1) Travel abroad
          d. Right to vote
             (1) Basic principles
       6. "Takings" Clause
          a. Taking v. Regulation
          b. Land use restrictions
             (1) Temporary restriction

Constitutional Law

VI. EQUAL PROTECTION OF THE LAWS — 33
    A. CONSTITUTIONAL BASIS — 33
        1. Source
        2. Relationship between Substantive Due Process and Equal Protection
            a. Substantive due process
            b. Equal protection
    B. THREE STANDARDS OF REVIEW — 33
        1. Strict Scrutiny
        2. Middle-tier, or Intermediate, Scrutiny
        3. Rational Basis Scrutiny
    C. PROVING DISCRIMINATORY CLASSIFICATIONS — 34
        1. Intentional Discrimination Required
            a. Facial discrimination
            b. Discriminatory application
            c. Discriminatory motive
    D. SUSPECT CLASSIFICATIONS — 34
        1. Race and National Origin
            a. Racial (or ethnic) classifications
            b. School segregation
                (1) Busing
            c. Affirmative Action
            d. Racial gerrymandering
        2. Alienage
        3. Illegitimacy
            a. Wrongful death
            b. Workmen's compensation
            c. Welfare benefits
            d. Intestate succession
        4. Gender
            a. Discrimination against women
            b. Discrimination against men
            c. Benign sex discrimination
        5. Age
        6. Poverty
        7. Mental retardation

VII. PRIVILEGES AND IMMUNITIES CLAUSES — 38
    A. PRIVILEGES AND IMMUNITIES UNDER THE 14TH AMENDMENT — 38
        1. Constitutional provision
        2. Scope
    B. PRIVILEGES AND IMMUNITIES UNDER ARTICLE IV, SECTION 2 — 38
        1. Constitutional provision
        2. Scope
            a. Improper discrimination
            b. Permissible discrimination

VIII. RETROACTIVE LEGISLATION — 40
    A. THE CONTRACT CLAUSE — 40
        1. Constitutional provision
            a. Retroactive state legislation

		b. Police power limitation	
		c. Modern applications	
	B.	**EX POST FACTO LAWS**	**40**
		1. Constitutional provision	
		a. Retroactive effects	
	C.	**BILLS OF ATTAINDER**	**40**
		1. Constitutional provision	
		2. Definition	
		a. Application	
IX.	**1ST AMENDMENT FREEDOMS**		**41**
	A.	**FREEDOM OF RELIGION AND SEPARATION OF CHURCH AND STATE**	**41**

    1. Constitutional provision
    2. General application
    3. Aid to parochial school students
        a. Textbooks
        b. Furnishing standardized tests
        c. Essential municipal services
        d. Health services
        e. Furnishing remedial and therapeutic services
        f. State income tax deduction for education expenses
            (1) Contrast
        g. Sign-language interpreters
    4. Direct aid to parochial schools and church-related institutions
        a. Hospitals
        b. Colleges
        c. Elementary and secondary schools
            (1) Teacher salaries
    5. Tax consequences
        a. Property tax exemptions
        b. Tax deductions
        c. Tax exemptions
        d. Vouchers
    6. Religious activities in public schools
    7. Incidental government action benefiting religion
    8. Ceremonies and displays
        a. Opening prayers
        b. Religious displays

	B.	**SCOPE OF FREE EXERCISE CLAUSE**	**45**

    1. In general
    2. Balancing test
        a. Strong state interest overriding "free exercise" claims
            (1) Polygamy
            (2) Child labor
            (3) Selective service
            (4) Denial of veterans' benefits to conscientious objectors
            (5) Sunday closing laws
            (6) Taxes
            (7) Wearing religious attire
            (8) College Scholarships

Constitutional Law

      b. "Free exercise" claims overriding weak state interest
         (1) Compulsory school attendance
         (2) Unemployment compensation
         (3) Door-to-door solicitation
    3. Status of Free Exercise Clause today
      a. Intentional interference with religion
      b. Unintentional interference with religion

C. FREEDOM OF EXPRESSION   **47**
    1. Constitutional provision
      a. Application to states
    2. Distinction between regulation of speech content and regulation of time, place, and manner of speech conduct
    3. Regulation of speech content
      a. Symbolic speech
         (1) Example
         (2) Compare
      b. Clear and present danger
         (1) Symbolic speech
      c. Fighting words
         (1) Overbreadth and vagueness
         (2) Hate crimes
      d. Defamation
         (1) Defamation of public officials and public figures
         (2) Nonmedia defamation of a private individual
         (3) Invasion of privacy
         (4) Opinion
      e. Obscenity
         (1) Pandering
         (2) Methods of regulating related areas
             (a) Zoning ordinances
             (b) 21st Amendment
      f. Child pornography
         (1) Sale and distribution
         (2) Private possession
         (3) Virtual child pornography
      g. Commercial speech
         (1) Modern test
         (2) Examples
             (a) Drug prices
             (b) Contraceptives
             (c) Attorney advertising
             (d) "Board Certified"
             (e) Billboards
             (f) Illegal or deceptive advertising
             (g) Newsracks
             (h) Beer bottle labels
         (3) Advertisement of harmful, yet lawful, products
      h. Funding restrictions
      i. Restrictions about discussing abortion

4. Regulation of the time, place and manner of speech
   a. Public forums
   b. Nonpublic forums
   c. Private property
      (1) Use of loudspeakers
      (2) Solicitation
      (3) Unwanted mail
   d. Requirement to include all political candidates in debates
   e. Licensing
      (1) Statute "void on its face"
      (2) Statute valid on its face
   f. Injunctions
      (1) Ex parte injunctions
5. Special procedural rules/Facial attacks
   a. Prior restraints
      (1) Presumption
      (2) Forms of prior restraint
   b. Exceptional cases in which prior restraints allowed
      (1) National security
      (2) Classified military information
      (3) Obscenity
      (4) Film censorship
   c. Overbreadth doctrine
   d. Vagueness doctrine
6. Freedom of Association
   a. Regulations upon public employment
      (1) In general
      (2) Modern test
   b. Examples
   c. Loyalty oaths
7. Freedom of the Press
   a. Right to attend trials
   b. "Gag" orders
   c. Newspersons' privilege
   d. Broadcasting regulations
   e. Cable programming
   f. Publication of illegally obtained information
   g. Prior restraints
8. Bar membership

SUMMARY QUESTIONS   60
Question by Question Capsule Outline   60
Constitutional Law Questions   66
Constitutional Law Explanatory Answers   137

MULTISTATE ISSUE GRAPHS   171

INTRODUCTION

Kaplan PMBR Finals: Core Concepts and Key Questions is a law school preparatory series from one of the leading companies for preparing for the Bar exam. It is designed to provide students with focused study to succeed on their law school exams. Remember that *Kaplan PMBR* is not simply another commercial outline series. Rather each edition consists of several integrated sections. This edition contains a substantive outline, capsule summary outlines, objective law school exam questions, essay exam questions, and fully detailed explanatory answers.

Finals is designed to be used as a pre-exam study aid. You should be aware that most law schools are now implementing objective and essay questions on their final examinations. In the past virtually all law school exams were written solely in an essay format. Now the trend is to test students with objective and subjective questions.

Objective questions on exams eliminate the subjectivity of essay grading. They provide uniformity and a basis for reliable grading. Law schools are also recognizing the necessity to prepare students for the Multistate Bar Examination (commonly referred to as the "MBE"). The MBE is a uniform, national, 200-question multiple choice exam covering the six subject areas of Torts, Contracts, Real Property/Future Interests, Evidence, Constitutional Law, and Criminal Law/Procedure.

Finals is designed as a national law school study aid. Many of the questions and answers follow the majority rule of law in effect in most jurisdictions. Many of the rationales and explanations refer to the national norm. This is to make the series as applicable as possible for students across the country.

This edition includes 150 multiple choice questions to review Constitutional Law. The questions require knowledge of the black letter law and some legal reasoning skills. Reviewing the questions will help you prepare for your exams and assist you in your comfort with the black letter law.

Kaplan and PMBR wish you the best of luck on your exams and in your legal career.

OUTLINE

I. THE NATURE OF JUDICIAL REVIEW

A. ORGANIZATION OF THE COURTS IN THE FEDERAL SYSTEM

1. **Federal Court System**

    a. **Source of federal judicial power:** Art. III, section 1 provides that the "judicial power of the United States shall be vested in one Supreme Court and in such inferior Courts as the Congress may from time to time ordain and establish."

    b. **Scope of federal judicial power:** Art. III, section 2 limits the jurisdiction of the federal courts to: (1) cases, in law and equity, arising under the Constitution, Laws of the United States and Treaties; (2) cases affecting ambassadors, public ministers and consuls; (3) cases of admiralty and maritime jurisdiction; (4) controversies to which the United States shall be a party; (5) controversies between two or more states; (6) cases between a state and citizens of another state; and (7) cases between citizens of different states ("diversity of citizenship" cases).

    c. **Limitation of the 11th Amendment on federal court jurisdiction:** The 11th Amendment prohibits the citizens of one state from suing ***their own state or*** another state in federal court without the state's consent.

    (1) The 11th Amendment recognizes the states and their governmental immunity.

    (2) The concept of governmental immunity, or sovereign immunity means that the government may not be sued without its consent. ***Note, however, that subdivisions of a state (e.g., cities, towns and counties) do not have immunity from suit under the 11th Amendment.***

    (3) The 11th Amendment applies not only to diversity suits but to federal question cases as well.

    (4) Despite Congress's enumerated powers under Article I, section 8, the 11th Amendment will nonetheless serve as a restriction to prohibit federal court adjudication against a state. [*Seminole Tribe of Florida v. Florida* 517 U.S. 44 (1996) held that Congress could not use Article I to circumvent the limitations placed on federal jurisdiction and therefore could not allow an Indian tribe to sue a state in federal court].

    Compare: Pursuant to its enforcement powers under the post-Civil War amendments (13th, 14th, and 15th), Congress can authorize private suits by individuals to compensate for past acts of discrimination. [*Fitzpatrick v. Bitzer*, 427 U.S. 445 (1979)].

    d. **Exceptions to the application of the 11th Amendment:**

    (1) **Suits against state officials:** The 11th Amendment does *not* bar suits against state officials for abusing their power in enforcing an *un*constitutional state statute. [*Ex parte Young*, 209 U.S. 123 (1908)].

(2) **Suits against state subdivisions:** The 11th Amendment does not bar suits against state subdivisions (e.g., cities, towns or counties). [*Lincoln County v. Luning*, 133 U.S. 529 (1890)].

(3) **Distinction:** The 11th Amendment does not bar federal suits brought by one state against another state, or suits brought by the federal government against a state.

(4) **Damages barred, not injunctions:** The 11th Amendment bars suits for damages, but does not bar most suits for injunctions, e.g. a private citizen may sue to enjoin a state official from acting in violation of the plaintiff's federal constitutional rights.

(5) **Expansion of 11th Amendment immunity:** After their *federal* court suit was dismissed on 11th Amendment grounds, a group of probation officers sued the state in *state* court claiming they were owed overtime pay under the federal Fair Labor Standards Act. The Court denied relief and held that state governments may not be sued in *state* court without their consent. Despite the lack of any express constitutional provisions in this area, the Court reasoned that state sovereign immunity "inheres in the system of federalism established by the Constitution." [*Alden v. Maine*, 119 S. Ct. 2240 (1999)] Similarly, state workers alleging age discrimination under the Federal Age Discrimination in Employment Act may not sue their employers (i.e., the State) because Congress lacks the power to override the States' 11th Amendment immunity from federal lawsuits [*Kimel v. Board of Regents* 528 U.S. 62 (2000)].

(6) **Suits to recover under the ADA:** The Supreme Court recently held that suits in federal court by state employees to recover money damages by reason of the State's failure to comply with Title I of the ADA are barred by the Eleventh Amendment. *Board of Trustees of Univ. of Ala. v. Garrett,* 121 S. Ct. 555 (2001).

(7) **State Consents:** A state may consent to suit in federal court. However, no consent will be found unless the state clearly waives its Eleventh Amendment immunity. A state may only waive its Eleventh Amendment immunity ***expressly and unequivocally*** (or by voluntarily invoking a federal court's jurisdiction). A state will ***not*** be held to have implied or constructively waived its immunity simply because Congress provides that a state will be subject to private suit if it engages in certain federally regulated conduct (such as infringing a federally granted patent) and the state voluntarily elects to engage in that conduct. [*College Savings Bank v. Florida Prepaid Postsecondary Education Expense Board*, 527 U.S. 666 (1999), ***overruling*** *Parden v. Terminal Railway*, 377 U.S. 184 (1964)].

(8) **11th Amendment today:** Complete preclusion of all jurisdiction may occur in certain instances—probation officers owed money under federal law cannot sue for it in either federal or state court; states can infringe patents or copyrights and thus violate federal law, but cannot be sued in either federal or state court. Remember, however, that state officials can be sued for injunctive relief, but injured plaintiffs have no damage remedy against state governments.

B. THE UNITED STATES SUPREME COURT

1. **Jurisdiction of the Supreme Court**

   a. **Original jurisdiction:** Under Art. III, section 2, the Supreme Court has original jurisdiction "in all cases affecting ambassadors, other public ministers and consuls and those in which a state shall be a party." Congress may neither enlarge nor restrict the Supreme Court's original jurisdiction. [*Marbury v. Madison,* 5 U.S. 137 (1803)].

   b. **Appellate jurisdiction:** Art. III, section 2 further provides that "in all other cases before mentioned, the Supreme Court shall have appellate jurisdiction, both as to law and fact, with such exceptions, and under such regulations as the Congress shall make."

   (1) **Power of judicial review:** The Supreme Court early held that it has the power to review state court decisions, in order to insure that the states would act in conformity to the U.S. Constitution. [*Martin v. Hunter's Lessee,* 14 U.S. 304 (1816); to hold acts of the other branches of the federal government (i.e., Executive and Congress) unconstitutional [*Marbury v. Madison, supra*]; and to hold state statutes unconstitutional. [*Fletcher v. Peck,* 10 U. S. 87 (1810)].

   (2) **Statutory regulation of appellate jurisdiction:** Under 28 U.S. C. section 1257, there are two methods for invoking Supreme Court appellate jurisdiction: (i) by appeal (where jurisdiction is mandatory) and (ii) by writ of certiorari (discretionary review where four or more justices vote to hear the case).

   (a) **Appeal:** Prior to 1988, obligatory review on appeal took place when a state court held a federal statute or treaty invalid, or upheld the validity of a state statute; or when a federal court held against the validity of a federal statute or treaty. Note: In 1988, Congress eliminated these types of obligatory review on appeal. Now, decisions of 3-judge federal district courts may be heard by the Supreme Court (also referred to as "USSC") by appeal (for example, a decision seeking injunctive relief).

   (b) **Certiorari:** Since the two categories of decisions noted above which were subject to obligatory review on appeal have been eliminated, practically all decisions from state supreme courts and federal courts are now reviewable by a writ of certiorari.

   Grounds for certiorari: 1) cases involving conflicts between different federal courts of appeal; 2) cases involving conflicts between the highest courts of two states, or the highest state court and a federal court of appeals; 3) cases from state courts or U.S. courts of appeal involving important, yet unresolved, issues.

2. **Limitations on Jurisdiction of Federal Courts**

   a. **Case or controversy requirement:** Art. III, section 2 limits the jurisdiction of federal courts to "cases" and "controversies." A "case" or "controversy" is a real and substantial dispute which touches the legal relations of parties having adverse

Constitutional Law

interests and which can be resolved by a judicial decree of a conclusive character. [*Aetna Life Insurance Co. v. Haworth,* 300 U.S. 227 (1937)].

(1) **No advisory opinions:** The Supreme Court will not give advisory opinions to either the President or Congress re: the constitutionality of some proposed action or legislation. Note, however, that state courts may be allowed to render advisory opinions.

(2) **Declaratory judgments:** The prohibition against advisory opinions does not preclude federal courts from granting declaratory judgments. A declaratory judgment is a decision where the court is requested to determine the legal effect of proposed conduct without awarding damages or injunctive relief. However, the legal questions may not be too abstract or hypothetical.

b. **Mootness:** If the controversy or matter has been resolved, then the case will be dismissed as moot. An ***actual case or controversy*** must exist at all stages of the litigation. [*Liner v. Jafco,* Inc. 375 U.S. 301 (1964)].

(1) **Collateral legal consequences:** Although the principal issue in the lawsuit has been resolved, if a party still has an interest in resolving collateral (or lesser) matters, the case will not be dismissed. In *Powell v. McCormick,* 395 U.S. 486 (1969), for example, Representative Powell had regained his seat in Congress at the time of Supreme Court review, but the case was *not* moot because the issue of his entitlement to backpay was still unresolved.

(2) **Where injury is capable of repetition.** A pregnant woman's suit challenging the constitutionality of a state abortion statute was held not to be moot even though she was no longer pregnant at the time the case reached the Court. Since pregnancy is "capable of repetition, yet evading review," it is a practical impossibility to achieve appellate review in such cases before the claims of the same plaintiff, or other plaintiffs who are members of the same class, become moot. [*Roe v. Wade,* 410 U.S. 113 (1973)].

c. **Ripeness:** The controversy must be ripe for decision. Otherwise the federal courts will decide constitutional issues before it is necessary to do so. Note the distinction between mootness and ripeness, ***whereas mootness bars consideration of claims after they have been resolved; ripeness bars consideration of claims before they have fully developed.***

(1) **Absence of real threat of harm:** A case may be dismissed as unripe where a statute has never been enforced and there is no real threat that it ever will be. [*Poe v. Ullman,* 367 U.S. 497 (1961) — anticontraceptive law had not been enforced for over 50 years despite "ubiquitous, open, public sales"]. Conversely, the Supreme Court did rule on the constitutionality of a statute prohibiting the teaching of evolution in public schools even though the statute had not been enforced. [*Epperson v. Arkansas,* 393 U.S. 97 (1968)].

(2) **No claim of harm:** The Court dismissed a claim against the Army's data gathering activities, because there was no showing that the Army's surveillance system resulted in any specific present harm or threat of future harm to the complainants. [*Laird v. Tatum,* 408 U.S. 1 (1972)]. Similarly, in *O'Shea v. Littleton,* 414

U.S. 488 (1974), the Court refused to grant equitable relief because there was no evidence that the pattern of racial discrimination (re: the constitutionality of bail and sentencing practices in the Cairo, Illinois court system) threatened the plaintiffs who were not in imminent danger of being prosecuted.

d. **Abstention:** The federal court may "abstain" or refuse to hear a particular case when there are undecided issues of state law presented. **Rational:** The doctrine permits the state court to resolve issues of state law thereby making a decision of the constitutional issue unnecessary. Thus, proper deference is paid to the state court system and harmonious federal-state relations are furthered. [*Railroad Commission v. Pullman,* 312 U.S. 496 (1941)].

   (1) **Where state law is vague or ambiguous:** The federal court may "abstain" if the meaning of a state law or regulation is unclear. Therefore, the state court may interpret the statute so as to avoid the constitutional issue. [*Harris County Commissioners' Court v. Moore,* 420 U.S. 77 (1975)].

   (2) **Pending state criminal proceedings:** Where state criminal proceedings are pending, the federal court will "abstain" in a suit seeking an injunction against the state prosecution, absent a showing of bad faith harassment on the part of the (state) prosecutors. [*Younger v. Harris,* 401 U.S. 37 (1971)].

   (3) **Analogous pending state civil proceedings:** The principle of *Younger v. Harris* was extended to cases where (1) state civil proceedings (i.e., injunction against operation of a state public nuisance statute used to close a porno movie house) had commenced. [*Huffman v. Pursue,* Ltd., 420 U.S. 592 (1975)]; and (2) where civil contempt hearings had begun. [*Judice v. Vail,* 430 U.S. 327 (1977)].

e. **Standing:** Art. III requires that a person litigating a constitutional question must show (1) injury in fact and (2) causation (i.e., proof that the relief sought will redress the harm or injury which is alleged).

   (1) **Injury in fact:** The plaintiff must show a direct and personal injury by the action that he (or she) is complaining about. Where the plaintiff has not suffered any personal injury or harm, then he (or she) does not have standing. [*Sierra v. Morton,* 405 U.S. 727 (1972)]. The injury must be caused by the violation of a duty affecting the plaintiffs rights arising under the ***constitution or federal law.***

   (2) **Causation ("But For" test):** Art. III requires that the plaintiff must show that his (or her) injury was causally connected to the challenged action and that the relief sought will prevent or redress the injury. [*Simon v. Eastern Kentucky Welfare Rights Organization,* 426 U.S. 26 (1976) — no proof that denial of hospital services was caused by or traced to an allegedly invalid I.R.S. rule].

   (3) **Specialized problems of standing**

      (a) **Taxpayer's standing:** As a general rule, federal taxpayers do not have standing to challenge allegedly unconstitutional federal expenditures on the ground that their interest in such expenditures is too remote

"to have any stake in the outcome." [*Frothingham v. Mellon,* 262 U.S. 447 (1923)].

Exception: In 1968 the Supreme Court held that a federal taxpayer had standing to challenge federal expenditures to aid parochial schools where there was a *nexus* (or logical link) between the taxpayer and the claim sought to be adjudicated. [*Flast v. Cohen,* 392 U.S. 83 (1968)]. Note: The *Flast v. Cohen, supra,* principle, however, has not been extended to other areas of government spending. See *United States v. Richardson,* 418 U.S. 166 (1974) — where a federal taxpayer was denied standing to challenge a statute regulating the C.I.A.; and *Schlesinger v. Reservists Committee to Stop the War,* 418 U.S. 208 (1974) — where citizens did not have standing to challenge a senator's or representative's membership in Armed Forces Reserve as violating Art. I, sect. 6 forbidding the same from "holding any office under the United States."

(b) **Third party standing — Raising the rights of others:** Under the traditional view, a litigant lacks the standing to assert the rights of third parties not before the court. [In *Tileston v. Ullman,* 318 U.S. 44 (1943) — a physician did not have third party (*jus tertii*) standing to attack a state anticontraceptive statute on the grounds that it prevented him from giving professional advice to his patients].

Exceptions: In certain situations, the Court has permitted a party to raise the constitutional rights of a third party.

  i. **Where special relationship exists between the claimant and third party:** The Court acknowledged the right of a physician to raise the rights of his patients in challenging an abortion ruling because of the close relationship between the doctor and his patient, and also because the patient was unable to bring suit on her own behalf [*Singleton v. Wulff,* 428 U.S. 106 (1976)]; also in *Craig v. Boren,* 429 U.S. 190 (1976) — a vendor of beer had standing (*jus tertii*) to assert the rights of males under the age of 21 against a law prohibiting the sale of beer to them; and in *Carey v. Population Services International,* 431 U.S. 678 (1977) — a seller of contraceptives has standing to assert the rights of potential purchasers against a law prohibiting the sale of such devices.

  ii. **Where third party is unable to bring suit on his (or her) own behalf:** In *NAACP v. Alabama,* 357 U.S. 449 (1958), for example, the NAACP was permitted to raise the right of freedom of association of its members, in a suit to require disclosure of membership lists, because the issue of the confidentiality of membership could not be raised by the members themselves without destroying that confidentiality.

  iii. **Associations:** An association has standing to assert the claims of its members, even if the association has not suffered any injury itself, if (a) the members would otherwise have standing to sue in their own right, (b) the interest asserted is germane to the association's purpose and (c) neither the claim asserted nor the relief requested would require participation by the individual members in the lawsuit. [*Hunt v. Washington Apple Advertising Commission,* 432 U.S. 333 (1977)].

f. **Justiciability — Political Questions:** In *Baker v. Carr,* 369 U.S. 186 (1962), the Supreme Court, in holding that a federal court action to compel reapportionment of a state legislature did not present a political question, set forth the following relevant factors which a court should take into consideration in determining if the political question doctrine will apply: (1) whether there is "a textually demonstrable constitutional commitment of the issue to a coordinate political department"; or (2) a "lack of judicially discoverable and manageable standards for resolving it"; or (3) "the impossibility of deciding without an initial policy determination of a kind clearly for non-judicial discretion"; or (4) "the impossibility of a court's undertaking independent resolution without expressing lack of respect due coordinate branches of government"; or (5) "an unusual need for unquestioning adherence to a political decision already made"; or (6) "the potentiality of embarrassment from multifarious pronouncements by various departments on one question."

Rationale: There are two principal factors related to the political question doctrine. First, considerations (1), (4), (5) and (6) enumerated above are rooted in the separation of powers. On the other hand, considerations (2) and (3) recognize the limitations of the judiciary to resolve certain types of controversies.

Example: In *United States v. Nixon,* 418 U.S. 683 (1974), the ability of a grand jury to subpoena documents in the possession of the President against a claim of executive privilege did not present a political question apart from a claim based on national security.

Other areas of political questions: decisions in regard to the impeachment process; the amendment ratification process; the President's power to unilaterally terminate a treaty; foreign affairs; Guaranty Clause issues under Article IV. Note, however, that issues dealing with reapportionment and gerrymandering—defining political districts for partisan, or discriminatory, purposes—are not political questions and may be heard by the federal judiciary.

g. **Adequate and independent state ground:** Although a state court decision involves a federal question, if the state court judgment can be supported on an adequate and independent state ground, the Supreme Court will *not* take jurisdiction. To do so would be tantamount to rendering an "advisory opinion." [*Herb v. Pitcairn,* 324 U.S. 117 (1945)]. Unlike other doctrines of judicial review, which apply to the entire federal judiciary, adequate state grounds only applies to the United States Supreme Court.

How the Doctrine Works: Suppose a state court holds that a state law is unconstitutional as violating both the state and federal constitutions. Where the state "substantive" ground upon which the decision was based is independent of the federal constitution, the doctrine of adequate state grounds will apply and the USSC will not hear the case. Alternatively, in the case where the state court reached its decision by interpreting the state ground as being co-extensive with

the federal constitution (or relied on federal law in piggy-backing its state claim on the federal constitution), then no clear, independent state ground exists, so the doctrine will not apply and the USSC will hear the case. [*Michigan v. Long*, 463 U.S. 1032 (1983)]. Finally, adequate state grounds has a "procedural" component as well. Suppose the plaintiff lost in state court for failing to comply with some state procedural rule. If the USSC finds the state procedural rule to be "adequate" (fundamentally fair under due process analysis), then the doctrine of adequate state grounds will also apply to foreclose Supreme Court review.

II. SEPARATION OF POWERS

A. THE POWERS OF CONGRESS

1. **Legislative Power — In General:** Art. I, section 1 provides "All legislative powers herein granted shall be vested in a Congress of the United States...." Legislative power is primarily the power to make laws, but incidental to that power is the right to conduct investigations, hearings and consider matters upon which legislation may be enacted, and do all other things "necessary and proper" to the enactment of legislation.

    a. **Express powers:** Art. I, section 8 specifically grants a variety of powers to Congress including the powers to lay and collect taxes, to borrow money on the credit of the United States, to regulate commerce with foreign nations and among the several states, to declare war, to raise and support armies, and to provide and maintain a navy.

    b. **Implied powers:** The last clause in Art. I, section 8, the "necessary and proper" clause, gives Congress the power "to make all laws which shall be necessary and proper for carrying into execution the enumerated powers and all other powers vested in this Constitution in the Government of the United States or any department or office thereof." In *McCulloch v. Maryland,* 4 Wheat 316 (1819), this clause was viewed as a significant expansion of the specific powers by Chief Justice Marshall who held that the power to establish a national bank was "necessary and proper" under Congress's power to regulate the federal currency. Thus, the "necessary and proper" clause has become the source of the doctrine of implied powers.

    c. **Enabling clauses:** The enabling clauses of the 13th, 14th and 15th Amendments give Congress the power to enforce those amendments by "appropriate legislation."

2. **Commerce Power:** In accordance with the holding in *Gibbons v. Ogden, 9* Wheat 1 (1824), many of the early cases used various criteria to restrict the power of Congress to regulate "commerce among the states" as "commerce which concerns more states than one." Today, Congress can regulate "channels" of interstate commerce (highways, waterways, and air traffic), instrumentalities of interstate commerce (cars, trucks, ships, airplanes, etc.), and activities which "substantially affect" interstate commerce.

    a. **Modern view:** Under the so-called "affectation doctrine," Congress now has the power to regulate any activity, whether carried on in one state or many, which has any appreciable effect (whether directly or indirectly) on interstate commerce. This doctrine was first formulated in *National Labor Relations Board v. Jones and*

Laughlin Steel Co., 301 U.S. 1 (1937) — which upheld the constitutionality of the Wagner Act in requiring collective bargaining in all industries "affecting" interstate commerce; and expanded in *United States v. Darby Lumber,* 312 U.S. 100 (1941) — which upheld Congressional regulation of hours and wages of employees of an industry where only part of the goods produced were shipped in interstate commerce.

   (1) **Limitations:** Congress's plenary commerce power is not without limits. In *U.S. v. Lopez,* 514 U.S. 549 (1995), for the first time in over half a century, the Court struck down a federal law as being beyond the scope of the commerce power. Specifically, the federal law made it a crime for any individual knowingly to possess a firearm in a school zone. Since gun possession in schools is neither itself a "commercial" activity nor an activity that "substantially" affects interstate commerce, and since no "jurisdictional nexus" connecting gun possession to interstate commerce was expressed in the language of the statute, the majority held that Congress was acting beyond the limits of the Commerce Clause. *Lopez* reaffirmed the affectation doctrine.

b. **Regulation of local matters affecting commerce:** In *Wickard v. Filburn,* 317 U.S. 111 (1942), the Court held that federal commerce power could regulate the amounts of wheat which a farmer grew on his own land and intended wholly for his own consumption. Since such consumption removes a demand for other commodities, it may have a substantial effect on interstate commerce.

c. **Racial segregation and discrimination:** The Commerce Clause has also been used as the vehicle to uphold laws aimed at barring racial discrimination in activities connected with interstate commerce. Thus, Congress may prohibit racial discrimination in private restaurants if a substantial portion of the food consumed traveled in interstate commerce. [*Katzenbach v. McClung,* 379 U.S. 294 (1964)]; and in *Heart of Atlanta Motel v. United States,* 379 U.S. 241 (1964), the Court upheld provisions of the Civil Rights Act of 1964 barring discrimination in places of public accommodation (e.g., as applied to a motel) as "affecting" interstate commerce.

d. **Criminal statutes:** In *Perez v. United States,* 402 U.S. 146 (1971), the Court upheld, under the commerce power, a federal law prohibiting extortionate credit transactions (i.e., "loan sharking") on the ground that such transactions provide a major source of revenue for organized crime, and that organized crime, in turn, has an adverse effect upon interstate commerce.

e. **The 10th Amendment as a limitation on the commerce power:** The 10th Amendment, which provides that powers not delegated to the federal government are reserved to the states, serves as a very weak limitation on the federal commerce power today. Generally applicable federal laws whose effect serves to regulate the states (state businesses and/or employees) do not violate the 10th Amendment. [*Garcia v. San Antonio Metropolitan Transit Authority,* 469 U.S. 528 (1985) — applying federal minimum-wage and overtime provisions to employees of a municipally-owned mass-transit system is a valid exercise of the federal commerce power and does not violate the 10th Amendment].

Compare: However, the 10th Amendment does prevent Congress from interfering with a state's law-making processes. Congress may not "commandeer the legislative processes of the states by directly compelling them to enact and enforce a federal regulatory program." [*New York v. U.S.*, 505 U.S. 144 (1992) — USSC held invalid as violating the 10th Amendment a federal law which required the state of New York to pass legislation to arrange for the disposal of radioactive waste generated within its borders].

3. **Taxing power**

   a. **Constitutional grant and limitation:** Art. I, section 8 provides: "Congress shall have power to lay and collect taxes, duties, imposts and excises ..." This power, however, is subject to three specific limitations:

      (1) **Uniformity limitation:** Art. I, section 8 requires that all duties, imposts and excises (a term encompassing all indirect taxes) must be uniform throughout the United States. Note: Uniformity means geographic uniformity (i.e., what Congress has properly selected for taxation must be identically taxed in every state where it is found). As long as the tax is geographically uniform, it will be sustained even though it is not intrinsically uniform (i.e., different tax rates). In *Knowlton v. Moore,* 178 U.S. 41 (1900), for example, the Court sustained progressive rates of inheritance tax among the states.

      (2) **Direct tax limitation:** A direct tax is usually one imposed directly against property (e.g., *ad valorem* tax upon property) or one imposed against the person who is ultimately responsible for the tax burden (e.g., use tax). All "direct" taxes must be apportioned among the several states. Note: The 16th Amendment gives Congress the power to lay and collect taxes on incomes from whatever source derived, without apportionment among the several states.

      (3) **Export tax limitation:** Art. I, section 9, clause 5 provides: "No tax or duty shall be laid on Articles exported from any State." To qualify as an export, the goods must be "in channels of transportation bound for a foreign country." [*Dooley v. United States,* 183 U.S. 151 (1901)]. Note: Goods may be taxed while in the manufacturing stage, even though manufactured for export.

   b. **Use of taxing power for purposes of regulation:** In the past, Congress has used its taxing power as a necessary and proper means of achieving a regulatory effect. Generally, as long as Congress has the power to regulate the activity taxed, the tax can then be used as a regulating device rather than for revenue raising purposes. In *Sunshine Anthracite Coal Co. v. Adkins,* 310 U.S. 381 (1940), for example, the Court sustained a tax on coal producers who violated a fair competition law even though it was clearly designed to be a penalty rather than revenue raising.

      (1) **Doctrine of objective constitutionality:** Even when Congress does not have power to regulate the activity taxed, the tax will, nevertheless, be upheld if its "dominant intent" is revenue raising. Thus, even though the tax may have a substantial regulatory effect, if the tax in fact raises revenue ("objective" test) it will be valid. In *McCray v. United States,* 195 U.S. 27 (1904), the Court upheld as revenue raising a discriminatory tax on colored oleomargarine, even though Congress did not have the power to regulate its production directly.

(2) **Modern trend:** As a general rule, the modern judicial trend is to uphold any tax as valid if it is, in fact, a revenue raising measure. Although a tax on bookmaking activities had a regulatory effect, it was upheld as producing revenue (even though negligible in amount). [*United States v. Kahriger,* 345 U.S. 22 (1953)].

4. **Spending power:** Art. I, section 8, clause 1 provides that "Congress shall have the power to lay and collect taxes ... to pay the debts and provide for the common defense and general welfare of the United States."

   a. **Modern view:** In *United States v. Butler,* 297 U.S. 1 (1936), the Court construed the General Welfare Clause as a limitation on Congress's taxing and spending powers and not as an independent source of congressional power. In other words, Congress's power to tax and spend must be exercised for the "general welfare" of the United States.

   b. **Use of spending power to regulate:** By exercising its spending power, Congress can require states to comply with specified conditions in order to qualify for federal funds.

      (1) *Oklahoma v. Civil Service Commission,* 330 U.S. 127 (1947) — Congress conditioned further grants of highway funds upon resignation of state highway administrator who was also state Democratic Party chairman.

      (2) *South Dakota v. Dole,* 483 U.S. — (1987) — the court rejected South Dakota's 10th and 21st amendment arguments and upheld Congress's action of withholding federal highway funds from states permitting the purchasing of alcoholic beverages by individuals under the age of 21.

   c. **Spending power and election reform:** The Federal Election Campaign Act, which limited the amount a candidate could spend if he (or she) accepted money from the federal government, is a valid exercise of the power to spend for the "general welfare." In *Buckley v. Valeo,* 424 U.S. 1 (1976), the Court sustained the power of Congress to finance elections since this would reduce the harmful effect of candidates' reliance on large private contributions.

5. **War and Defense Powers**

   a. **Congressional provisions:** According to Art. I, section 8 Congress has the following powers with respect to war and defense: (1) power to declare war; (2) power to raise and support Armies; (3) power to provide and maintain a Navy; and (4) power to organize, arm, discipline and call forth the militia.

   b. **Scope of war power:** The war power confers upon Congress very broad authority to initiate whatever measures it deems necessary to provide for the national defense in peacetime as well as in wartime. Thus, the military draft and selective service systems have repeatedly been upheld. [*United States v. O'Brien,* 391 U.S. 367 (1968)]; similarly, the power of Congress to initiate wage, price and rent control of the civilian economy during wartime has been sustained [*Yakus v. United States,* 321 U.S. 414 (1944)]; and the exclusion of civilians from certain restricted areas during wartime. [*Korematsu v. United States,* 323 U.S. 214 (1944)].

c. **Military courts:** Art. I, section 8, clause 14 grants Congress the power to establish military courts and tribunals. Since military courts are not Article III courts, the accused in court-martial proceedings is not entitled to the same procedural safeguards as set forth in the Bill of Rights (i.e., right to jury trial, grand jury indictment). Rather, an accused is safeguarded by the procedures provided in the Uniform Code of Military Justice.

   (1) **Review by civilian courts:** Although civilian courts have no general power of review over court-martial proceedings, there can be a limited examination of the regularity of such proceedings by a civilian court. [*Burns v. Wilson,* 339 U.S. 103 (1950)].

   (2) **Jurisdiction:**

   (a) Military courts have jurisdiction over offenses committed by servicemen (or servicewomen) on a military post or area under military control, or for service connected offenses committed elsewhere.

   (b) Military courts have jurisdiction over **current** members of the armed forces, even while on a pass or on leave. Jurisdiction is determined by the **status** of the individual as an armed service member not the service-connectedness of the offense [*Solario v. U.S.,* 55 U.S. Law Week 5038 (1987), overruling *O'Callahan v. Parker,* 395 U.S. 258 (1969)].

   (c) As long as civilian courts are available, military courts are denied jurisdiction over civilians and their dependents. [*Ex parte Milligan,* 71 U.S. 2 (1866) — a military tribunal did not have jurisdiction to try and convict an Indiana citizen who was not a member of either the Union or Confederate armed forces].

6. **Investigatory Power:** Although Congress does not have any express constitutional power to investigate, the "necessary and proper" clause permits Congress to conduct investigations incident to its legislative power. [*McGrain v. Daugherty,* 273 U.S. 135 (1927)].

   a. **Scope of investigatory power:** Congress's investigatory power is quite broad, and it may extend to any matter within a "legitimate legislative sphere." [*Eastland v. United States Servicemen's Fund,* 421 U.S. 491 (1975) — the Speech and Debate Clause forbids the courts from enjoining members of Congress or their aides from issuing subpoenas or conducting their inquiry].

   b. **Enforcement of investigatory power:** Where a witness fails to appear after being summoned before a congressional committee or fails to answer a question posed by such a committee, Congress may either (1) cite the witness for contempt or (2) refer the matter to the United States Attorney General for prosecution.

   c. **Defenses available to a witness who refuses to answer questions before a congressional committee:** Generally, a witness can raise (1) the privilege against self-incrimination, or (2) lack of due process safeguards or (3) interference with the 1st Amendment rights to privacy and freedom of association. In *Gibson v. Florida Legislative Committee,* 372 U.S. 539 (1963), for example, the Court upheld the

refusal of a member of the NAACP to release membership lists to a legislative committee because there was not a sufficient nexus between the investigation and the records sought.

7. **Property Power:** Article IV, section 3 provides that Congress shall have the power "to dispose of and make all needful rules and regulations respecting the territory or other property belonging to the United States."

8. **Power of Eminent Domain:** Although the Constitution does not expressly give Congress the power of eminent domain, the power to take property is "implied in aid of the other powers granted to the federal government." [*Kohl v. United States,* 91 U.S. 367 (1876)].

    a. **Limitation on power of eminent domain:** The 5th Amendment provides, in part, that "... nor shall private property be taken for public use, without just compensation."

9. **Admiralty and Maritime Power:** The Court has determined that Article III, section 2 and the "necessary and proper" clause give Congress complete and plenary power to fix and determine the maritime laws throughout the country. [*Southern Pacific Co. v. Jensen,* 244 U.S. 205 (1917)].

10. **Bankruptcy Power:** Art. I, section 8, clause 4 grants Congress the power "to establish uniform laws on the subject of bankruptcies throughout the United States."

11. **Postal Power:** Art. I, section 8, clause 7 provides that Congress shall have the power "to establish post offices and post roads."

12. **Copyright and Patent Power:** Art. I, section 8, clause 8 gives Congress the power "to promote the progress of science and useful arts, by securing for limited times to authors and inventors the exclusive right to their respective writings and discoveries."

13. **Speech and Debate Clause:** Art. I, section 6, clause 1 provides that "senators and representatives shall not be questioned in any other place for any speech or debate in either house." The Speech and Debate Clause protects legislators (and their aides) against criminal or civil proceedings for "legislative acts." See *United States v. Johnson,* 383 U.S. 169 (1966) and *Gravel v. United States,* 408 U.S. 606 (1972). Members of Congress, however, can be liable based on defamation for issuing press releases or newsletters which injure reputation.

    a. **Scope of immunity:** The clause does not bar prosecution for taking a bribe to influence legislation. [*United States v. Brewster,* 408 U.S. 501 (1972)]. The clause, however, only insulates members of Congress for "acts that occur in the regular course of the legislative process."

B. **EXECUTIVE POWER**

1. **As Chief Executive:** Art. II, section 1 provides that "the executive power shall be vested in the President." This provision confers broad authority in the President to execute the laws of the United States. Although there are few enumerated powers

Constitutional Law

expressly granted to the President under Article II, much of the President's domestic and foreign powers are implied. The Court has emphasized strongly that the President has no power to make the laws, but has the power to execute them.

a. **Appointment power:** Art. II, section 2 gives the President the power, "with the advice and consent of the Senate," to nominate and appoint all "ambassadors, other public ministers and consuls, Judges of the Supreme Court, and all other officers of the United States, whose appointments are not herein otherwise provided for."

Note: The presidential appointment power should be construed as a limitation on the congressional appointment power. Although Congress can appoint officials to its legislative committees, it cannot appoint members to any agency or commission with administrative powers. [*Buckley v. Valeo*, 424 U.S. 1 (1976) — where an attempt to vest the power to appoint members of the Federal Elections Commission in the Speaker of the House was held unconstitutional].

Federal executive officers: The President can appoint—and Congress cannot—federal executive officers (principal or high-level officials such as ambassadors and cabinet members). Congress, however, can delegate the appointment of "inferior" officers (including special prosecutors) to either 1) the President or 2) the judiciary or 3) heads of departments (Cabinet members).

b. **Removal power:** Although the Constitution is silent with respect to removal power, it is generally agreed that the President may remove any executive appointee without cause (*i.e.* an ambassador). The President must have cause, however, to remove executive officers having fixed terms and officers performing judicial or quasi-judicial functions (*i.e.* Federal Trade Commissioner). Congress has no power to summarily remove an executive officer. [*Bowsher v. Synar*, 478 U.S. 714 (1986)]. Federal judges cannot be removed by either Congress or the President during "good behavior"; formal impeachment proceedings would be required for removal.

c. **Obligation to report:** Art. II, section 3 provides that the President "shall from time to time give Congress information on the state of the union, and recommend to their consideration such measures as he shall judge necessary and expedient." This obligation has evolved into the annual "State of Union" address given by the President.

(1) **Veto power:** Under Art. I, section 7 once Congress has approved legislation, the President is granted 10 days in which to act upon it. Unless he vetoes it within the 10 day period, the proposed legislation will become law. Note that the President can "pocket veto" a bill passed at end of the Congressional term by not signing it. A "line-item veto", which gives the President the power to cancel statutory provisions of new federal legislation, has been held unconstitutional as violating the Presentment Clause of Article I, Section 7. [*Clinton v. City of New York*, 118 S. Ct. 2091 (1998)].

(2) **Override of veto:** Article 1, section 7 provides that Congress has the power to override a veto by a two-thirds vote of each house.

(3) **No other legislative power:** In *Youngstown Sheet and Tube Co. v. Sawyer,* 343 U.S. 579 (1952), the Court invalidated a presidential order directing seizure of steel mills to prevent a threatened strike.

d. **Pardon power:** Article II, section 2 gives the President the power "to grant reprieves and pardons for offenses against the United States, except in cases of impeachment."

(1) **Caveat:** The President's power to pardon is limited to federal offenses (or "offenses against the United States"). Note that the President does *not* have the power to grant pardons for state crimes.

e. **Executive privilege:** The President has an absolute privilege to refuse to disclose information relating to military, diplomatic or sensitive national security secrets. However, other confidential communications between the President and his advisors are only *presumptively* privileged. [See *United States v. Nixon,* 418 U.S. 683 (1974)].

2. **As Commander-in-Chief:** Article II, section 2 provides that "the President is the Commander-in-Chief of the army and navy, and of the militia of the several states when called into federal service by Congress."

   a. **Military powers:** The President has the power to deploy military forces without a formal declaration of war [*Prize Cases,* 2 Black 635 (1863)]; and he (or she) has the power to seize private property during wartime [*United States v. Pewee Coal Co.,* 341 U.S. 114 (1951) — coal mines were seized to prevent nationwide strike]; however, the President does not have the power to declare war.

   b. **Unsettled areas:** Certain issues remain unclear today, such as whether the President may commit forces, without congressional approval, to aid a U.S. ally under attack (although provisions in certain defense treaties would authorize such intervention), or whether the President may order a preemptive strike in anticipation of an enemy attack. Clearly, the President may commit troops to repel a sudden attack on the United States.

3. **International Affairs**

   a. **Treaty power:** Under the Supremacy Clause, Article IV, section 2, the President has the power to make treaties with foreign nations "by and with the advice and consent of two-thirds of the Senate." In accordance with the Supremacy Clause, treaties "are the supreme law of the land; and the judges of every state shall be bound thereby, anything in the laws or constitution of any state to the contrary notwithstanding." Note: Treaties take precedence over any conflicting state law (regardless of whether it precedes or follows the enactment of the state law). [*Nielsen v. Johnson,* 279 U.S. 47 (1929)].

   (1) **Self-executing treaties:** A treaty is "self-executing" when it takes effect without the necessity of any action by Congress [*Missouri v. Holland,* 252 U.S. 416 (1920) — a treaty with Canada concerning migratory birds was held valid since it regulated matters which were beyond Congressional regulation under the Commerce Clause].

(2) **Not self-executing treaties:** A treaty is "not self-executing" when it requires Congress to pass federal legislation to implement its provisions. An example of such a treaty would be the human rights provision of the United Nations Charter.

(3) **Distinction:** "Self-executing" treaties are considered the supreme law of the land; whereas "not self-executing" treaties are *not* part of the supreme law of the land and thus do not supersede existing federal and state statutes without further action by Congress.

b. **Executive agreements:** The President has the power to enter into executive agreements and compacts with foreign nations. Such agreements are valid and prevail over any inconsistent state law. [*United States v. Belmont,* 301 U.S. 324 (1937)].

(1) **Ratification by Congress unnecessary:** Executive agreements are the sole responsibility of the President, and need not be ratified by Congress.

C. **INTERBRANCH CHECKS UPON THE EXERCISE OF FEDERAL POWER**

1. **Congressional limits on the executive**

    a. **Impeachment power:** Article II, section 4 provides that the "President, Vice President and all civil officers of the United States shall be removed from office on impeachment for, and conviction of, treason, bribery or other high crimes and misdemeanors." The House of Representatives is entrusted with the sole power to impeach; while the Senate is conferred with the power to try impeachments. A two-thirds vote is required for conviction.

    b. **Legislative veto:** In *Immigration & Naturalization Service v. Chadha,* 103 S. Ct. 2764 (1983), the Supreme Court held that a legislative veto violated the constitutional requirements of the separation of powers, and, therefore, it was unconstitutional.

        (1) **Example:** In relation to the Gramm-Rudman Balanced Budget Act, the court held that a provision therein authorizing the Comptroller General of the United States, a member of the legislative branch, to direct the *execution* of the Act's specific budget reductions (rather than the President), was tantamount to a congressional veto and violated the separation of powers [*Bowsher v. Synar,* 478 U.S.—(1986)].

    c. **Investigatory power:** As indicated earlier, under the Necessary and Proper Clause, Congress has the implied power to make investigations concerning all matters upon which Congress has jurisdiction.

    d. **Delegation to executive:** On numerous occasions Congress has delegated to the President broad authority to effect structural changes in the executive branch (i.e., agencies such as the Department of Health, Education, and Welfare, the Environmental Protection Agency, and the Nuclear Regulatory Commission).

    e. **Appropriations power:** Where Congress by legislative act explicitly directs the President to spend appropriated money, the President has no power to impound (i.e., refuse to spend or delay spending) the authorization of such funds.

2. **The President's power to veto or to withhold action under a statute:** As noted previously, Article 1, section 7 requires that every act of Congress shall be approved and signed by the President before it can become law, or being disapproved, must be passed by a two-thirds vote of each House.

3. **Judicial restraints upon President and Congress:** Under Article III, section 2, the federal judiciary is the ultimate arbiter of cases whose disposition depends upon construction of the Constitution, an act of Congress, or a federal treaty (and cases or controversies arising thereunder).

III. THE RELATION OF THE NATION AND THE STATES IN THE FEDERAL SYSTEM

A. NATURE AND SCOPE OF FEDERAL AND STATE POWERS

1. **In General:** The fundamental principle of federalism is the co-existence of the national government and the state governments. The basic structure of governmental powers as contained in the United States Constitution may be summarized as follows: (1) those powers which are exclusively given to the federal government; (2) those powers reserved to the states under the 10th Amendment; and (3) those powers which can be exercised concurrently by both the federal and state governments.

   a. **Exclusive federal powers:** The Constitution expressly provides that certain federal powers are "exclusive." Article 1, section 10, for example, specifies that "no state shall enter into any treaty, alliance ... or coin money ... or lay any imposts or duties on imports or exports ..."

   b. **Exclusive state powers:** The 10th Amendment provides that "the powers not delegated to the United States by the Constitution, nor prohibited by it to the states, are reserved to the states respectively."

   c. **Concurrent federal and state powers:** The Supremacy Clause, Article VI, section 2, has the effect of invalidating any state laws which conflict with the Constitution, treaties or other laws of the United States. Note, however, that the states are free to regulate areas (of federal power) where Congress has not yet acted. [*Sturges v. Crowinshield,* 17 U.S. 122 (1819) — state bankruptcy law was upheld since no federal bankruptcy law had yet been enacted].

   d. **No general police power:** While each has a general police power, there is no federal police power (the federal government must legislate through one of its enumerated powers, whereas the states may regulate any health, safety, welfare, morals, or aesthetics interests through their respective 10th Amendment police powers. In practice, however the federal government routinely passes criminal statutes and gives law enforcement powers to various agencies.

      (1) **General welfare clause:** Congress has the power to "lay and collect taxes ... to pay the debts ... and provide for the ... general welfare". In other words, Congress can *tax and spend* for the general welfare, but the general welfare clause is not an independent source of federal power.

Constitutional Law

- (2) **Necessary and proper clause:** Congress has the power to "make all laws which shall be necessary and proper for carrying into execution" its enumerated powers. The necessary and proper clause can be used to achieve constitutionally permissible objectives, but it is not an independent source of federal power.

B. INTERGOVERNMENTAL IMMUNITIES

1. **Immunity of federal government**

   a. **In general:** In accordance with *McCulloch v. Maryland, supra,* the federal government and its agencies are immune from state taxation and state regulation. Moreover, the federal government and its agencies are immune from suits by private individuals except where it allows itself to be sued (e.g., the federal Tort Claims Act).

      (1) **Postal Service:** U.S. Postal Service is part of Federal Government rather than separate anti-trust "person" under the Sherman Act and therefore is not subject to antitrust liability. [*U.S. Postal Service v. Flamingo Industries (USA) Ltd.,* 2004].

   b. **Taxation of the federal government by the state:**

      (1) **Tax on independent contractors:** Although states may not tax the federal government as an entity, states may nevertheless collect a nondiscriminatory tax on persons who deal or contract with the federal government. [*James v. Dravo Contracting Co.,* 302 U.S. 134 (1937) — a nondiscriminatory gross receipts tax applied to a contractor performing work for the federal government upheld].

      (2) **State sales tax:** In *Alabama v. King & Boozer,* 314 U.S. 1 (1941) a state sales tax on goods purchased by a contractor who had a "cost-plus" contract with the federal government was upheld. Note, however, that such sales taxes will be invalidated if the legal incidence of the tax falls on the United States itself.

      (3) **State property tax:** A state property tax was upheld as applied to a building owned by the United States, but used by a contractor. [*Detroit v. Murray Corp.,* 355 U.S. 489 (1958)].

      (4) **State income tax:** A state income tax as applied to the salaries of federal employees domiciled within the state held valid. [*Graves v. O'Keefe,* 306 U.S. 466 (1939)].

   c. **Regulation of the federal government by the state:** As a general rule, ***the Supremacy Clause impliedly prevents the states from regulating the activities of agents or instrumentalities of the federal government which interfere with the government's ability to carry out its federal functions.*** [*Johnson v. Maryland,* 254 U.S. 51 (1920)] — state cannot require a U.S. postal employee to obtain a state driver's license to deliver the mail]; nor can a state require a federal contractor to obtain a state license to construct facilities at an Air Force base located within the state [*Miller Inc. v. Arkansas,* 352 U.S. 187 (1956)].

      (1) **State regulation of federal lands:** Under Article IV, section 3, clause 2, ***Congress has the power "to dispose of and make all needful rules and regulations***

respecting the territory or other property belonging to the United States." Thus, federal lands (e.g., military bases, Indian reservations, F.B.I. offices) are subject to the authority of the federal government, except to the extent that Congress has ceded jurisdiction to the state.

2. **Immunity of state government**

   a. **Immunity against suits:**

      (1) **Suits by the federal government:** The federal government or one of its agencies (or instrumentalities) may sue a state without its consent. In which case, the United States Supreme Court has original and concurrent jurisdiction. In practice, the USSC has rarely interpreted this amendment to give positive authority to states. Accordingly students are much more likely to be tested on the explicit limitation set forth below.

      (2) **Suits by a sister state:** A state may be sued by a sister state without its consent. In which case, the United States Supreme Court has original and exclusive jurisdiction.

      (3) **Suits by a private citizen:** As a general rule, the 11th Amendment prohibits citizens of one state to sue another state in federal court. This rule has been extended to prohibit suits by a citizen of a state against his (or her) own state. **Exceptions:** (1) a state may be sued if it consents to the suit; or (2) where a state officer has abused his power by acting beyond the scope of his authority [*Ex parte Young, supra*].

   b. **Immunity against federal regulation:** In *National League of Cities v. Usery*, 426 U.S. 833 (1976) the Court attempted to set affirmative limits on the Commerce power in situations where federal regulation directly impaired a state's ability to perform integral operations that were traditional governmental functions — federal labor law held inapplicable to regulation of minimum wages and hours of state employees. The basis of state sovereignty in *Usery* was the 10th Amendment reserved powers. In 1985 *Usery* was overruled by *Garcia v. San Antonio Metropolitan Transit Authority*, 469 U.S. 528 (1985) — municipal ownership and operation of a mass transit system held subject to federal regulation. *Garcia* stated that "the attempt to draw boundaries of state regulatory immunity in terms of 'traditional governmental functions' is not only unworkable but inconsistent with established principles of federalism." *Note:* Federal labor law held applicable under the Commerce Clause to state-owned railroad engaged in interstate commerce [*United Transportation Union v. Long Island Railroad Co.*, 455 U.S. 678 (1982)].

   c. **Immunity against federal taxation:** Under the modern view, ***a state now enjoys immunity from federal taxation if the tax is applied to either (1) unique state activities or (2) to essential governmental functions.*** Note, however, that where a state engages in a proprietary business (i.e., one which is similar in nature to a business operated by a private individual) then the state may be taxed to the same extent as the private citizen.

Constitutional Law

C. THE AUTHORITY RESERVED TO THE STATES

1. **Source of power:** The 10th Amendment provides that the "powers not delegated to the United States by the Constitution, nor prohibited by it to the states, are reserved to the states respectively, or to the people."

   a. **Constitutional limitations:** Article 1, section 10 specifically prohibits any state from: (1) making treaties with other nations; (2) coining money; (3) passing a bill of attainder; (4) enacting an *ex post facto* law; (5) impairing the obligation of contracts; (6) laying any duty on imports or exports, except where it is necessary for executing its inspection laws; (7) engaging in war; or (8) maintaining a peacetime army.

2. **State regulation of interstate commerce:** Obviously, the Commerce Clause gives Congress the power to regulate interstate commerce. Where Congress, however, has not enacted legislation, the states are free to regulate local transactions affecting interstate commerce subject to certain limitations. This doctrine is generally known as the Dormant Commerce Clause, or the negative implications doctrine. State regulation must be 1) non-discriminatory and 2) impose no undue burden on interstate commerce, using a balancing test.

   a. **Basic test:** In the absence of federal regulation, states may regulate interstate commerce subject to the following set of judicially imposed limitations:

   (1) **Discrimination:** If the purpose or effect of the regulation is to discriminate against commerce from another state (i.e., where the state law is designed to protect local economic interests at the expense of out-of-state competitors) it will be invalid [*Dean Milk Co. v. City of Madison,* 340 U.S. 349 (1951) — state law discriminated against out-of-state suppliers by requiring all milk sold in the city to be processed and bottled locally]; and in *City of Philadelphia v. New Jersey,* 437 U.S. 617 (1978) a New Jersey statute prohibiting the importation of out-of-state rubbish was held unconstitutional because it discriminated in favor of local trash collectors. Furthermore, a city or county may not protect its own local economic interests by discriminating against **both** out-of-state and out-of-town producers [*Fort Gratiot Sanitary Landfill v. Michigan Department of Natural Resources*, 504 U.S. 353 (1992) — state law preventing each county from accepting solid waste generated from outside the county, absent express consent, held impermissible discrimination against interstate commerce].

   Market participant exception: *When a state acts as a market participant, not as a market regulator, it is not prohibited from buying only from or selling only to local businesses* [*Reeves v. Stake,* 447 U.S. 429 (1980)]; or as a market participant a state may discriminate against nonresidents by hiring local residents to work on public construction projects [*White v. Massachusetts Council of Construction Employers,* 103 S. Ct. 1042 (1983)].

   (2) **Nature of activity regulated:** If the matter regulated requires uniform national regulation, then no state regulation is permissible. [*Cooley v. Board of Wardens,* 53 U.S. 299 (1851)].

   (3) **Balance of interests test:** Here, the Court will balance the objective and purpose of the state law against the burden on interstate commerce. If the

benefits of the state law outweigh the burden on interstate commerce, then the regulation will generally be upheld.

b. **Factors determining constitutionality of state regulation:**

(1) **Police power:** Traditionally, *it is within the state's police power to enact legislation for the protection of the health, safety and welfare of its citizens.* A Detroit smoke abatement ordinance which affected ships traveling in interstate commerce was upheld as a valid health measure. [*Huron Portland Cement Co. v. City of Detroit,* 352 U.S. 440 (1960)].

(2) **Burden cannot outweigh state interest:** If a state regulation furthers no ostensible benefit and imposes a substantial burden on interstate commerce, it will likely be held unconstitutional. A state law limiting the length of trucks traveling on Wisconsin highways was held unconstitutional because the regulation unduly burdened interstate trucking, and the state failed to demonstrate any significant safety benefit [*Raymond Motor Transportation, Inc. v. Rice,* 434 U.S. 429 (1978)]; also in *Bibb v. Navajo Freight Lines, Inc.,* 359 U.S. 520 (1959) an Illinois statute requiring all trucks to be equipped with a new type of contour mudguards (instead of the flat mudguards permitted in all other states) was declared unconstitutional because it placed an unreasonable burden on interstate carriers; and an Arizona statute limiting the length of trains traveling through the state was similarly invalidated because of the substantial burden the law placed on interstate railroads. [*Southern Pacific Co. v. Arizona,* 325 U.S. 761 (1945)].

(3) **Public health measures:** Generally, public health measures (e.g., quarantine and inspection laws) are upheld as long as they do not discriminate against or unduly burden interstate commerce. [*Hannibal & St. Joseph Railroad v. Husen,* 95 U.S. 465 (1877)].

D. **RESERVED STATE POWER IN TAXATION**

1. **General Principles:** As a general rule, *state taxation of interstate commerce is permissible as long as the tax does not discriminate against or unduly burden interstate commerce.* If the taxing measure discriminates against or imposes an impermissible burden on interstate commerce, it will be invalidated under the Commerce Clause. In determining the validity of a state tax affecting interstate commerce, the Court will generally consider the following four factors:

a. **Nexus requirement:** There must be a *"substantial nexus"* between the activity taxed and the taxing state. In other words, the taxpayer must have "sufficient contacts" or presence within the taxing state. [*Braniff Airways v. Nebraska Board of Equalization,* 347 U.S. 590 (1954) — airline company, although it owned no property in state, had a nexus because it made eighteen regularly scheduled flights each day from a rented depot]. A "substantial nexus" is more than "minimum contacts" under the Due Process Clause. [*Quill Corp v. North Dakota,* 504 U.S. 298 (1992) — where an interstate seller solicits within a state by mail and ships orders either by mail or common carrier, minimum contacts are satisfied, but not the substantial nexus which is required by the Commerce Clause].

b. **Apportionment:** The tax must be *"fairly apportioned."* In *Norfolk & Western Railway v. Missouri Tax Commission,* 390 U.S. 317 (1968), the Court invalidated an apportionment based upon track mileage within the state, as compared to total track mileage, which resulted in a disproportionate tax because the railroad had an unusually high amount of track in taxing state. Note that the taxpayer has the burden to prove unfair apportionment.

c. **Discrimination:** The tax must not *"discriminate"* against interstate commerce. A tax favoring local commerce over interstate commerce will be invalidated under the Commerce Clause unless authorized by Congress. [*Prudential Insurance Co. v. Benjamin,* 328 U.S. 408 (1946) — pursuant to its commerce power, Congress may validate a state tax that discriminates against interstate commerce].

   (1) **Privileges and immunities clause:** Article IV, section 2 prohibits state taxes that discriminate against nonresidents [*Austin v. New Hampshire,* 420 U.S. 656 (1975) — invalidated income tax on nonresidents, that exempted local residents, as discriminatory and violative of privileges and immunities].

d. **Relationship to services rendered:** The tax must be *"fairly related to the services provided"* by the taxing state. [See *Complete Auto Transit, Inc. v. Brady,* 430 U.S. 274 (1977)].

2. **Various types of state taxes:**

   a. **Ad valorem property taxes:** States are not permitted to levy an *ad valorem* tax on "goods" which happen to be in the taxing state on the tax day, if those goods are still in the course of transit. [*Standard Oil Co. v. Peck,* 342 (1952)]. However, the validity of such *ad valorem* property taxes as applied to "instrumentalities of commerce" (e.g., airplanes or railroad cars) depends upon (1) whether there is a taxable situs (or nexus) within the state and (2) whether the tax is fairly apportioned to the amount of time the equipment is in the state.

   b. **Sales and use taxes:** A sales tax is a tax upon the transfer of title of goods consummated within the state. On the other hand, a use tax is a tax upon the use of goods within the state which were purchased outside the state.

      (1) **Sales tax:** If the sale is consummated within the state (even though the buyer takes the goods outside the state), such a tax is valid. If, however, the sale is made to a buyer outside the state (i.e., if the seller delivers the goods to an out-of-state buyer), then the sales tax is invalid.

      (2) **Use tax:** The ability of a state to collect such a tax usually depends upon whether the interstate seller (who receives goods from outside the state) has a sufficient nexus within the taxing state. Where the seller maintains offices within the taxing state (or even sends salesmen into the state as employees or independent contractors), there is a sufficient nexus even though the use tax was imposed on interstate mail order sales. [*National Geographic Society v. California Board of Equalization,* 430 U.S. 551 (1977)]. In contrast, if no sales office is maintained in the state, and all selling is done by mail, then there is

not a sufficient nexus with the taxing state to justify the collection of a use tax. [*National Bellas Hess, Inc. v. Department of Revenue,* 386 U.S. 753 (1967)].

    c. **"Doing Business" taxes:** These types of taxes (variously referred to as "privilege," "occupation," "franchise," "license," "gross receipts" or "net income" taxes) can be measured by either a flat annual fee or by a graduated rate based in proportion to the amount of revenue derived from the taxing state. As a general rule, such taxes must "relate to the benefits" conferred by the taxing state upon the interstate business. [*Evansville-Vanderburgh Airport Authority v. Delta Airlines,* 405 U.S. 707 (1972) — a fee applied to airport users held constitutional because it bore a reasonable relationship to use of the facilities by the passengers].

    d. **Net income taxes:** A state has the right to apply a net income tax upon an interstate company (or nonresident) engaged in business in the taxing state. Again, it is necessary that the tax be fairly apportioned and nondiscriminatory. [*Northwestern States Portland Cement Co. v. Minnesota,* 358 U.S. 450 (1959) — net income tax levied on interstate company engaged in business within taxing state upheld].

    e. **Flat license fee on "drummers":** Generally, a flat license fee levied upon "drummers" (or solicitors), who solicit local orders to be filled from goods shipped interstate, is unconstitutional. [*Nippert v. Richmond,* 327 U.S. 416 (1946)].

    f. **License tax on "peddlers":** Conversely, a state may levy a license tax on a "peddler" (or itinerant salesman) who actually sells and delivers goods within the state. As long as such taxes are applied equally to local businessmen, they will be upheld as nondiscriminatory.

E. NATIONAL POWER TO OVERRIDE STATE AUTHORITY

1. **Supremacy clause:** Pursuant to Article VI, section 2, the Supremacy Clause provides that the Constitution, treaties and laws of the United States are "the supreme law of the land." In general, *a federal law will supersede any state law which is in direct conflict.* Furthermore, Congress can preempt any state law in an area where the federal intent is to occupy the field.

    a. **Similarity between state and federal statutes:** Where Congress does not intend to occupy the field completely, then the states may enact similar legislation. [*Colorado Anti-Discrimination Commission v. Continental Air Lines, Inc.,* 372 U.S. 714 (1963)—a state statute prohibiting racial discrimination held valid even though there was an identical federal law]; also in [*Huron Portland Cement Co. v. Detroit supra,* a municipal smoke abatement statute was held valid although it imposed stricter standards than the federal regulation].

    b. **Greater state protection permitted:** *Where Congress has legislated merely to establish certain minimum standards (such as in the areas of health and safety requirements pertaining to food and drugs, or regulation of roads and highways), then the states are free to enact more stringent standards than those mandated by federal law.*

Constitutional Law

IV. PROTECTION OF INDIVIDUAL RIGHTS

A. **"STATE ACTION" AND THE ROLE OF THE FEDERAL JUDICIARY**

1. **14th Amendment:** In accordance with the 14th Amendment, "no state shall ... abridge the privileges or immunities of citizens of the United States; nor deprive any person of life, liberty or property without due process of the law; nor deny to any person within its jurisdiction the equal protection of the laws."

    a. **Application:** By its terms, the 14th Amendment applies to actions taken by the state. It does not restrict purely private action. [*Shelley v. Kraemer*, 334 U.S. 1 (1948) — the Court held that the 14th Amendment does not apply to private action, however discriminatory or wrongful].

    b. **13th Amendment:** The 13th Amendment prohibits any badge or incident of slavery or involuntary servitude. The 13th Amendment can be used to proscribe purely private acts of racial discrimination without the requirement of state action. For example, Congress, through its enabling clause (i.e. "by appropriate legislation"), can prohibit a private employer from discriminating in hiring practices on the basis of race. *Patterson v. McLean Credit Union*, 491 U.S. 164 (1989).

2. **State Action Requirement:** The Constitution prohibits only governmental conduct which infringes upon protected individual rights. "State Action" is a threshold requirement of governmental conduct which must be satisfied before private acts may be punished under the 14th and 15th Amendments. State action can be found in the actions of private individuals under either of two theories: 1) "public function—where a private entity is carrying on activities traditionally and exclusively performed by the state; or 2) significant state involvement. Examples of state action:

    a. **Where the private activity performs an exclusive public function:**

        (1) **Company towns:** In *Marsh v. Alabama,* 326 U.S. 501 (1946), a private company owned an entire town and posted signs prohibiting peddlers. A member of the Jehovah's Witnesses was arrested and convicted of violating a state trespass law which made it a crime "to enter or remain on the premises of another." The Supreme Court reversed the trespass conviction because the town's streets, although privately owned, were really the equivalent of city streets. The Court held that the company's actions were in violation of the 1st and 14th Amendments because neither a state nor a private owner can totally ban the expression of free speech. On the contrary, in *Hudgens v. NLRB,* 424 U.S. 507 (1976), the Court ruled that the "company town" rationale did not apply to a privately owned shopping center.

        (2) **Elections:** In *Smith v. Allwright,* 321 U.S. 649 (1944), the Court held that since elections were exclusively public functions, a political party could not racially discriminate against blacks by excluding them from voting in a primary election.

    b. **State involvement:** Where there is ***"significant state involvement"*** in private discrimination, then the 14th Amendment may be applicable. In *Burton v. Wilmington Parking Authority,* 365 U.S. 715 (1961) a restaurant owner, whose business was

located in a building owned by the city, was prohibited from discriminating against racial minorities ("symbiotic relationship"); also in *Shelley v. Kraemer, supra,* state court enforcement of restrictive covenants (prohibiting sale of property to Blacks) was held to constitute sufficient state involvement to trigger "state action."

(1) **No significant state involvement:** The mere closing of a municipal swimming pool did not constitute "state action" even though nearby private facilities were discriminating. [*Palmer v. Thompson,* 403 U.S. 217 (1971)]; likewise in *Moose Lodge No. 107 v. Irvis,* 407 U.S. 163 (1972) granting a liquor license to a private club which racially discriminated against Blacks did not significantly involve the state so as to constitute "state action;" termination of service to a customer without notice or a hearing by a utility company under heavy state regulation was found not to constitute "state action" [*Jackson v. Metropolitan Edison*, 419 U.S. 345 (1974)].

V. DUE PROCESS AND THE INCORPORATION OF PORTIONS OF THE BILL OF RIGHTS

A. **INCORPORATION OF THE BILL OF RIGHTS:** As originally enacted, the Bill of Rights (i.e., the first ten amendments to the U.S. Constitution) were applicable only to the federal government, not to the states. In 1868, the 14th Amendment was adopted, which provided: "Nor shall any state make or enforce any law which shall abridge the privileges or immunities of citizens of the United States; nor shall any state deprive any person of life, liberty, or property without due process of law; nor deny to any person within its jurisdiction the equal protection of the laws."

1. **14th Amendment Privileges and Immunities Clause:** A few years after the 14th Amendment was adopted, the Court held that the fundamental rights set forth in the Bill of Rights were *not* privileges and immunities of national citizenship. [*Slaughterhouse Cases,* 83 U.S. (16 Wall.) 36 (1873) — this decision effectively rendered the 14th Amendment Privileges and Immunities Clause powerless in protecting individual rights from state abridgment]. In 1999, the Court indicated that the 14th Amendment Privileges and Immunities Clause (along with the fundamental right to travel) could possibly serve as a justification to challenge a state's denial to new residents of full unemployment benefits until a specified waiting period has been satisfied.

   a. **New revival:** In *Saenz v. Roe*, 119 S. Ct. 1518 (1999), the Court struck down a California law that limited the payment of welfare benefits for first-year residents to the amount they would have received from the former state. The law violated the right to travel freely from state to state which, the Court said, is protected by the 14th Amendment Privileges and Immunities Clause as a right of national citizenship.

2. **14th Amendment Due Process Clause:** Although the Court in *Adamson v. California,* 332 U.S. 46 (1947) rejected the notion that the Due Process Clause incorporated *all* of the Bill of Rights, under the doctrine of selective incorporation the following specific provisions are now applicable to the states:

   a. The 1st Amendment freedom of speech, freedom of press, the right to assemble, the right to petition the government, the free exercise of religion, and the prohibition against the establishment of religion.

b. The 4th Amendment provisions guaranteeing the right to be free from unreasonable searches and seizures. [*Ker v. California*, 374 U.S. 23 (1963)].

c. The 5th Amendment protection against double jeopardy [*Benton v. Maryland*, 395 U.S. 784 (1969)], privilege against self-incrimination [*Malloy v. Hogan*, 378 U.S. 1 (1964)], and requirement of just compensation when private property is taken for public use.

d. The 6th Amendment rights guaranteeing the accused in criminal prosecutions a speedy and public trial [*Klopfer v. North Carolina*, 386 U.S. 213 (1967)], the right to confront and cross-examine witnesses [*Pointer v. Texas*, 380 U.S. 400 (1965)], the right to counsel [*Gideon v. Wainwright*, 372 U.S. 335 (1963)], the right to a jury trial and the right to a jury trial in criminal cases [*Duncan v. Louisiana*, 391 U.S. 145 (1968)].

e. The 8th Amendment prohibition against cruel and unusual punishment.

f. Most of the Bill of Rights safeguards have been "selectively incorporated" to the states under the Due Process Clause of the 14th Amendment. Major guarantees *not* incorporated include the 5th Amendment right to a grand jury in criminal cases, and the 7th Amendment right to a jury trial in civil cases.

3. **Scope of the Due Process Clause:**

    a. **Person:** The Due Process (and Equal Protection) Clause(s) of the 14th Amendment protects the rights of "persons" (and not merely "citizens").

    b. **Corporation:** A corporation is considered a "person" for purposes of due process and equal protection. Note, however, that a corporation is *not* entitled to the privilege against self-incrimination.

    c. **Aliens:** Aliens are considered "persons" for purposes of due process and equal protection.

4. **Procedural due process:** Both the 5th and 14th Amendments protect against ***the deprivation of "life, liberty or property without the due process of the law."*** Where there is a deprivation of one's "life", "liberty" or "property" interests, then the individual is entitled to the procedural safeguards (i.e., some form of *notice* and *hearing*).

    a. **Deprivation of liberty:**

        (1) **Freedom from bodily restraints:** State must grant parolee evidentiary hearing when it revokes parole (or probation). [*Morrissey v. Brewer*, 408 U.S. 471 (1972)].

        (2) **Defamation by government:** Liberty found in the effect of a state law which authorized the police to post the names of "excessive drinkers" in liquor stores. [*Wisconsin v. Constantineau*, 400 U.S. 433 (1971)].

        (3) **Physical punishment:** Corporal punishment of pupils in a school did invade a liberty interest. [*Ingraham v. Wright*, 430 U.S. 651 (1977)].

(4) **Commitment to a mental institution:** An adversary hearing must be provided adults before commitment to a mental institution against their will. Minor children have a liberty interest in not being confined unnecessarily for medical treatment. In this case, a screening by a neutral factfinder is required. [*Parham v. J.R.*, 442 U.S. 584 (1979)].

(5) **Injury to reputation:** Injury to one's good reputation is not a deprivation of a liberty interest. [*Paul v. Davis*, 424 U.S. 693 (1976)].

(6) **Competency to stand trial:** The Federal Government may administer antipsychotic drugs against the Defendant's will in order to render him or her competent to stand trial, so long as the treatment is medically appropriate, without substantial side effects, and is necessary to **significantly further important governmental** trial related interests. [*Sell v. United States*, 2004].

b. **Property interests:**

(1) **Public education:** There is a constitutionally protected property interest in the entitlement to continued attendance at a public school. [*Goss v. Lopez*, 419 U.S. 565 (1975) — a significant suspension for disciplinary reasons (e.g., 10 day duration) cannot be imposed without at least a minimum form of hearing]. On the other hand, no prior evidentiary hearing is required when a student is dismissed for academic reasons. [*Board of Curators v. Horowitz*, 435 U.S. 78 (1978)].

(2) **Continued welfare benefits:** A property interest has been found in the right to continued welfare benefits. [*Goldberg v. Kelly*, 397 U.S. 254 (1970) — where the applicant met statutory criteria].

(3) **Retention of driver's license:** A state may not revoke a driver's license without a hearing. [*Bell v. Burson*, 402 U.S. 535 (1971)].

(4) **Public employment:** There is a property interest if the employment is under a tenure system, or there is a clear understanding, either express or implied that the employee can be terminated only for "cause." [*Perry v. Sindermann*, 408 U.S. 593 (1972)].

Compare: In *Bishop v. Wood*, 426 U.S. 341 (1976), however, the Court held that there was *no* property interest where a police officer held his position "at the will of" the public employer. Also, there is *no* property interest when a state refuses to renew a fixed-term contract. [*Board of Regents v. Roth*, 408 U.S. 564 (1972)].

(5) **Prejudgment garnishment:** Prejudgment attachment or garnishment of wages, without notice or hearing, violates procedural due process. [*Sniadach v. Family Finance Corp.*, 395 U.S. 337 (1969)].

Compare: Note, however, that procedural due process is *not* required where there is no "state action". [*Flagg Brothers v. Brooks*, 436 U.S. 149 (1978) — lien creditor privately sells goods to foreclose a warehouseman's lien].

(6) **Distinguish:** A due process property interest does not arise when an individual is first applying for employment; however, if the person has already been getting benefits, he has a property interest in continuing the receipt of those benefits.

(7) **Forfeiture of property:** Due process is satisfied where the government sends a certified letter to an inmate's prison to notify the inmate that property seized will be forfeited, because such an action is "reasonably calculated, under the circumstances, to apprise interested parties of the pendency of the action and afford them an opportunity to present their objections." Actual notice is not required. *Dusenbery v. United States*, 122 S. Ct. 694 (2002).

(8) **Business licensing:** First Amendment and due process requires that licensing scheme for adult businesses provide applicants challenging denial of license with *"prompt judicial determination"* of constitutionality of denial, as opposed to mere prompt access to judicial review [*Littleton, Colo. v. Z.J. Gifts*, 2004].

c. **Type of process required:** Once it is determined that there is a sufficient deprivation of life, liberty or property, the next step is to decide what process is required. In order to determine what procedural safeguards are necessary, the Court looks to the following factors as set forth in *Mathews v. Eldridge*, 424 U.S. 319 (1976).

(1) The private interest that will be affected by the official action.

(2) The risk of an erroneous deprivation of such interest through the procedures used.

(3) The magnitude of the government's interest, including the fiscal and administrative cost of a hearing.

Example: In *Curators v. Horowitz, supra,* the Court held that a full hearing was not required for the dismissal of a medical student from a state medical school for academic deficiency because the decision was an evaluative one, made by faculty officers and outside practitioners.

Example: In *Ingraham v. Wright, supra,* the Court held that it was not necessary for a public school to give a student a hearing *before* imposing corporal punishment.

Example: In *Mackey v. Montrym,* 443 U.S. 1 (1979) the Court ruled that a temporary suspension of a driver's license without a hearing, where the driver refused to take a breathalyzer test, was valid because he had a right to an immediate hearing following the suspension.

Compare: Note, however, that a prior hearing was required in *Morrissey v. Brewer, supra,* before parole could be revoked; and a prior hearing was required in *Goldberg v. Kelly, supra,* before welfare benefits could be terminated.

d. **Irrebuttable presumptions:** In recent cases, the Supreme Court has held that it is a violation of procedural due process for a tribunal to foreclose issues by conclusively presuming them to be true.

   (1) **Civil proceedings:** In *Cleveland Board of Education v. LaFleur,* 414 U.S. 632 (1974), the Court held that a statutory presumption that a pregnant school teacher was physically incapable of performing her duties was unconstitutional; also, in *Stanley v. Illinois,* 405 U.S. 645 (1972) a state law requiring children of unwed fathers to become wards of the court was invalidated because its statutory effect was to create a conclusive presumption that unwed fathers were unfit parents.

   (2) **Criminal cases:** A statutory presumption that possession of marijuana was conclusive proof that the drug had been imported was invalidated in *Leary v. United States* (1969) — because marijuana is frequently grown in this country as well as abroad.

5. **Substantive due process**

   a. **Economic regulation:** In the past, the doctrine of substantive due process was frequently used to invalidate state laws that arbitrarily and unreasonably regulated economic activity. Where a state statute is reasonable, on the other hand, it is within the state's police power to regulate economic activity. [*Lemieux v. Young,* 211 U.S. 489 (1909) — upholding validity of "blue sky" laws regulating the sales of stocks and securities]. Since the New Deal, the USSC has not struck down an economic regulation on substantive due process grounds. Such an economic regulation will be upheld if it is rationally related to a legitimate government interest.

   b. **Fundamental rights:** *Modernly, substantive due process applies to regulations affecting fundamental rights. Strict scrutiny review applies to laws which burden the exercise of fundamental rights — 1) the right to vote; 2) the right to travel; 3) the right to privacy; and 4) all 1st Amendment rights (since they are deemed "fundamental").* The following areas represent some of the categories which fall under the penumbra of privacy:

   (1) **Contraceptives:** In *Griswold v. Connecticut,* 381 U.S. 479 (1965), the Court invalidated a state law prohibiting the use of contraceptive devices (thus recognizing a right of marital privacy); also, in *Eisenstadt v. Baird,* 405 U.S. 438 (1972), the Court expanded the *Griswold* decision and held that the right to use contraceptives belonged to single as well as married persons; and, similarly, in *Carey v. Population Services International,* 431 U.S. 678 (1977), the Court invalidated a state law that prohibited the sale of contraceptives to adults except through a licensed pharmacist.

   (2) **Abortion:** *Planned Parenthood of Southeastern Pennsylvania v. Casey,* 505 U.S. 833 (1992) largely reshaped the law of abortion which stood for so many years under *Roe v. Wade,* 410 U.S. 113 (1973). The *Casey* holding rejected the trimester approach of *Roe* and instead adopted an "undue burden" standard. An undue burden exists where the purpose or effect of a state law places

Constitutional Law

substantial obstacles in the way of a woman's right of access to seek an abortion before the fetus attains viability (*i.e.* viability occurs in the last trimester). A woman has a protected privacy interest in choosing to have an abortion before viability. Subsequent to viability, the Court reaffirmed *Roe* in concluding that the "State may regulate, and even proscribe abortion except where it is necessary for the preservation of the life or health of the mother." Whereas the state has a countervailing interest in protecting potential life, it has no right to ban all pre-viability abortions. Rather than apply strict scrutiny, the Court chose to apply the "undue burden" test.

(a) **Consent requirements:** Neither spousal notification nor spousal consent are required before a woman may obtain an abortion. [*Planned Parenthood of Missouri v. Danforth*, 428 U.S. 52 (1976)]. However, parental consent may be required before an unemancipated woman under the age of 18 obtains an abortion, or the state may allow a "judicial bypass" whereby a minor may obtain an abortion with the consent of a judge. [*Hodgson v. Minnesota*, 497 U.S. 417 (1990)].

(b) **Public funding:** There is no constitutional right for indigent women to obtain government funding to finance abortions. [*Maher v. Roe*, 432 U.S. 464 (1977)]. Furthermore, a state may prohibit all use of public facilities and publicly-employed staff in performing abortions. [*Webster v. Reproductive Health Services*, 492 U.S. 490 (1989)].

(c) **Late-term abortion:** Where a Nebraska statute prohibited "deliberately and intentionally delivering into the vagina a living unborn child, or a substantial portion thereof, for the purpose of performing a procedure that the person performing such procedure knows will kill the unborn child and does kill the unborn child," such a statute was unconstitutional because it did not provide an exception for the health of the mother and forbade a very common dilation and evacuation procedure used in most second-trimester abortions as well as a more infrequently used one. [*Stenberg v. Carhart*, 120 S. Ct. 2597 (2000)].

(3) **Family relations:** *A fundamental right exists for related persons to live together*. [*Moore v. City of East Cleveland*, 431 U.S. 494 (1977)* — a zoning ordinance which prohibited members of the extended family from living in a single household violated strict scrutiny]. **This fundamental right does not apply to unrelated persons** [*Belle Terre v. Borass*, 416 U.S. 1 (1974)], but does extend to homosexuals. [*Bowers v. Hardwick*, 478 U.S. 186 (1986), was overruled by *Lawrence v. Texas*, in which the Court held that a statute making it a crime for a person to engage "in deviate sexual intercourse with another individual of the same sex" furthered no legitimate state interest that could justify its intrusion into private sexual conduct of consenting adults. The Court stated that such a statute violated a liberty interest protected by 14th Amendment's due process clause. 123 S. Ct. 2472 (2003)]; However, parents may limit the visitation of non-parents, even that of grandparents; in the visitation context, the right to family relations does not extend beyond the immediate family. [*Troxel v. Granville*, 120 S. Ct. 2054 (2000)].

(4) **Private education:** Parents have a right to privately educate their children outside the public school system. [*Pierce v. Society of Sisters*, 268 U.S. 510 (1925)].

(5) **Marriage:** *The right to marry is deemed fundamental. Any substantial interference with that right must be necessary to further a compelling interest.* [*Zablocki v. Redhail*, 434 U.S. 374 (1978)].

(6) **Obscene material:** The right to possess obscene material in the privacy of one's home is protected under the holding in *Stanley v. Georgia*, 394 U.S. 557 (1969), but good luck in getting it there: The government can severely restrict the sale, purchase, receipt, transport, and distribution of obscene materials both in stores and through the mail. Furthermore, the state can criminalize even the private possession of child pornography. [*Osborne v. Ohio*, 495 U.S. 103 (1990)].

(7) **The right to die:** The right of a terminally ill or comatose person to choose to die is not presently a fundamental right. Nevertheless, it is an established due process "liberty" interest that a person may not be forced to undergo unwanted medical procedures, such as life- support. [*Cruzan v. Missouri Department of Health*, 497 U.S. 261 (1990)]. However, the state has a countervailing interest in preserving life. A terminally ill patient has no "liberty" interest in committing suicide. See *Vacco v. Quill*, 117 S. Ct. 2293 (1997) — where assisted suicide is illegal but refusal of medical treatment artificially to prolong life is legal, no constitutional violation; *Washington v. Glucksberg*, 117 S. Ct. 2258 (1997) — imposition of criminal liability on anyone who helps another to commit suicide constitutional under the Fourteenth Amendment.

Exam tip: In the area of fundamental right of privacy, the Court is traditionally slow to act and hesitant to expand the scope of protected privacy rights.

c. **Right to travel:** The interstate Privileges and Immunities Clause, Article IV, section 2, and the Commerce Clause mutually enforce the right of every citizen to travel freely from state to state [*Griffin v. Breckenridge,* 403 U.S. 88 (1971)]. The right of individuals to move freely from state to state is fundamental. Durational residency requirements for dispensing government benefits are subject to strict scrutiny. The following are examples: a 1-year waiting period before receiving welfare benefits or state-subsidized medical care is invalid; reasonable residency requirements are valid for obtaining a divorce as well as for obtaining reduced tuition at state universities.

(1) **Travel abroad:** The right to international travel is not absolute and may be subject to certain restrictions (e.g., passport requirement); and Congress may authorize the President to restrict travel to certain countries or danger areas. [*Zemel v. Rusk,* 381 U.S. 1 (1965) — *Cuban* passport denied].

d. **Right to vote:** The fundamental right of U.S. citizens over age 18 to vote extends to all federal, state, and local elections, as well as to primaries. Strict scrutiny review is used to adjudicate restrictions on the right to vote. However, reasonable restrictions on age, residency (*e.g.* 30 days is valid), or payment of filing fees require only minimum rational basis scrutiny.

Constitutional Law

(1) Basic principles:

(a) A rule of *"one-person, one-vote"* is generally followed. Whenever the government attempts to establish a new apportionment or redistricting scheme, fairly exact mathematical equality between districts is required so as not to dilute the fundamental right to vote.

(b) There must be equality in the *distribution* of the right to vote.

Examples:

i. Imposition of a poll tax as a prerequisite to vote violates equal protection and is unconstitutional. [*Harper v. Virginia Board of Elections*, 383 U.S. 663 (1966)].

ii. Limiting voting for school board elections to parents of school children and/or property owners is unconstitutional [*Kramer v. Union Free School District*, 345 U.S. 662 (1969)].

iii. Exception: Voting can be limited only to landowners for a special purpose "water-storage district" (which cannot enact laws or perform government functions. [*Ball v. James*, 451 U.S. 355 (1981)].

6. **"Takings" Clause:** The 5th Amendment provides that private property shall not be taken for public use *without just compensation*. This prohibition applies to the states as well through the 14th Amendment. Property can be taken by various methods: eminent domain; inverse condemnation; or police power (whereby no compensation need be paid). Where client trust accounts draw interest, that interest is the client's private property for the purposes of the Fifth Amendment Takings' Clause and cannot be applied to state programs for indigents where actual interest would be generated. [*Phillips v. Washington Legal Foundation*, 118 S. Ct. 1925 (1998); *Brown v. Legal Foundation of Washington*, 123 S. Ct. 1406 (2003)].

a. **Taking v. Regulation:** Where the state validly regulates for health, safety, or welfare purposes under its police power, then the government action merely amounts to a regulation without payment of compensation. A taking generally results where there is an actual appropriation, destruction, or permanent physical invasion of one's property. [*Loretto v. Teleprompter Manhattan CATV Corp.*, 455 U.S. 904 (1982) — ordinance requiring landlords to install cable television wires in all rental units (physical occupation)].

b. **Land use restrictions:** *In order not to constitute a taking, a land use regulation must substantially advance a legitimate state interest and not deny the owner all reasonable economically viable use of his land.* [*Lucas v. South Carolina Coastal Council*, 505 U.S. 1003 (1992) — state zoning law was passed after the owner purchased the property, and held to constitute a taking because the law precluded him from erecting any permanent structure on his land]. To analyze regulations which merely decrease economic value, the Court uses a balancing test to determine if there is a taking.

(1) **Temporary restriction:** When looking at whether a taking has occurred, a court will look at both dimensions of a property interest (metes and bounds and

term of years). A temporary restriction causing a diminution in value (such as a 32 month moratorium on development in an area) is not a taking of the parcel as a whole, because the property will recover value when the prohibition is lifted, and thus a regulation will not "permanently deprive" the owner of "all economic beneficial uses" of his land. *Tahoe-Sierra Preservation Council, Inc. v. Tahoe Regional Planning Agency*, 122 S. Ct. 1465 (2002).

VI. EQUAL PROTECTION OF THE LAWS

A. CONSTITUTIONAL BASIS

1. **Source:** The 14th Amendment provides that "no state shall ... deny to any person within its jurisdiction the equal protection of the laws."

2. **Relationship between Substantive Due Process and Equal Protection:** The guarantee of substantive due process assures that a law will be fair and reasonable, not arbitrary. Equal protection review is triggered where persons similarly situated are treated differently.

    a. **Substantive due process:** Substantive due process review applies where a law affects the rights of ***all*** persons with respect to a specific activity (*e.g.* state law prohibits the sale of birth control devices, except by prescription).

    b. **Equal protection:** Equal protection review applies where a law affects the rights of ***some*** persons with respect to a specific activity (*e.g.* state law prohibits the sale of birth control devices to unmarried persons, except by prescription).

B. THREE STANDARDS OF REVIEW

1. **Strict Scrutiny:** *Under the strict scrutiny standard, the burden of persuasion is on the government to prove that the measure being challenged is necessary to further a compelling interest.* The word "necessary" means that there is no less restrictive alternative means available. There must be a very close "fit" between the means and the end. The government usually fails to prove its burden under strict scrutiny, so the Equal Protection challenge to the law is generally a winning argument (*i.e.* the law is presumptively invalid). *Strict scrutiny review applies to 1) suspect classes — race, alienage, and national origin; 2) fundamental rights — right to vote, right to travel, right to privacy; and 3) protected 1st Amendment rights.*

2. **Middle-tier, or Intermediate, Scrutiny:** *Under the middle-tier standard, the burden of persuasion is generally placed on the government to prove that the measure being challenged is substantially related to an important interest.* The key term, "substantially related", means that an exceedingly persuasive justification must be shown. Middle-tier scrutiny is much closer to strict scrutiny than it is to rational basis. *Intermediate scrutiny applies to classifications based on the following quasi-suspect areas: 1) gender and 2) illegitimacy*; also, a similar, though not identical, test is used for 3) content neutral time, place, manner regulation of free speech.

3. **Rational Basis Scrutiny:** *Under the rational basis standard of review, the burden of persuasion is on the plaintiff to show the measure being challenged is not*

Constitutional Law

rationally related to any legitimate interest. Rational relationship is a minimal requirement which means that the law cannot be arbitrary or unreasonable. Practically any police power regulation which furthers a health, safety, or welfare purpose will be found "legitimate". For this reason, laws scrutinized under rational basis are almost always upheld. From the plaintiff's standpoint rational basis is traditionally a default test (*i.e.* an equal protection challenge under rational basis is generally a losing argument). ***Rational basis review applies to all classifications not falling under strict or intermediate scrutiny, namely such classifications as those based on age, poverty, wealth, mental retardation, necessities of life (food, shelter, clothing, medical care), and social and economic welfare measures.***

C. PROVING DISCRIMINATORY CLASSIFICATIONS

1. **Intentional Discrimination Required:** Discriminatory intent (*i.e.* purposeful, invidious discrimination) must be shown to trigger strict or intermediate scrutiny. Mere discriminatory effect is insufficient. Discriminatory intent may be shown facially, or as applied, or where a discriminatory motive exists.

   a. **Facial discrimination:** Facial discrimination arises where a law, by its very language, creates distinctions between classes of persons (*e.g.* only white, male U.S. citizens may apply for positions with the state police department).

   b. **Discriminatory application:** A facially neutral law can be applied in a discriminatory manner. Where the challenger can show a discriminatory purpose, the law will be invalidated. [*Yick Ho v. Hopkins*, 118 U.S. 356 (1886) — law prohibiting operation of laundries in wooden buildings most of which were owned by Chinese individuals, but granting discretionary exemptions, held invalid].

   c. **Discriminatory motive:** Where a law which appears neutral on its face and in its application has a disproportionate effect on a particular class of persons, strict or middle-tier scrutiny will apply only if the Court finds a ***discriminatory purpose*** exists. [*Washington v. Davis*, 426 U.S. 229 (1976) — the fact that Black applicants on a police qualifying test scored lower than White applicants did not per se prove a discriminatory purpose in hiring practices, so strict scrutiny review was not triggered and no Equal Protection violation was found].

D. SUSPECT CLASSIFICATIONS

1. **Race and National Origin:** Strict scrutiny applies to classifications based on race and national origin. Such laws will be presumptively invalid, absent a showing by the state that the measure is necessary to a compelling interest.

   a. **Racial (or ethnic) classifications:** A state law prohibiting interracial marriages was held unconstitutional [*Loving v. Virginia*, 388 U.S. 1 (1967)]; and a state law prohibiting interracial cohabitation was held invalid. [*McLaughlin v. Florida*, 379 U.S. 184 (1964)].

   b. **School segregation:** In *Brown v. Board of Education*, 347 U.S. 483 (1954), which overruled *Plessy v. Ferguson*, 163 U.S. 537 (1896), the Court held that deliberate "de jure" segregation violates equal protection. Also, various plans to hinder desegregation have been deemed unconstitutional, including the closing of all public schools. [*Griffin v. County School Board of Prince Edward County*, 377 U.S. 218 (1964)] and in [*Norwood v. Harrison*, 413 U.S. 455 (1973)], the Court held public aid to private segregated schools (such as tuition grants and exclusive use of public facilities) unconstitutional.

   (1) **Busing:** School boards have an affirmative duty to eliminate intentional racial segregation of schools. Court-ordered busing is constitutional where it is implemented to remedy past discrimination in a particular school system. Court-ordered busing is a temporary measure which must be terminated once the vestiges of past discrimination have been eliminated. [*Board of Education v. Dowell*, 498 U.S. 237 (1991)]. Also, the proper purpose of court-ordered busing must be to remedy past discrimination, not to attract non-minority students from outside districts to achieve integration.

c. **Affirmative Action:** In *Richmond v. Croson*, 488 U.S. 469 (1989), the USSC first held that minority set-asides established by state or local governments for construction projects—*i.e.* programs where a fixed percentage of publicly-funded money is awarded to minority-owned businesses—are subject to strict scrutiny review and must be narrowly tailored to justify a compelling interest. Subsequently, in *Adarand Construction, Inc v. Pena*, 515 U.S. 200 (1995) the Court set forth a clear rule that ***any race-based affirmative action program designed to remedy past discrimination—whether enacted by a state municipality, or even the federal government—is subject to strict scrutiny***. This rule applies to any "benign", or compensatory, program by any government entity which either ***favors*** or ***discriminates against*** racial or ethnic minorities. Other general principles include the following:

   (1) Remedying past discrimination in a particular government institution is generally viewed as a compelling interest, but attempting to remedy general, societal injustice through affirmative action is not.

   (2) Race or ethnic origin may be considered as a factor in admissions programs — *U.C. Regents v. Bakke*, 438 U.S. 265 (1978) — ***but use of "quota" systems (as opposed to hiring "goals") is disfavored and will almost always be struck down as not being necessary to promote racial equality or educational diversity.*** *Bakke* was affirmed in *Grutter v. Bollinger*, 123 S. Ct. 2325 (2003) (school may take race into account as one of many factors in making admissions decisions); but see *Gratz v. Bollinger*, 123 S. Ct. 2411 (2003) (school may not use quota system to enroll minority students, even if expressed purpose is to remedy past discrimination and create a diverse student body).

   (3) Discrimination by private employers is not subject to equal protection review, but may be restricted under the 13th Amendment or the Commerce Clause.

d. **Racial gerrymandering:** Where it can be shown that race was the "predominant factor" in defining the borders of new election districts (rather than contiguity, compactness, or community interest), then such a plan will violate strict scrutiny absent a showing by the state that the scheme was narrowly tailored to serve a compelling interest. [*Miller v. Johnson*, 515 U.S. 900 (1995)].

2. **Alienage:** Although alienage is not a "suspect" classification per se, the Court will generally apply the strict scrutiny test where a state law discriminates against aliens.

Constitutional Law

Examples: A state law prohibiting aliens from owning land was invalidated in *Oyama v. California*, 332 U.S. 633 (1948); and a state law denying commercial fishing licenses to resident aliens, who were ineligible for citizenship, held invalid [*Takahashi v. Fish & Game Commission*, 334 U.S. 410 (1948)]; and in *Nyquist v. Mauclet*, 432 U.S. 1 (1977), the Court invalidated a state law that excluded financial assistance for higher education to aliens who were eligible for U.S. citizenship as not furthering any "compelling state interest."

Exception: States may discriminate against aliens where participation in the functioning of government is involved: New York statute requiring state police officers to be citizens held valid. [*Foley v. Connelie*, 435 U.S. 291 (1978)]; also, aliens may be denied positions as public school teachers because they may influence students' views toward government and the political process. [*Ambach v. Norwick*, 441 U.S. 68 (1979)].

Illegal Aliens: The USSC has not held illegal aliens to be a suspect class. Rational basis analysis applies. However, note that in *Plyler v. Doe*, 457 U.S. 202 (1982), the Court determined that illegal alien children have a right to free public elementary and secondary education.

Note: Remember that federal classifications based upon alienage are not subject to the strict scrutiny test, because Congress has broad plenary power to regulate immigration. Thus, in *Mathews v. Diaz*, 426 U.S. 67 (1976), Congress established a 5-year residency requirement for federal Medicare benefits that disqualified many resident aliens. On the other hand, in *Hampton v. Moo Sun Wong*, 426 U.S. 88 (1976), the Court barred discrimination against aliens in federal civil service employment.

3. **Illegitimacy:** Distinctions drawn between legitimate and illegitimate children are subject to an intermediate, or "quasi-suspect," standard. [*Mathews v. Lucas*, 427 U.S. 495 (1976)]. As a result, it is now close to the "almost suspect" standard used for gender discrimination. [*Mills v. Habluetzel*, 102 S. Ct. 1549 (1982) — classifications must be "substantially related to an important state interest"]. Classifications which favor legitimates and disfavor illegitimates are generally struck down since the overriding government interest in this area is not to punish the offspring of an illicit relationship.

   a. **Wrongful death:** In *Levy v. Louisiana*, 391 U.S. 68 (1968), the Court struck down a state law which permitted legitimate children (but not illegitimate children) to maintain a wrongful death action.

   b. **Workmen's compensation:** Similarly, in *Weber v. Aetna Casualty and Surety Company*, 406 U.S. 164 (1972), the Court invalidated a state law that excluded illegitimate children from sharing equally with other children in worker's compensation death benefits.

   c. **Welfare benefits:** Likewise, illegitimate children are entitled to welfare benefits. [*New Jersey Welfare Rights Organization v. Cahill*, 411 U.S. 619 (1973)].

   d. **Intestate succession:** Illinois intestacy statute which excluded illegitimate children from inheriting from their intestate fathers was declared unconstitutional. [*Trimble v. Gordon*, 430 U.S. 762 (1977)]: however, in *Lalli v. Lalli*, 439 U.S. 259

(1978), the Court upheld a New York intestacy statute which required the paternity of the father be proved during his lifetime, as serving an important state interest in promoting a just or orderly disposition of property at death.

Note: As with federal classifications based upon alienage, the Supreme Court has been more lenient in applying an intermediate standard of scrutiny to illegitimacy under federal law than under state law. The Court upheld a federal law granting immigration preferences to legitimate children in *Fiallo v. Bell,* 430 U.S. 787 (1977) — within Congress's plenary power to regulate immigration.

4. **Gender:** Classifications based on gender are *"quasi-suspect" and violate equal protection unless they are "substantially related to important government interests."* [*Craig v. Boren,* 429 U.S. 190 (1976) — Oklahoma statute which permitted the sale of beer to females over 18 years old, but forbade the sale of the beverage to males between 18 and 21 held invalid as *not* substantially related to any important government objectives]. Middle-tier review applies whether the classification is invidious (intended to harm) or benign (intended to help, or intended to remedy past discrimination). Intentional, or purposeful, discrimination is required to trigger middle-tier scrutiny; just as was discussed regarding race, discriminatory effect alone is insufficient. Statutes which reinforce archaic gender-based stereotypes will almost certainly be struck down. Based on an important recent decision, the Court will apply intermediate scrutiny in a quite rigorous manner such that the ***government*** must prove gender discrimination and show that an "exceedingly persuasive justification" exists. [*U.S. v. Virginia*, 518 U.S. 515 (1996)].

    a. **Discrimination against women:** In recent decisions, the Court has held unconstitutional under equal protection all laws discriminating against women. A state law giving preference to men over women (who were equally qualified) to be administrators of decedents' estates held unconstitutional in *Reed v. Reed,* 404 U.S. 71 (1971)]; also in *Frontiero v. Richardson,* 411 U.S. 677 (1973) discrimination in military benefits to servicewomen held invalid.

    b. **Discrimination against men:** The Court has held unconstitutional under equal protection laws discriminating against men. [*Craig v. Boren, supra];* also, the Court struck down a law authorizing alimony payments upon divorce to women but not to men. [*Orr v. Orr,* 440 U.S. 268 (1979)]; and in *Caban v. Mohammed,* 441 U.S. 380 (1979) — the Court invalidated a New York law which permitted an unwed mother, but not an unwed father, to block the adoption of their child]; and recently in *Mississippi University for Women v. Hogan,* 102 S. Ct. 3331 (1982), the Court held the exclusion of males from a state nursing school violated a male applicant's right to equal protection.

    Caveat: Note, however, that in some cases laws discriminating against men have been upheld when "substantially related to important government objectives." In *Rostker v. Goldberg,* 453 U.S. 57 (1981), for example, the Court upheld the registration of males and not females for conscription by the military because Congress, pursuant to its military powers, has determined that this was necessary to further important government interests; also, in *Michael M. v. Sonoma County Superior Court,* 450 U.S. 464 (1981), statutory rape laws which punished the male participant (but not the female accessory) upheld because it furthered an important state interest in preventing teenage pregnancy.

    c. **Benign sex discrimination:** Such laws are generally upheld as being substantially related to the important governmental objective of ameliorating past gender-based discrimination. Thus, in *Califano v. Webster,* 430 U.S. 313 (1977), Social Security statutes and tax exemptions that entitle women to greater benefits were upheld; also, a navy discharge procedure which required male officers, who were twice denied promotion, to be automatically discharged (whereas female officers were not) was upheld in *Schlesinger v. Ballard,* 419 U.S. 498 (1975), because in the past men were afforded greater promotional opportunities than women.

5. **Age:** Age is not a "suspect" classification. The Court has upheld the validity of a Massachusetts statute requiring police officers to retire at age 50, even though they may be as physically fit as younger officers. [*Massachusetts Board of Retirement v. Murgia,* 427 U.S. 307 (1976)]. Thus, laws and other governmental action against the elderly are judged by the traditional (or "rational basis") test.

6. **Poverty:** The Court has held that "poverty standing alone is not a suspect classification." [*Harris v. McRae,* 448 U.S. 297 (1980)]; and in *James v. Valtierra,* 402 U.S. 137 (1971), the Court upheld a state law that required approval by a local referendum as a prerequisite for the construction of low-rent public housing projects.

7. **Mental retardation:** In *City of Cleburne v. Cleburne Living Center,* 473 U.S. 432, (1985), the Court held that mental retardation is not a "quasi-suspect" classification, and that the rational basis standard of review is applicable.

VII. PRIVILEGES AND IMMUNITIES CLAUSES

A. PRIVILEGES AND IMMUNITIES UNDER THE 14TH AMENDMENT

1. **Constitutional provision:** The 14th Amendment provides that "No state shall make or enforce any law which shall abridge the privileges or immunities of citizens of the United States."

2. **Scope:** The Court ruled early in the *Slaughterhouse Cases, supra,* that the Privileges and Immunities Clause of the 14th Amendment had very limited application. Among the privileges and immunities of *national* citizenship which are protected include: the right to travel from state to state; to petition Congress for redress of grievances; to vote for national offices; to enter public lands; to be protected while in custody of U.S. marshals; and the right to assemble peaceably. [*Twining v. New Jersey, 211* U.S. 78 (1908)]. Corporations and aliens are not protected under the 14th Amendment Privileges and Immunities Clause.

B. PRIVILEGES AND IMMUNITIES UNDER ARTICLE IV, SECTION 2

1. **Constitutional provision:** Article IV, section *2,* which is sometimes referred to as the Comity Clause, provides: "The citizens of each state shall be entitled to all privileges and immunities of citizens in the several states."

2. **Scope:** This clause prohibits states from discriminating against nonresidents (based upon the fact that they do not reside in the state) with respect to "essential activities" or "fundamental rights." Corporations and aliens are not "citizens" for purposes of the Article IV Privileges and Immunities Clause.

   a. **Improper discrimination:** The following have been held to be *invalid forms of nonresident discrimination:*

      (1) State statute requiring a nonresident commercial fisherman to pay a $2,500 license fee to fish offshore, while a resident fisherman paid only a $25 license fee. [*Toomer v. Witsell,* 334 U.S. 385 (1948) — state law invalid because it discriminated against nonresidents who were pursuing their livelihood (i.e., commercial fishermen)].

      (2) Commuter tax applied to nonresidents who entered New Hampshire to work (while New Hampshire residents were exempt from tax) held invalid. [*Austin v. New Hampshire,* 420 U.S. 656 (1975)].

      (3) State statute imposing residency requirements on women seeking an abortion. [*Doe v. Bolton,* 410 U.S. 179 (1973) — held invalid because an individual has a fundamental right to seek medical care].

      (4) Alaska law requiring employers to give hiring preference to state residents held invalid. [*Hicklin v. Orbeck,* 437 U.S. 518 (1978) — discrimination against nonresidents adversely affected an "essential activity" (namely, their pursuit of a livelihood)].

   b. **Permissible discrimination:** Remember that the Privileges and Immunities Clause does not protect a nonresident against all forms of discrimination. *The following types of (nonresident) discrimination have been upheld:*

      (1) State statute requiring a nonresident to pay $225 for a recreational hunting license, while a resident hunter paid only a $9 license fee. [*Baldwin v. Montana Fish and Game Commission,* 436 U.S. 371 (1978) — discrimination permitted because it is within a state's police power to regulate recreational, noncommercial, activities].

      (2) Discrimination against nonresidents will be given special consideration if its purpose is the preservation of natural, state-owned resources. [*Sporhase v. Nebraska,* 102 S. Ct. 3456 (1982) — involving scarce water resources].

      Exam tip: Discrimination against *citizens* or *residents* in regard to an essential economic right or liberty triggers the Article IV Privileges and Immunities Clause, whereas general economic discrimination against a business or entity is more often viewed using Commerce Clause analysis.

VIII. RETROACTIVE LEGISLATION

A. **THE CONTRACT CLAUSE**

1. **Constitutional provision:** Article 1, section 10, provides: "No state shall pass any law impairing the obligation of contracts."

    a. **Retroactive state legislation:** The principal reason for the inclusion of the Contract Clause in the Constitution was to prevent *state legislatures* from passing retroactive laws impairing an existing contractual obligation. As such, the Contract Clause applies only to state legislation, not to state court decisions. Nor does the Contract Clause apply to the federal government.

    b. **Police power limitation:** A private contract can be modified by the legislature under its police power when it is necessary 1) to serve an important and legitimate public interest and 2) the regulation is a reasonable and narrowly tailored means of promoting that interest. Thus, during the Depression a statute imposing a moratorium on mortgage foreclosures was upheld. [*Home Building & Loan Association v. Blaisdell,* 290 U.S. 398 (1934) — impairment of contract was necessary to preserve economic stability.] In determining whether a contract may be modified, the Court will consider (1) the severity of the impairment and (2) the importance of the public interest to be served. [*Allied Structural Steel Co. v. Spannaus,* 438 U.S. 234 (1978)].

    c. **Modern applications:** In *United States Trust Co. v. New Jersey,* 431 U.S. 1 (1977), the Court held that New York and New Jersey violated the Contract Clause by permitting the Port Authority to use funds to subsidize public transportation in violation of a previous statutory covenant to private bondholders. Also, in *Allied Steel, supra,* the court recognized the validity of police power limitations on the Contract Clause, and invalidated state pension reform legislation which increased the obligation of companies under preexisting pension plans.

B. **EX POST FACTO LAWS**

1. **Constitutional provision:** There are two ex post facto clauses in the Constitution which prevent both the state and federal governments from passing retroactive criminal laws. Article I, section 9, clause 3, provides that: "No ... ex post facto law shall be passed"; and Article I, section 10, clause 1 provides: "No state shall pass any ex post facto law."

    a. **Retroactive effects:** In general, *a statute retroactively alters the criminal law if (1) it makes criminal an act that was not a crime when committed, or (2) prescribes greater punishment for a crime after its commission, or (3) decreases the amount of evidence required for conviction or (4) extends limitations period for crime as to which previously applicable limitations period has already expired.*

C. **BILLS OF ATTAINDER**

1. **Constitutional provision:** Article I, section 9, clause 3 states: "No bill of attainder shall be passed"; and Article I, section 10, clause 1 provides: "No state shall pass any bill

of attainder." These two provisions prevent both federal and state legislatures from passing bills of attainder.

2. **Definition:** *A bill of attainder is a legislative act that inflicts punishment without a judicial trial* upon named individuals or an easily ascertainable group for past conduct.

   a. **Application:** The Court held that a provision in the Landrum-Griffin Act making it a crime for a member of the Communist Party to act as an officer of a labor union to be the equivalent of legislative punishment, and hence a bill of attainder. [*United States v. Lovett,* 328 U.S. 303 (1946)]; however, in *Nixon v. Administrator of General Services,* 433 U.S. 425 (1977), the Court held that legislation authorizing government control of various presidential papers and tape recordings did not constitute a bill of attainder, because the act was nonpunitive.

IX. 1ST AMENDMENT FREEDOMS

A. **FREEDOM OF RELIGION AND SEPARATION OF CHURCH AND STATE**

   1. **Constitutional provision:** The 1st Amendment provides that "Congress shall make no law respecting an establishment of religion or prohibiting the free exercise thereof."

   2. **General application:** Where a government program prefers one religion, or one religious sect, over others, strict scrutiny analysis will be applied. [*Board of Education v. Grumet,* 512 U.S. 687 (1994)] — creation of special public school district boundaries so as to educate disabled Jewish children was held unconstitutional as not narrowly tailored to a compelling interest]. On the other hand, where the legislation or government program contains no religious or sect preference, the Court will follow the 3-part test under *Lemon v. Kurtzman,* 403 U.S. 602 (1971): 1) the statute must have a secular purpose; 2) the primary effect or purpose must neither advance nor inhibit religion; and 3) the statute must not foster excessive government entanglement with religion.

   3. **Aid to parochial school students:** The following government assistance programs have been upheld as constitutional. These programs which provide aid to *all elementary and secondary students (including parochial school students) have been held to "pass" the three-prong test*:

      a. **Textbooks:** In *Board of Education v. Allen,* 392 U.S. 236 (1968), the Court permitted the state to furnish textbooks to *all* students (including those attending parochial schools) because there was little entanglement, and the primary effect was secular.

      b. **Furnishing standardized tests:** Furnishing standardized secular examinations to parochial school students held valid. [*Wolman v. Walter,* 43 3 U.S. 229 (1977) — because the materials did not contain any religious content].

      c. **Essential municipal services:** Providing bus transportation to and from school for *all* students (including those attending parochial schools) held valid. [*Everson v. Board of Education,* 330 U.S. 1 (1947) — purpose and effect essentially secular];

also, such necessary municipal services (e.g., police and fire protection) can be provided to churches and church-related institutions.

d. **Health services:** Public health services (including a school lunch program) can be provided to *all* students, since their purpose and effect are secular. [*Lemon v. Kurtzman,* 403 U.S. 602 (1971)].

e. **Furnishing remedial and therapeutic services:** In *Mitchell v. Helms,* 120 S. Ct. 2530 (2000), the Supreme Court held that the *Wolman* case, *supra,* was overruled insofar as it prohibited government-run remedial and therapeutic services in the parochial schools. It held that Chapter 2 of the 1981 Education Consolidation and Improvement Act, which channels federal funds to local education agencies to acquire, for use in public and private schools, instructional and educational materials, including library and media materials and computer software and hardware, had a secular purpose and did not have the effect of advancing religion, either by resulting in governmental indoctrination or by defining recipients by reference to religion, and therefore did not violate the First Amendment's Establishment Clause.

f. **State income tax deduction for education expenses:** A state statute permitting *all* parents, in computing their state income tax, to deduct expenses incurred in providing "tuition, textbooks and transportation" for their children in elementary and secondary schools (including parochial schools) upheld. [*Mueller v. Allen,* 77 L.Ed. 2d 721 (1983) — primary effect not sectarian since the deduction is available to all parents].

   (1) **Contrast:** Grants to parents: Giving tax deductions or tuition grants to parents whose children attend parochial schools held unconstitutional as violating the Establishment Clause. [*Committee for Public Education v. Nyquist,* 413 U.S. 756 (1973) — primary effect was to promote religious activity].

g. **Sign-language interpreters:** A public school may pay for an interpreter for a deaf child at a religious high school in a program which aids disabled students in both public and private schools without reference to religion. [*Zobrest v. Catalina Foothills School District,* 509 U.S. 1 (1993)].

4. **Direct aid to parochial schools and church-related institutions:**

   a. **Hospitals:** Federal grants to church-affiliated hospitals for maintenance and care of indigent patients held valid. [*Bradfield v. Roberts,* 175 U.S. 291 (1899)].

   b. **Colleges:** The Court has been very permissive of aid to church-related colleges. [*Tilton v. Richardson,* 403 U.S. 672 (1971) — upholding government grants for construction of buildings at church-affiliated colleges].

   c. **Elementary and secondary schools:** Most government programs providing *direct aid* to parochial schools have been held to violate the Establishment Clause, because they involve "excessive government entanglement" with religion.

      (1) **Teacher salaries:** Grants to parochial schools for salaries of teachers of secular subjects held invalid, because of the risk of "excessive government

entanglement." [*Lemon v. Kurtzman, supra*].; on the contrary, grants to church-related colleges are permissible because their instructors are thought to be restrained by the various academic disciplines (e.g., sociology, biology); and their students are older, more mature and less susceptible to indoctrination.

5. **Tax consequences:**

   a. **Property tax exemptions:** In *Walz v. Tax Commission*, 397 U.S. 664 (1970), the Court upheld the validity of a property tax exemption for religious institutions. Neither the purpose nor effects of such an exemption is regarded as secular, because it is the equivalent of exempting other charitable organizations.

   b. **Tax deductions:** Tax deductions given to reimburse tuition expenses only for parents of children in religious schools is invalid. However, if a tax deduction is given to ***all*** parents based on actual expenditures for children attending any public, private, or religious school, it will be upheld. [*Mueller v. Allen*, 463 U.S. 388 (1983)].

   c. **Tax exemptions:** A tax exemption from sales and use taxes available only for the sale of ***religious*** magazines and books violates the Establishment Clause as an endorsement of religion. [*Texas Monthly v. Bullock*, 489 U.S. 1 (1989)].

   d. **Vouchers:** Voucher program that allows parents to send their children to parochial or religious schools with state aid instead of to failed public schools allowed because aid is neutral with respect to religion to broad class of citizens, defined without reference to religion, who direct aid to religious schools as result of their own independent and private choice. [*Zelman v. Simmons-Harris*, 122 S. Ct. 2460 (2002)].

6. **Religious activities in public schools:** As a general rule, religious activities conducted in public schools violate the Establishment Clause because their primary purpose is to promote religion. The following practices in public schools have been held to be invalid:

   a. **Prayer and Bible reading in public schools held invalid.** [*Engel v. Vitale*, 370 U.S. 421 (1962)].

   b. Posting the Ten Commandments on the walls in public school classrooms held ***invalid***. [*Stone v. Graham*, 449 U.S. 39 (1980)].

   c. Anti-evolution laws prohibiting the teaching of Darwinian principles in public schools held ***invalid***. [*Epperson v. Arkansas*, 393 U.S. 97 (1968)].

   Exception: A state university regulation prohibiting the use of school facilities by a registered student religious organization (whereas facilities were available to other student groups) has been held to be in violation of freedom of free speech under the 1st Amendment. [*Widmar v. Vincent*, 454 U.S. 263 (1981) — equal access to school facilities did not violate Establishment Clause]. Also, the Supreme Court recently held that prohibiting a religious club from meeting in a public school amounted to religious viewpoint discrimination and violated the Free Speech Clause of the First Amendment. Furthermore, permitting the club to meet on school grounds would not be a violation of the Establishment Clause. *Good News Club v. Milford Central*

Constitutional Law

School, 121 S. Ct. 2093 (2001); see also *Lamb's Chapel v. Center Moriches Union Free School District*, 113 S. Ct. 2141 (1993) (prohibition against showing religious films at a school violated free speech); *Rosenberger v. Rector and Visitors of the University of Virginia*, 115 S. Ct. 2510 (1995) (university's refusal to fund a student publication because it addressed issues from a religious perspective violated free speech); *Board of Regents of University of Wisconsin System v. Southworth*, 120 S. Ct. 1346 (2000) (state university's viewpoint-neutral allocation of mandatory student activities fee to political and ideological groups as part of program to facilitate extracurricular student speech does not violate First Amendment rights of students who object to subsidizing those groups' activities).

d. An Alabama law authorizing a period of silence "for meditation or voluntary prayer" was held invalid as an establishment of religion [*Wallace v. Jaffree*, 472 U.S. 38 (1985)].

e. A public school may not sponsor a rabbi or other cleric to conduct even a non-denominational prayer as part of a graduation ceremony. [*Lee v. Weisman*, 505 U.S. 577 (1992)]; Furthermore, where high school students were allowed to vote on whether a student-delivered "invocation" or "message" would take place at school football games, such an activity would be forced on all those present and therefore violated the First Amendment Establishment Clause. [*Santa Fe Independent School District v. Doe*, 120 S. Ct. 2266 (2000)].

7. **Incidental government action benefiting religion:** In *McGowan v. Maryland*, 366 U.S. 420 (1961), Sunday closing laws were upheld; but in *Larkin v. Grendel's Den, Inc.* 459 U.S. 116 (1982), a state statute giving churches and schools the power to veto applications for liquor licenses within a 500-foot radius of the church or school held unconstitutional, because of "excessive government entanglement."

8. **Ceremonies and displays:**

    a. **Opening prayers:** A state legislature may employ a chaplain to conduct an opening day prayer [*Marsh v. Chambers*, 463 U.S. 783 (1983)]; however, a state court judge may not conduct such a daily prayer. [*North Carolina v. Constangy*, 59 LW 2294 (1991)].

    b. **Religious displays:** Displays which celebrate the holiday season without favoring one religion over another are generally upheld. The government cannot permit the type of display which a reasonable observer would conclude constitutes an *endorsement* of religion. The context surrounding the display is a key factor in determining its validity. [*Lynch v. Donnelly*, 465 U.S. 668 (1984) — a nativity scene surrounded by two plastic reindeer, a Santa Claus, and a "Season's Greetings" banner, taken as a whole, celebrated the holiday season and was held not to violate the Establishment Clause].

    Compare: In *Alleghany County v. ACLU*, 492 U.S. 573 (1989), a display of only a creche (but no other symbols nearby — "Season's Greetings" banner, Chanukah menorah) prominently displayed by a private religious group in the county courthouse violated the Establishment Clause.

Compare: Placing a cross in a state-owned park immediately in front of the State Capitol was held not to violate the Establishment Clause — no endorsement of religion since the park had long been used by a variety of groups to conduct expressive activities. [*Capitol Square Review Board v. Pinette*, 515 U.S. 753 (1995)].

B. SCOPE OF FREE EXERCISE CLAUSE

1. **In general:** A person's religious beliefs are absolutely protected. The government may not punish an individual by denying benefits or imposing burdens based on religious belief. [*Cantwell v. Connecticut,* 310 U.S. 296 (1940)]; also, a West Virginia statute compelling a flag salute held unconstitutional. [*West Virginia State Board of Education v. Barnette,* 319 U.S. 624 (1943) — state cannot require affirmation of a belief]. Similarly, state cannot require a person to carry a message on his (or her) license plate (e.g., "Live Free or Die") which offends one's religious belief. [*Wooley v. Maynard,* 430 v.s. 705 (1977)]. Furthermore, the government may not determine the reasonableness (*i.e.* "truth" or "falsity" where a person says, "I talked to God") of one's religious beliefs, but it may determine sincerity. [*U.S. v. Ballard,* 332 U.S. 78 (1944)]. Also, public employment may not be conditioned on taking an oath based on a religious belief.

2. **Balancing test:** Conduct in furtherance of one's religious beliefs, however, may sometimes be regulated. Where an ***individual's conduct is motivated by his (or her) religious belief***, the state may regulate or prohibit the activity if there is an "important" or "compelling" state interest.

    a. **Strong state interest overriding "free exercise" claims:**

    (1) **Polygamy:** State law outlawing polygamy upheld. [*Reynolds v. United States,* 98 U.S. 145 (1878)].

    (2) **Child labor:** Massachusetts child labor statute can be applied against an employer who permits a 12-year-old child to sell religious literature on the street.

    (3) **Selective service:** As a matter of military policy, the Court has upheld a Selective Service Act exemption for "conscientious objectors." [Gillette v. United States, 401 U.S. 437 (1971)].

    (4) **Denial of veterans' benefits to conscientious objectors:** Conscientious objectors who perform alternate civilian service can be denied veterans' benefits. [*Johnson v. Robison,* 415 U.S. 361 (1974)].

    (5) **Sunday closing laws:** The Court has upheld such laws because it furthers the state interest in providing a common day of rest. [*Braunfeld v. Brown,* 366 U.S. 599 (1961) — upheld even though they placed Orthodox Jews and others who observe a religious holiday on Saturday at an economic disadvantage].

    (6) **Taxes:** Social Security tax applied to an Amish employer held valid, even though his beliefs forbade payment and receipt of benefits. [*United States v. Lee,* 102 S. Ct. 1051 (1982)].

Constitutional Law

- (7) **Wearing religious attire:** The Court struck down a free exercise challenge by a Jewish Air Force cadet who violated uniform dress requirements by wearing a yarmulke while on duty [*Goldman v. Weinberger*, 475 U.S.—(1986)].

- (8) **College Scholarships:** State regulation making devotional theology majors ineligible for state-funded scholarship awards does not suggest animus toward religion or impose more than relatively minor burden on program participants [*Locke v. Davey*, 2004]

b. **"Free exercise" claims overriding weak state interest:**

- (1) **Compulsory school attendance:** The Court invalidated a law (as it applied to the Amish community) requiring children to attend school until age 16. [*Wisconsin v. Yoder*, 406 U.S. 205 (1972)].

- (2) **Unemployment compensation:** A state cannot deny unemployment benefits to a person whose religious faith commands the observance of Saturday as the Sabbath. [*Sherbert v. Verner*, 374 U.S. 398 (1963) — upholding right of individual not to accept "suitable work" on the Sabbath].

- (3) **Door-to-door solicitation:** Although this area will be covered more fully in the section on "free speech," the Court held a Connecticut statute forbidding door-to-door solicitation as it applied to Jehovah's Witnesses unconstitutional. [*Cantwell v. Connecticut*, 310 U.S. 296 (1940)].

3. **Status of Free Exercise Clause today:** Although free exercise is a protected 1st Amendment right, the Court does not automatically apply strict scrutiny. The key is to determine if the government action intentionally or unintentionally interferes with religion.

   a. **Intentional interference with religion:** Where the government purposely interferes with particular conduct because it is dictated by religious beliefs, strict scrutiny analysis will be applied and the law will be presumptively invalid as a Free Exercise Clause violation. In *Church of the Lukumi Babalu Aye, Inc v. Hialeah*, 508 U.S. 520 (1993), a city ordinance banned all animal sacrifice done in a public or private ritual not for the primary purpose of food consumption ("kosher" slaughter was permitted). The primary purpose of the law was not to prevent cruelty to animals, but to abolish the sacrificial rituals of a particular Cuban Santeria religious sect. Such purposeful interference was struck down 9–0 using strict scrutiny.

   b. **Unintentional interference with religion:** Where a neutral government regulation of general applicability produces merely an incidental burden on religiously motivated conduct, strict scrutiny is not applied. Moreover, where the government regulation is a generally-applicable criminal prohibition, the law will routinely be upheld. In *Employment Division v. Smith*, 494 U.S. 872 (1990), the state of Oregon criminalized the possession of peyote as a means of strengthening its drug and narcotics enforcement policy. No exemption was made for American Indians who used peyote for their religious rituals. The Court upheld the law without applying either strict scrutiny or a balancing test, since the regulation was a generally applicable ban, not motivated by any desire to burden religious conduct.

C. **FREEDOM OF EXPRESSION**

1. **Constitutional provision:** The 1st Amendment provides "Congress shall make no law ... abridging the freedom of speech, or of the press; or of the people peaceably to assemble, and to petition the government for a redress of grievances."

    a. **Application to states:** The 1st Amendment has also been held applicable to the states through the Due Process Clause of the 14th Amendment. [*Gitlow v. New York,* 268 U.S. 652 (1975)].

2. **Distinction between regulation of speech content and regulation of time, place, and manner of speech conduct:** In general, government regulations aimed directly at the content of speech are likely to be held invalid unless necessary to a compelling state interest and narrowly drawn to meet that interest. [*Virginia Pharmacy Board v. Virginia Consumer Council*, 425 U.S. 748 (1976) — USSC struck down state ban on advertising prices of prescription drugs as being "content-based", and held that the speech was being regulated because of the government's fears about how consumers would respond to its communicative impact]; The First Amendment is violated where legal services attorneys may not represent clients seeking welfare benefits in cases that "involve an effort to amend or otherwise challenge existing law." [*Legal Services Corporation v. Velazquez*, 121 S. Ct. 1043 (2001)]; but see [*National Endowment for the Arts v. Finley*, 118 S. Ct. 2168 (1998) — federal statute that required the National Endowment for the Arts to "tak[e] into consideration general standards of decency and respect for the diverse beliefs and values of the American public" in judging grants on basis of "artistic excellence and artistic merit," 20 USC 954(d)(1), was not viewpoint specific and, therefore, did not facially violate the First Amendment's Free Speech Clause. Furthermore, such requirements were not void for vagueness because the statute was not considered criminal or regulatory.]. On the other hand, government regulations not aimed at content, but at protecting "content-neutral" interests (such as regulating the time, place and manner of speech) are generally upheld unless the restrictions unduly constrict the flow of free speech. A three-part test (akin to middle-tier scrutiny) is used whereby 1) the government regulation must further an important (significant) government interest, 2) the regulation must be narrowly tailored, and 3) alternative channels of communication must be left open.

3. **Regulation of speech content:** Strict scrutiny applies to restrictions on "protected" speech. On the other hand, there are several areas of "unprotected" speech where the content can be regulated if certain requirements are met:

    a. **Symbolic speech:** Symbolic speech—communication where the conduct/medium itself is the message—may be restricted if the regulation 1) furthers an important government interest which is 2) unrelated to the suppression of speech, and 3) the burden on speech is no greater than necessary. [*U.S. v. O'Brien*, 391 U.S. 367 (1968)].

        (1) **Example:** Ban on public nudity, including nude dancing in adult entertainment establishments, held constitutional in order to protect the important government interest in morality — which was unrelated to the suppression of speech. [*Barnes v. Glen Theatres, Inc.*, 501 U.S. 1030 (1991)].

(2) **Compare:** Students wearing black armbands to protest the Vietnam War was held protected speech. [*Tinker v. Des Moines Independent Community School District*, 393 U.S. 503 (1969)]. Federal prohibition against burning the American flag held unconstitutional because the regulation was content specific since it was an attempt to preserve the flag as a symbol of national unity. [*U.S. v. Eichman*, 496 U.S. 310 (1990)].

b. **Clear and present danger:** The constitutional guarantees of free speech do not permit state regulation "except where the speech is directed to *inciting or producing imminent lawless action, and is likely to incite or produce such action.*" [*Brandenburg v. Ohio*, **395 U.S. 444 (1969)**].

(1) **Symbolic speech:** The political message conveyed by students wearing black armbands to protest the Vietnam War was held "protected" in *Tinker v. Des Moines Independent Community School District,* 393 U.S. 503 (1969). However, the Court refused to extend First Amendment protection to a high school student's lewd and offensive campaign speech delivered at a school assembly [*Bethel School District No. 403 v. Fraser,* 478 U.S.—(1986)].

c. **Fighting words:** Words likely to incite an ordinary citizen to acts of immediate physical retaliation may be punished. [*Chaplinsky v. New Hampshire,* 315 U.S. 568 (1942)* — upholding the conviction of a Jehovah's Witness who had been involved in a fight after calling a policeman "a Goddamned racketeer" and "a damned Fascist"]. Note: To fall within this category, the speech must be more than annoying or offensive; there must be a genuine likelihood of imminent violence by a hostile audience.

(1) **Overbreadth and vagueness:** "Fighting words" statutes are subject to facial invalidity if the conduct proscribed is vague (*i.e.* "opprobrious words") or overbroad.

(2) **Hate crimes:** "Fighting words" statutes designed only to punish certain viewpoints are unconstitutional. [*R.A.V. v. St. Paul,* 505 U.S. 377 (1992) — USSC struck down an ordinance that punished only those fighting words that "insult or provoke violence on the basis of race, religion, or gender"; *but see Virginia v. Black,* 123 S. Ct. 1536 (2003) — where a statute prohibits cross burning with the intent to intimidate, such a statute may be consistent with the First Amendment, especially because cross burning is "such a virulent form of intimidation."].

d. **Defamation:** Constitutional restrictions apply to defamatory speech where the plaintiff is either public official or public figure, or where the defamatory statement involves a matter of public concern. In these instances, the plaintiff must prove the state law requirements of defamation, plus *falsity* of the statement and *fault*. As to fault, public officials and public figures must prove malice, whereas private person plaintiffs need to only show negligence for matters of public concern (matters of private concern require only proof by plaintiff that the defamatory statement was made).

(1) **Defamation of public officials and public figures:** In order for a public official (or public figure) to recover for defamation, the plaintiff must establish

that the false statement was made with "actual malice" (i.e., knowledge of the falsity or reckless disregard for the truth). [*New York Times v. Sullivan*, 376 U.S. 254 (1964) — public official standard; and *Gertz v. Robert Welch, Inc.*, 418 U.S. 323 (1974) — rule extended to public figures].

(2) **Nonmedia defamation of a private individual:** Speech "on matters of purely *private* concern," such as the operations of credit reporting agencies, is not encompassed by the principles of *Gertz* or *Sullivan*. In this case, a private figure plaintiff may recover according to common law defamation principles [*Dun & Bradstreet, Inc. v. Greenmoss Builders, Inc.*, 472 U.S. 749 (1985)].

(3) **Invasion of privacy:** In *Time v. Hill*, 385 U.S. 374 (1967), the Court held that a plaintiff suing a media defendant for false light privacy concerning a matter of public interest must prove malice. In addition, the Court said that a newspaper or broadcaster cannot be held for publishing truthful information obtained from the public record. [*Cox Broadcasting Co. v. Cohn*, 420 U.S. 469 (1975) — plaintiff sued television station for broadcasting the fact that his daughter was a rape victim].

(4) **Opinion:** In *Milkovich v. Lorain Journal Co.*, 497 U.S. 1 (1990), the Court ruled that pure opinion may be actionable where it is sufficiently factual to be susceptible of being proven true.

e. **Obscenity:** Obscenity is unprotected speech. To be obscene, a three part test must be satisfied under *Miller v. California*, 413 U.S. 15 (1975):

i.) the material, taken as a whole, must appeal to the prurient interest in sex applying contemporary community standards (no national standard is used);

ii.) the material must depict sexual conduct in a patently offensive way (state law determines what is patently offensive); and

iii.) the material must lack serious literary, artistic, political, or scientific value (a national reasonable person standard is used — *Pope v. Illinois*, 481 U.S. 497 (1987).

(1) **Pandering:** The manner in which allegedly obscene materials are advertised and sold may be probative of their "prurient" appeal. [*Ginzburg v. United States*, 383 U.S. 463 (1966)].

(2) **Methods of regulating related areas:**

(a) **Zoning ordinances:** Narrowly drawn zoning ordinances may be used to restrict the location of adult theatres [*City of Renton v. Playtime Theatres, Inc.*, 475 U.S. 41 (1986)]. Furthermore, where a city finds through a study that crime rates increase in areas with high concentrations of adult operations, it is reasonable for it to regulate to lessen the concentration of these types of businesses. *Los Angeles v. Alameda Books*, 122 S. Ct. 1728 (2002).

Constitutional Law

- (b) **21st Amendment:** Live sexual entertainment and adult films may be regulated by the 21st Amendment in establishments licensed by the state to serve liquor, without satisfying the *Miller* test.

f. **Child pornography:** Child pornography is clearly unprotected speech. It may be regulated even without satisfying the *Miller* test because of the state's compelling interest in protecting its minor children.

  (1) **Sale and distribution:** Sale and distribution of visual depictions of sexual conduct involving children may be prohibited. [*N.Y. v. Ferber*, 456 U.S. 942 (1982)].

  (2) **Private possession:** A state may criminalize even the private possession of child pornography in one's home. [*Osborne v. Ohio*, 495 U.S. 103 (1990)].

  (3) **Virtual child pornography:** Recently, the Supreme Court held that a statute which outlawed not only actual child pornography but also virtual child pornography (in which no real children were depicted) was overly broad and violated the First Amendment. [*Ashcroft v. Free Speech Coalition*, 122 S. Ct. 1389 (2002).]

g. **Commercial speech:** As a general rule, commercial speech is afforded 1st Amendment protection. However, it can be prohibited as to false or deceptive advertising, as well as to harmful or illegal products.

  (1) **Modern test:** To determine the constitutionality of *lawful* commercial speech, the Court applies a 3-part test under *Central Hudson Gas v. Public Service Commission*, 447 U.S. 557 (1980): The regulation must

    i.) serve a substantial interest; and

    ii.) directly advance the interest; and

    iii.) be narrowly tailored to serve that substantial interest. Note, in this step, only a reasonable "fit" between the means and the end is required, rather than use of the least restrictive means.

  (2) **Examples:**

    (a) **Drug prices:** State cannot place an absolute ban on the advertisement of drug prices by a pharmacist. [*Virginia State Board of Pharmacy v. Virginia Citizens Consumer Council*, Inc., 425 U.S. 748 (1976)].

    (b) **Contraceptives:** Federal law making it a crime to send unsolicited advertisements for contraceptive devices held invalid. [*Bolger v. Youngs Drug Products*, 77 L.Ed.2d 469 (1983)].

    (c) **Attorney advertising:** A state cannot prohibit attorneys from advertising routine legal services at stated fees. [*Bates v. State Bar of Arizona*, 433 U.S. 350 (1977)]; and a state supreme court rule prohibiting an attorney from mailing new office opening announcements to persons "other than lawyers, clients, friends or relatives" held invalid. [*In re R.M.J.*, 455

U.S. 191 (1982)]; however, a state may discipline lawyers for "in-person" solicitation of clients for personal gain, because of the potential for over-reaching. [*Ohralik v. Ohio State Bar Association,* 436 U.S. 447 (1978)].

(d) Because the commercial speech doctrine does not protect fraudulent speech, and because such a statute reasonably advances the state's interest in protecting the public, a state can prevent doctors from claiming to be "board certified" in a medical specialty unless the certifying organization meets certain state standards. [*American Academy of Pain Management v. Joseph*, 2004 WL 19824 (9th Cir. 2004)].

(e) **Billboards:** It is within a state's police power to prohibit billboards carrying commercial advertising. [*Metromedia, Inc. v. City of San Diego,* 453 U.S. 490 (1981) — *city may regulate all billboards for purposes of highway safety and aesthetics;* however, it may not distinguish between different types of messages]. Also, it is unclear whether a *total* ban on billboards would be upheld.

(f) **Illegal or deceptive advertising:** A state may prohibit commercial advertising of matters which are illegal (e.g., prostitution), or advertising which is untruthful, misleading or deceptive. [*Pittsburgh Press Co. v. Pittsburgh Commission on Human Relations,* 413 U.S. 376 (1973) — newspaper enjoined from running help-wanted ads headed "male" or "female" because such classifications violated prohibitions against sex discrimination under a local ordinance].

(g) **Newsracks:** City ban on newsracks placed on sidewalks to distribute commercial publications (while allowing newsracks to sell newspapers) held invalid since there was no reasonable "fit" between the type of advertising being regulated and the state interest in reducing litter and promoting aesthetics. [*Cincinnati v. Discovery Network, Inc.*, 507 U.S. 410 (1993)].

(h) **Beer bottle labels:** Federal ban prohibiting beer bottle labels from displaying the alcoholic content held invalid as a violation of the brewer's free speech rights. Since the law applied only to labels, not to advertising, and only to beer, not to wine and spirits, it did not directly advance the government's interest in preventing "strength wars". [*Rubin v. Coors Brewing Co.*, 514 U.S. 476 (1995)].

(3) **Advertisement of harmful, yet lawful, products:** Clearly, advertising of unlawful products can be prohibited. However, as to advertising of harmful, yet lawful, products — *i.e.* "vice advertising" such as cigarettes, liquor, and gambling — it seems unlikely that the governments can completely ban truthful advertising of any lawful product or service.

(a) In *44 Liquormart, Inc v. Rhode Island*, 517 U.S. 484 (1996), the majority of Justices held that a complete ban on truthful, nonmisleading commercial speech is invalid — ban prohibiting *all* advertisement of liquor prices, except for price tags displayed on the merchandise, enacted in order to protect the public and decrease alcohol consumption by discouraging price wars, was held unconstitutional.

Constitutional Law

  (b) Note that the 21st Amendment, which allows the states to regulate liquor and liquor establishments within the state's borders, may not be used as a constitutional basis to override the protection on commercial speech afforded by the 1st Amendment.

 h. **Funding restrictions:** Where Congress prohibited funding to a legal services organization if that organization represented clients in an effort to amend or otherwise challenge existing welfare law, such a prohibition violated the First Amendment. In such cases, the attorney speaks on behalf of a private, indigent client, and such speech cannot be classified as governmental speech. *Legal Services Corp. v. Velazquez*, 121 S. Ct.1043 (2001).

 i. **Restrictions about discussing abortion:** On the other hand, in *Rust v. Sullivan*, 111 S. Ct.1759 (1991), in which a restriction prohibiting doctors employed by federally funded family planning clinics from discussing abortion with their clients was upheld, the Court held that the counseling activities amounted to governmental speech.

4. **Regulation of the time, place and manner of speech:** The government may place reasonable restraints on the time, place, and manner of speech in public areas such as streets, sidewalks, and parks — places historically associated with expressive conduct (*i.e.* picketing, leafleting, and broadcasting). In this section, the focus is not on the "content" or "message" of the speech, but rather its "conduct" or "method".

 a. **Public forums:** A 3-part test is used to determine the constitutionality of time, place, manner regulations of speech and assembly in public places. The regulation must be:

  (1) content neutral (as to both subject matter and viewpoint, i.e. the regulation cannot prefer some messages over others);

  (2) narrowly tailored to serve a significant (important) government interest; and

  (3) must leave open alternative channels of communication. Note that this test is very close to middle-tier scrutiny. For example, an ordinance prohibiting picketing on the sidewalk in front of a particular residence has been upheld. [*Frisby v. Schultz*, 487 U.S. 474 (1988) — the ordinance did not attempt to regulate the message (content neutral), only applied to a single residence (narrowly tailored to protect the homeowner's privacy interest), and did not prohibit picketing in other areas of the neighborhood (left open alternative channels). However, in a case where a bar applicant protested in front of a state bar official's home, the 6th Circuit held that where there was no time, place or manner restriction in place, peaceful targeted residential picketing is protected by under the Free Speech clause. [*Dean v. Byerley*, 2004 WL 34841 (6th Cir. 2004)]; On the other hand, where a statute established an 8-foot wide "buffer zone" around a health clinic and denied picketers the right to "knowingly approach," hand a leaflet to, display a sign to, or talk to anyone within the buffer zone, the statute was constitutional because it was content neutral, narrowly tailored, and left open alternatives channels of communication. [*Hill v. Colorado*, 120 S. Ct. 2480 (2000)]; *See also Thomas v. Chicago Park District*, 122 S. Ct. 2528 (2002) — where an ordinance gave a list of 13

reasons for which permit could be denied, such a list was constitutional where it encouraged speech and did not give park authorities "unbridled discretion" to censor speech.

b. **Nonpublic forums:** Speech-related activities at nonpublic forums, such as military bases, jails, government workplaces, and mailboxes) can be regulated by reasonable time, place, manner regulations. The test used by the Court requires a government regulation to be

(1) viewpoint neutral, and

(2) reasonably related to a legitimate interest.

(a) Certain types of public property (such as jailhouses) that are not open to general public can be regulated more substantially. [*Adderley v. Florida*, 385 U.S. 39 (1966) — state may prohibit demonstrations on jailhouse grounds]; also military bases may be closed to political speeches and distribution of leaflets. [*Greer v. Spock*, 424 U.S. 828 (1976) — purpose of a military base is to train soldiers, not to provide a public forum]. A city may sell space for commercial advertising on city buses, but refuse to sell such space for political advertising. [*Lehman v. Shaker Heights*, 418 U.S. 298 (1974)]. A public school may not deny use of its facilities to religious groups if other public and private groups are allowed similar access. [*Lamb's Chapel v. Center Moriches Union Free School District*, 508 U.S. 672 (1992)].

c. **Private property:** The owner of *a private shopping center is not required to allow access thereto for purposes of picketing and/or leafleting*. [*Hudgens v. NLRB*, 424 U.S. 507 (1976) — overruling *Amalgamated Food Employees v. Logan Valley Plaza*, 391 U.S. 308 (1968)]; however, a state's constitution may be interpreted to protect such expressive activity in a shopping center's public areas. [*Pruneyard Shopping Center v. Robins*, 447 U.S. 74 (1980)].

(1) **Use of loudspeakers:** In the interests of protecting privacy, a state may restrict the volume of sound, or the hours during which amplifiers may be used. [*Kovacs v. Cooper*, 336 U.S. 77 (1949) — upholding the validity of a New Jersey ordinance prohibiting loud and raucous noises].

(2) **Solicitation:** The Court has held that a ***complete ban on door-to-door solicitation is unnecessary***, because a homeowner can protect his privacy by posting a "No Solicitors" sign. [*Martin v. Struthers*, 319 U.S. 141 (1943)]; and, an ordinance requiring door-to-door solicitors or canvassers to identify themselves to local authorities was upheld in the interests of crime prevention. *Hynes v. Mayor of Oradell*, 425 U.S. 610 (1976). However, the Supreme Court recently held that a city may not require persons canvassing door to door to register with the mayor's office and receive a permit where the canvassing consists of religious proselytizing (such as that done by Jehovah's Witnesses), anonymous political speech, and the distribution of handbills. Such a requirement is in violation of the First Amendment. *Watchtower Bible & Tract Soc. of N.Y., Inc. v. Village of Stratton*, 122 S. Ct. 2080 (2002). *See also Murdock v. Pennsylvania*, 63 S. Ct. 870 (1943); *Schneider v. State*, 60 S. Ct. 146 (1939); *Thomas v.*

Collins, 65 S. Ct. 315 (1945). Furthermore, charitable solicitations for funds in residential neighborhoods are generally protected; [See *Schaumburg v. Citizens for a Better Environment,* 444 U.S. 620 (1980) — an ordinance banning door-to-door solicitations by charitable organizations that fail to use at least 75% of their receipts for charitable purposes held unconstitutional under the "less restrictive means" test]. Face-to-face solicitation of funds at an airport terminal, which is a nonpublic forum, may be prohibited, but not a total ban on distribution of literature. *International Society for Krishna v. Lee*, 505 U.S. 672 (1992).

(3) **Unwanted mail:** The Court has upheld the constitutionality of a federal law which permits the Post Office, upon a householder's request, to order a mailer to stop all future mailings to that addressee. [*Rowan v. United States Post Office*, 397 U.S. 728 (1970) — recognizing that householder's right to privacy outweighs the mailer's 1st Amendment right to speech].

d. **Requirement to include all political candidates in debates:** Where a public television station excluded a candidate who had not generated much interest in favor of major party candidates, such exclusion was permissible because the selection criteria were content-neutral and met the requirements for speech in a non-public forum. [*Arkansas Educational Television Commission v. Forbes*, 118 S. Ct. 1633 (1998)].

e. **Licensing:** Another method the government frequently uses for regulating the time, place and manner of speech is to require a license or permit for such activities as a parade, demonstration or rally. Such a licensing statute is valid provided that it is (1) content neutral as applied, *i.e.* for protected speech, the message of the petitioners cannot be considered in granting or denying the permit, and (2) does not give licensing officials "unfettered discretion" to determine who may receive a permit. For example, a parade permit which required applicants to pay up to $1000 per day to cover anticipated costs of police security was held void on its face as a prior restraint. Also, as applied to a white supremacy group, the ordinance was not content neutral since unpopular speech is met with greater hostility, thus requiring more police protection. [*Forsyth County v. Nationalist Movement*, 505 U.S. 123 (1992)].

(1) **Statute "void on its face":** Where a statute is facially void (i.e., it gives the licensing officials unrestricted discretion), a speaker need not even apply for a permit. In which case, one may exercise his (or her) 1st Amendment rights on the public property without a permit. [*Staub v. Baxley,* 355 U.S. 313 (1958) — holding a speaker cannot be convicted for violating a facially invalid licensing statute].

(2) **Statute valid on its face:** On the other hand, if a statute is valid on its face (i.e., contains narrowly defined standards as to time, place, manner and duration), then the applicant must seek a permit. If the permit is denied (even arbitrarily), the applicant must appeal the adverse ruling to the proper administrative or judicial body. [*Poulos v. New Hampshire,* 345 U.S. 395 (1953) — one may not speak without a permit, and then raise the defense that the permit was improperly denied]. *See, e.g., Thomas v. Chicago Park District,* 122

S. Ct. 755 (2002) (where an ordinance requires users of a public forum to obtain a permit to hold a large-scale event there, such a scheme is permissible if the reasons for denying permits do not involve subject-matter censorship but are only content neutral time, place and manner restrictions and if the ordinance contains guidelines for officials to follow in conducting their review of the permits).

e. **Injunctions:** As a general rule, if one is enjoined from speaking, he (or she) must either obey the injunction or appeal it — unless the time is such that an appeal would effectively frustrate the exercise of his (or her) rights. [*Walker v. City of Birmingham,* 388 U.S. 307 (1967) — upholding contempt conviction for violating injunction; noting that an expedited appellate procedure was available].

(1) **Ex parte injunctions:** An ex parte injunction against 1st Amendment activity is generally invalid, except in an emergency. Such injunctions should be overturned on appeal.

5. **Special procedural rules/Facial attacks:**

a. **Prior restraints:** As a general rule, the government cannot suppress or restrain speech in advance of its publication or utterance.

(1) **Presumption:** There is a strong presumption against the constitutional validity of any system of prior restraint of expression. [*Bantam Books, Inc. v. Sullivan,* 372 U.S. 58 (1963)].

(2) **Forms of prior restraint:** The Court refused to permit the government to enjoin the publication of the Pentagon Papers. [*New York Times v. United States,* 403 U.S. 713 (1971)]; also, confiscation by the Post Office of mailed materials determined by the Postmaster General to be "obscene" held invalid. [*Bantam Books, supra*]; and injunction sought against media reporting of a criminal trial held invalid in *Nebraska Press Association v. Stuart,* 427 U.S. 539 (1976) — absent proof that there is a "clear and present danger that pretrial publicity would threaten a fair trial." *See also Republican Party of Minnesota v. White*, 122 S. Ct. 2528 (2002) — although the courts are meant to be politically neutral, a state cannot prevent judicial candidates from expressing their opinions on disputed legal or political issues; to do so is to restrict political speech based on content.

b. **Exceptional cases in which prior restraints allowed:**

(1) **National security:** A government agency can require prepublication review of writings related to employment of past or present employees. [*Snepp v. United States,* 444 U.S. 507 (1980) — where such review is necessary to protect national security].

(2) **Classified military information**

(3) **Obscenity:** The seizure of allegedly "obscene" materials *prior to distribution is a prior restraint,* and hence subject to constitutional safeguards. Students should be advised that for exam purposes, any case involving a search and

seizure is governed by the 4th Amendment. Thus, any "large scale" seizure of allegedly "obscene" materials must be preceded by a full adversary hearing and a judicial determination of obscenity. [*Quantity of Books v. Kansas,* 378 U.S. 205 (1964)]; however, the seizure of a *single* book or film to preserve as evidence in a criminal proceeding need only be made pursuant to a warrant based on a determination of probable cause by a neutral magistrate. [*Heller v. New York,* 413 U.S. 483 (1973)].

(4) **Film censorship:** Another form of prior restraint is the censorship or licensing of motion pictures prior to their exhibition. The Court has held that statutes requiring films to be submitted to a Board of Censors before showing them are constitutional if the following requirements are met: (1) the standards for the denial of a license must be narrowly drawn and reasonable; (2) when a license is denied, the censor must *promptly* seek an injunction [*Teitel Films v. Cusack,* 390 U.S. 139 (1968) — invalidating a statute which permitted a 50 day administrative process before the censor was required to institute judicial proceedings]; (3) the burden of proving that the material is "obscene" or otherwise unprotected is on the censor; and (4) there must be a prompt judicial determination. [*Freedman v. Maryland,* 380 U.S. 51 (1965)].

c. **Overbreadth doctrine:** Even when a state does have the power to regulate an area dealing with free speech, it must not do so "by means which sweep unnecessarily broadly and thereby invade the area of protected freedoms." [*NAACP v. Alabama,* 377 U.S. 288 (1964)]. Thus, the wording of a statute must be narrow and specific, and not overly broad so as to have a "chilling effect" upon protected speech. Note the following examples of *"overbroad"* statutes/regulations that were held to be unconstitutional:

(1) An ordinance making it unlawful "to curse or revile or to use obscene or opprobrious language toward or with reference" to a police officer performing his duties. [*Lewis v. City of New Orleans,* 415 U.S. 130 (1974) — invalid because the ordinance effectively punished all vulgar and offensive speech even though some of this speech may be protected by the 1st Amendment].

(2) An ordinance prohibiting speech that "stirs the public to anger, invites dispute" held to be overbroad. [*Terminiello v. City of Chicago,* 337 U.S. 1 (1949)].

(3) An ordinance requiring charitable organizations to use at least 75% of their receipts for "charitable purposes" held void. [*Schaumburg v. Citizens for a Better Environment, supra*].

(4) *But see Virginia v. Hicks*, 123 S. Ct. 2191 (2003) — A municipal housing authority's rule that required nonresidents who wished to engage in leafleting or demonstrating on housing authority's property to obtain permission from official with unfettered discretion not overbroad because it did not apply to sufficiently substantial amount of speech protected by First Amendment.

d. **Vagueness doctrine:** The "vagueness" doctrine is closely related to the "overbreadth" doctrine. In *NAACP v. Button*, 371 U.S. 415 (1963), the Court admonished that governmental regulations must be drawn "with narrow specificity." The following statutes have been ruled "void for vagueness":

(1) Statute making it a crime to "publicly mutilate, trample upon, deface or treat contemptuously the flag of the United States." [*Smith v. Goguen,* 415 U.S. 566 (1974) — "void for vagueness" because there is no "ascertainable standard" for defining "treat contemptuously"].

(2) Municipal vagrancy ordinance defining vagrants to include "rogues and vagabonds ... lewd, wanton, and lascivious persons ... persons wandering or straying around from place to place without any lawful purpose or objective" to be unconstitutional. [*Papachristou v. City of Jacksonville,* 405 U.S. 156 (1972) — void for vagueness].

(3) A city ordinance that defined "loitering" as "to remain in any one place with no apparent purpose," and gave police officers absolute discretion to issue dispersal orders to groups of two or more persons seen loitering in a public place if the officer reasonably believed that one of them was a criminal street gang member and made it a criminal offense to disobey such order. [*Chicago v. Morales*, 119 S. Ct. 1849 (1999)].

6. **Freedom of Association:** There is a close "nexus" between the freedoms of speech and association. The Supreme Court has acknowledged that "state action which may curtail (or have the effect of curtailing) the freedom to associate is subject to the closest scrutiny." Under the freedom to associate the court has struck down laws which prevented the NAACP from assisting individuals [*NAACP v. Button, supra*], and which prevented a labor union from assisting its members in retaining lawyers. [*Brotherhood of Railroad Trainmen v. Virginia,* 377 U.S. 1 (1964)]. On the other hand, where the Boy Scouts of America sought to exclude homosexuals from participating in the organization because of the organization's view that homosexual conduct was inconsistent with the values it sought to instill in youth members, such exclusion was constitutional under the organization's First Amendment right of expressive association [*Boy Scouts of America v. Dale*, 120 S. Ct. 2446 (2001)].

    a. **Regulations upon public employment:**

       (1) **In general:** *An individual cannot be denied public employment based upon membership in a political organization.* [*Keyishian v. Board of Regents,* 385 U.S. 589 (1967)—public employment cannot be denied members of the Communist Party].

       (2) **Modern test:** An individual may not be punished or deprived of public employment for political association unless: (1) he (or she) is an active member of a subversive organization; (2) such membership is with *knowledge of the illegal aims* of the organization; and (3) he (or she) has a *specific intent* to further those illegal ends (violent overthrow of the government). [*Scales v. United States,* 367 U.S. 203 (1961)].

    b. **Examples:**

       (1) In *United States v. Robel,* 389 U.S. 258 (1967), the Warren Court ruled a provision of the Subversive Activities Control Act was unconstitutionally overbroad by denying members of the Communist Party "employment in any defense facility."

(2) The Court invalidated political patronage dismissals by the Democratic Sheriff of Cook County. [*Elrod v. Burns,* 427 U.S. 347 (1976) — upholding the principle that one may not be excluded from public employment on the basis of political affiliation unless the proscribed organization is truly subversive].

(3) In *Brand v. Finkel,* 445 U.S. 507 (1980), the Court held that party affiliation is not an appropriate requirement for the position of public defender.

c. **Loyalty oaths:** In the past, the Court has chosen to deal with loyalty qualifications under the "vagueness" and "overbreadth" doctrines. Thus, in *Shelton v. Tucker,* 364 U.S. 479 (1960) the Court invalidated an Arkansas statute requiring teachers to file an affidavit listing "every organization to which they have belonged or regularly contributed within the preceding five years" as overbroad. Similarly, in *Cramp v. Board Of Public Instruction,* 368 U.S. 278 (1961) the Court invalidated a Florida statute requiring public employees to swear, "I have not and will not lend my aid, support, advice, counsel or influence to the Communist Party" as vague and ambiguous.

Compare: On the other hand, an oath that public employees will "support the Constitution of the United States and will oppose the overthrow of the government of the United States by force, violence, or by any illegal or unconstitutional means" was held valid in *Connell v. Higgenbotham,* 403 U.S. 207 (1971).

7. **Freedom of the Press:** The press has no greater freedom to speak than any ordinary member of the general public. The press has no special right of access to government information.

   a. **Right to attend trials:** The 1st Amendment guarantees both the public and the press a right to attend criminal trials; however, this right is not absolute and may be outweighed where the judge finds an "overriding" interest that cannot be accommodated by less restrictive means. [*Richmond Newspapers v. Virginia*, 448 U.S. 555 (1980)].

   b. **"Gag" orders:** A "gag" order, a pre-trial order prohibiting the press from publishing certain types of information, will almost never be held constitutional as a violation of 1st Amendment rights because the trial judge has other alternatives at his disposal (*i.e.* change of venue, postponement of the trial, careful **voir dire**, or restricting statements of the lawyers, police, and witnesses, etc). [*Nebraska Press Association v. Stuart*, 427 U.S. 539 (1976)].

   c. **Newsperson's privilege:** A newsperson has no 1st Amendment right to refuse to testify before a grand jury. [*Branzburg v. Hayes*, 408 U.S. 665 (1972)].

   d. **Broadcasting regulations:** In general, radio and television broadcasting can be more closely regulated than the press, due to the limited number of airwaves available. A radio broadcast of "patently offensive sexual and excretory speech" (even though not "obscene" under the *Miller* test) can be sanctioned to protect the privacy interests of children likely to be listening. [*FCC v. Pacifica Foundation*, 438 U.S. 726 (1978)].

e. **Cable programming:** The Court has held that cable television receives 1st Amendment protection somewhere between broadcast TV and newspapers. Where cable TV operators are subjected to content neutral regulations, intermediate scrutiny is applied. [*Turner Broadcasting System, Inc. v. FCC*, 512 U.S. 622 (1994)]. On the other hand, where content specific regulation is imposed, the Court has yet to pick a standard of review; however, the Court allows cable TV operators the right to ban "indecent"—describing sexual activities in a patently offensive manner—programming on channels which are leased outright to unaffiliated third parties (but not as to public access channels). [*Denver Area Educational Telecommunications Consortium, Inc. v. FCC*, 518 U.S. 727 (1996)].

f. **Publication of illegally obtained information:** The Supreme Court recently held that, where a radio commentator played a tape on his talk show that he had legally obtained, but which had been recorded by another person in violation of the law, such a publication was protected under the First Amendment. The Court reasoned that a stranger's illegal conduct does not suffice to remove the First Amendment shield from speech about a matter of public concern. [*Bartnicki v. Vopper*, 121 S. Ct. 1753 (2001)].

g. **Prior restraints:** As a general rule, any *prior* restraint of publication will be deemed illegal. That does not mean that after publication, there may not be civil or criminal consequences from the publication itself. When taking any test, make sure you understand the timing of the action in question; whether it takes place before or after publication is essential.

8. **Bar membership:** The state is permitted under the Due Process Clause to inquire into the qualifications and fitness of candidates for admission to the bar. However, a candidate cannot be denied admission for past membership in the Communist Party. [*Schware v. New Mexico Board of Bar Examiners*, 353 U.S. 232 (1957) — cannot infer "bad moral character" based on applicant's membership in the Communist Party 15 years prior to his application to the bar]; but the state can refuse bar membership to an applicant who refuses to answer questions (re: past Communist Party membership), if his refusal obstructs the bar examiner's investigation of his qualifications. [*Konigsberg v. State Bar of California*, 366 U.S. 36 (1961)].

   Modern view: Reaffirming the validity of *Konigsberg*, the Court held in *Law Students Civil Rights Research Council, Inc. v. Wadmond*, 401 U.S. 154 (1971) that a state can inquire into knowing membership in subversive organizations in screening its applicants for the bar. Thus, the 1st Amendment does not extend unlimited protection to a bar applicant who refuses to disclose his political affiliations.

   Residency Requirements: A residency requirement by the New Hampshire state bar requiring a Vermont resident to establish a home address in New Hampshire prior to being sworn in was held to be violative of the Privileges and Immunities Clause of Article IV, §2 [*Supreme Court of New Hampshire v. Piper*, 84 LEd 2d 205 (1985)].

QUESTION BY QUESTION CAPSULE OUTLINE

1. Presidential Powers
2. Presidential Powers
3. Commerce Clause
4. Federal Jurisdictional Matter
5. Presidential Appointment Power
6. Standing
7. Bill of Attainder
8. Aliens
9. State Statute re: Billboards
10. Contracts Clause
11. Foreign Affairs—Nonjusticiable Political Question
12. Commerce Clause
13. Nonjusticiable Political Question—House of Representatives Membership
14. State's Reserved Powers under Tenth Amendment
15. Supreme Court Review—Advisory Opinions
16. Freedom of Speech—Parade Permits
17. Freedom of Speech—Public Officials
18. Freedom of Speech—Picketing of Dwelling
19. Ripeness
20. Freedom of Religion—Establishment Clause
21. Freedom of Religion—Establishment Clause
22. Procedural Due Process
23. Congressional War Power Authority
24. Free Exercise Clause
25. Equal Protection Clause ("Rational Basis" Test)
26. Standing
27. Commerce Clause

28. Due Process—Burden of Persuasion
29. Supremacy Clause
30. Commerce Clause
31. Commerce Clause
32. Adequate and Independent State Grounds
33. Fundamental Rights
34. Police Power—Validity of State Statute
35. Commerce Clause—Less Restrictive Alternatives
36. Freedom of Speech—Speech Related Conduct
37. Fifteenth Amendment—Voting
38. Children of Illegal Aliens—Quasi-Suspect Status
39. State Police Power Authority
40. Equal Protection Clause—Voting
41. U.S. Supreme Court Review
42. Executive Privilege—Criminal Proceedings
43. Executive Power—Appointment of Officers
44. Establishment Clause
45. Abortion Statute
46. Private Discrimination under Fourteenth Amendment
47. Contract Clause
48. *Ex Post Facto* Clause
49. Presidential Pardon
50. U.S. Supreme Court—Jurisdiction
51. Treaty Power
52. Treaties—Conflicting State Action
53. Freedom of Press
54. *Ex Post Facto* Clause

Constitutional Law

55. Immunity—Federal Employee
56. Commercial Speech
57. *Ad Valorem* Taxation
58. Reserved Power—State Taxation of Property
59. Congress' Power to Regulate *Interstate* Commerce
60. State Statute Regulating Intrastate Commerce
61. President *Not* Empowered to Regulate *Interstate* Commerce
62. Gross Receipts Tax
63. License Tax
64. Excise Tax
65. Privileges and Immunities Clause
66. Restriction(s) on Rt. to be a Candidate for Public Office
67. Voting—Party Affiliation Statute
68. State Taxes—Military Personnel
69. Commercial Free Speech—Advertising for Contraceptives
70. Congressional Legislation Re: Local Matters
71. U.S. Supreme Court Review by *Certiorari*
72. Obscenity
73. Congress' Power to Legislate Over the District of Columbia
74. Due Process Clause—Housing Ordinance
75. State Police Powers
76. Pre-Emption Doctrine—Conflict Between State and Federal Laws
77. Compelling State Interest
78. Compelling State Interest—Burden of Proof Assigned to State
79. Bill of Attainder
80. Speech and Debate Clause
81. Privileges and Immunities Clause—Taxation of Non-Residents

Question by Question Capsule Outline

82. Privileges and Immunities Clause—Licenses
83. Power of Eminent Domain
84. Procedural Due Process—Eminent Domain
85. Due Process Clause—Rezoning Ordinance
86. Due Process Clause—Referendum Process
87. Due Process Clause—Housing Ordinance
88. Candidate Qualifications—Ballot Access Requirement
89. Government Regulation Constituting a Compensable Taking
90. Fourteenth Amendment—Enabling Clause
91. Freedom of Religion—Establishment Clause
92. Freedom of Religion—Establishment Clause
93. Freedom of Speech—Parade Permits
94. Freedom of Speech—State Police Power
95. Parade Permits— Discretion of Public Official
96. State Taxation
97. Equal Protection Clause
98. Right to Vote—Fifteenth Amendment
99. Equal Protection Clause
100. Police Power—Regulation of Employment
101. Equal Protection Clause—Sex Classification
102. Equal Protection Clause—Race Classification
103. Equal Protection Clause
104. Equal Protection Clause—Residency Requirement
105. Validity of State Statute—Police Power Basis
106. Equal Protection Clause—Alienage
107. Standing—Requirement of Actual Injury
108. General Welfare Clause

Constitutional Law

109. Equal Protection Clause—Alienage
110. Equal Protection Clause—Burden of Proof
111. Equal Protection Clause—Rational Basis Test
112. Interstate Commerce—Commerce Clause
113. Standing—"Actual Injury" Requirement
114. Individual Rights—Residency Requirements
115. First Amendment—Free Exercise Clause
116. Mootness
117. Freedom of Speech—Sound Amplification Equipment
118. Freedom of Speech
119. Freedom of Speech—Hostile Audience
120. Invasion of Privacy—Actual Malice
121. Federal Taxation
122. Vagueness "Overbreadth" Doctrine
123. Equal Protection Clause—Sex Discrimination
124. Residency Requirements—Compelling State Interest
125. Freedom of Speech—Private Shopping Center
126. "Overbreadth" Doctrine
127. Freedom of Speech—Symbolic Expression
128. Freedom of Religion—Free Exercise Clause
129. Due Process Clause—Deprivation of Property
130. Speech and Debate Clause
131. State Statute Restricting Use of Contraceptive Devices
132. Third-Party *(jus tertii)* Standing
133. Advertisement—Private Newspaper Refusal to Publish
134. Freedom of Religion—Free Exercise Clause
135. "Affectation Doctrine"—Commerce Power

Question by Question Capsule Outline

136. Obscene Material—Private Possession

137. Equal Protection Clause—"Suspect" Classifications

138. Legitimate State Interest—Statute Re: Auto Radar Detection Devices

139. Constitutional Provisions Applicable to Corporations

140. State Economic Regulation—Commerce Clause

141. State Regulation of Interstate Commerce

142. Contract Clause

143. State Police Power—Protection of Health, Safety and Welfare of Citizens

144. "Balance of Interests" Test—State Regulation/Burden on Interstate Commerce

145. Due Process Issue—Re: Student Dismissal from School

146. Due Process—Student Suspension

147. Gender Discrimination—Equal ProtectionViolation

148. Conflict Between Executive Order and Act of Congress

149. Equal Protection Clause—Denial of Licenses

150. Freedom of Speech

QUESTIONS

Question 1 is based on the following fact situation.

During the final days of Reagan's presidency, many of his Cabinet members began leaking rather embarrassing stories of the Chief Executive to the press. In one such story, which appeared in the *New York Post* newspaper, an unidentified Cabinet member was quoted as saying that Reagan pardoned George Steinbrenner, owner of the New York Yankees baseball team, for a previous felony conviction because Steinbrenner promised to give Reagan a lifetime pass to all future Yankee games. Upset by these news "leaks", Reagan in his last official act as President issued an executive order banning all executive employees from having conversations with members of the press unless prior permission had been obtained from an administrative supervisor. The executive order called for the dismissal of any employee willfully in violation of that order.

After Reagan left office, the press made repeated reference to the executive order and derisively referred to it as "the Reagan legacy." Nonetheless, after George Bush took office he promised to abide by the order. Thereafter, London Wainwright III, one of Vice-President Dan Quayle's senior advisors, leaked a story to the *Washington Post* stating that Quayle told staff members that the only reason he visited San Francisco following the earthquake was because he wanted to play golf at nearby Pebble Beach Country Club. The *Post* printed the story and named Wainwright as the source. In compliance with civil service regulations, a hearing was conducted and Wainwright was found to have violated the executive order barring unauthorized communications with print media. Based on the recommendation of the Civil Service Commission, Wainwright was summarily dismissed from his executive staff position.

1. Wainwright brings an appropriate action seeking reinstatement and challenges the constitutionality of the executive order. If this case reaches the U.S. Supreme Court, the justices should rule the executive order is

    (A) constitutional, because governmental employment is a privilege and not a right
    (B) constitutional, because the President has plenary power to set forth employment regulations for Executive Department employees
    (C) unconstitutional, because Congress, not the President, has authority to regulate the terms and conditions of federal employment
    (D) unconstitutional, because the President cannot broadly limit all executive employees' freedom of speech and association

Question 2 is based on the following fact situation.

A devastating earthquake measuring 8.5 on the Richter scale struck Tijuana, Mexico. The earthquake destroyed hundreds of homes and buildings. Thousands of residents were killed, injured and left homeless by the earthquake. Ernesto Zevillo Ponce de Leon, Mexico's president, sought the assistance of the United States in providing emergency aid.

President Clinton initially wanted to send troops from the United States military base in San Diego but learned that they were on maneuvers in the South Pacific. As a result, President Clinton issued an executive order directing members of the Border Patrol, a federal agency under the supervision of the Immigration and Naturalization Service (INS), in southern California to travel to Tijuana to engage in emergency rescue operations. The Border Patrol's main function is to patrol the border with Mexico to prevent illegal aliens from entering the United States.

2. Duke Duckworth, a member of the Border Patrol, refused to comply with the executive order and assist in the Mexico relief effort. He claims that participating in such operations in a foreign country is beyond the scope of his job responsibilities. Duke brings suit in federal court challenging the validity of President Clinton's executive order. Assuming Duke has adequate standing, the court should rule the executive order

   (A) valid, because as commander-in-chief the President has unfettered authority to require federal employees to participate in an international relief effort
   (B) valid, because employees of an executive agency can be required to perform such emergency functions
   (C) invalid, because the executive order is beyond the scope of presidential power absent congressional authorization
   (D) invalid, because the director of the INS, not the President, has the power to issue directives to the Border Patrol

Question 3 is based on the following fact situation.

On April 15, 1984, the SALT (Strategic Arms Limitations Talks) between the United States and the U.S.S.R. suddenly broke down at the insistence of the Russian Foreign Minister. Two weeks later, Congress passed an Act wherein the United States government would purchase and operate all of the nation's airlines.

3. In all likelihood, Congress's power to enact this legislation will derive from

   (A) its power to tax and provide for the general welfare
   (B) its power to raise and support an army and declare war
   (C) its power to regulate commerce
   (D) its power to make laws regarding territory and other property belonging to the United States

Questions 4–5 are based on the following fact situation.

Congress has recently passed the National Rent Control Act (henceforth referred to as NRCA), which is designed to make the stabilization of rents more effective throughout the United States. The NRCA will be applicable to all leasehold contracts hereafter entered into between landlords and tenants involving residential and commercial properties. The new federal law is intended to protect tenants from spiraling rents and "profiteering" by landlords without curtailing the supply of rental units or depriving landlords of substantial constitutional rights.

4. The new federal NRCA statute would be most clearly constitutional as applied to

   (A) the rental of a state owned office building by the state of Tennessee to a privately owned business
   (B) the rental of residential property located in the District of Columbia by an individual landlord to a family of six
   (C) the rental of an apartment located in the state of Oregon by the Portland Real Estate Company to an individual tenant
   (D) the rental of an office building to the government of the city of Picayune in the state of Mississippi by an individual landlord

5. To help administer the new federal NRCA statute Congress created a seven member agency, four members of which were appointed by the President, two by the Senate and one by the Speaker of the House. The agency was authorized to issue rules interpreting regulations prescribed under existing federal law. It was also authorized to issue "cease and desist" orders after hearings against landlords or leasing firms "intentionally engaged in profiteering." In this regard, violations of the "cease and desist" orders were made punishable by fine and/or imprisonment. Which of the following is the strongest constitutional argument against the authority of this agency?

   (A) Congress may not delegate to the agency power to make interpretations of existing federal laws.
   (B) Congress may not delegate to the agency power to make "cease and desist" orders, the violation of which are punishable by imprisonment.
   (C) Congress may not make enforcement of a federal law such as the NRCA in any governmental body other than U.S. Attorney General or the courts.
   (D) Congress may not retain the power to appoint even a minority of members of such an agency.

Question 6 is based on the following fact situation.

The U.S. Navy wanted to build a naval base on the north shore of the island of Oahu in Hawaii. Situated along the north shore of this island were coral reefs which are the home of the Hawaiian Hammerhead fish. The Hawaiian Hammerhead is a very unique and rare species of fish that is only found along the north shore area.

Congress conducted hearings as to whether to authorize the construction of the naval base. During the hearings one of the speakers who addressed the congressional committee was Professor Kingfish, a famous expert on oceanography and marine biology. Professor Kingfish vehemently opposed the naval plan and stated that the construction would in his opinion result in the extinction of the Hawaiian Hammerhead. Congress thereafter approved the construction of the naval base and passed a bill providing necessary authorization and funding for the project.

6. Professor Kingfish has filed an action in federal district court seeking to enjoin the construction of the naval base on ecological grounds. Does Professor Kingfish have adequate standing?

   (A) Yes, because he has a personal stake in the litigation.
   (B) Yes, because he is a recognized expert on marine biology and he testified at the congressional hearings.
   (C) No, because the suit presents a nonjusticiable political question.
   (D) No, because Professor Kingfish is not suffering any actual harm or injury.

Question 7 is based on the following fact situation.

Iris Fox is a licensed State Farm Insurance agent in the state of Cahuenga. Iris is one of 2,000 insurance agents licensed under the general licensing laws of the state. The Cahuenga state legislature recently passed a highly controversial bill that, inter alia, reduces "good driver" automobile insurance rates and prohibits price-fixing and discrimination by insurance companies. This bill passed despite a well financed and intense lobbying effort mounted by the insurance industry. After this law was enacted, Iris was interviewed by the *Cahuenga Chronicle* newspaper and publicly stated, "the legislature is a bunch of crooked, self-serving scumbags." After Iris's statement made newspaper headlines, the Cahuenga legislature enacted a statute providing that "the Cahuenga state insurance license of Iris Fox is henceforth revoked." Astonished by the legislature's action, Iris, who remains unrepentant, seeks your legal advice.

7. You should advise Iris that the Cahuenga statute revoking her state insurance license is

    (A) constitutional, because a state license is a privilege and not a right, and, therefore, it is not protected by the due process clause
    (B) unconstitutional, because it denies her the equal protection of the laws
    (C) unconstitutional, because it is a prohibited bill of attainder
    (D) unconstitutional, because it is a denial of a privilege or immunity protected by Article IV

Question 8 is based on the following fact situation.

You are counsel to a U.S. Senate Committee of which Senator X is Chairman. The Committee has held hearings on the problems of health care for senior citizens. Evidence at the hearings has indicated that thousands of elderly citizens die each year because they cannot afford proper medical and hospital treatment. Based on the evidence presented at these hearings, Senator X wishes to introduce a bill providing free medical and hospital care for all U.S. citizens 70 years of age and older. Senator X, however, intends to include a provision in the bill denying such medical and hospital care benefits to aliens (in the same age category) unless they have been legally admitted for permanent U.S. residency. Senator X has asked for your advice regarding his proposed bill. You are understandably concerned about the legality of the aliens proviso.

8. As such, which of the following is the strongest argument in support of the constitutionality of the provision disqualifying aliens from receiving such medical and hospital benefits?

    (A) Since the medical and hospital benefits will be paid for by the government, they are a privilege, not a right, and therefore they are not within the meaning of the Fifth Amendment.
    (B) The disqualifying provision does not unduly burden either interstate commerce or the right of aliens to travel freely from state to state.
    (C) The principles of equal protection apply against the states and not against the federal government.
    (D) The disqualifying provision is reasonably related to legitimate congressional objectives under its immigration, citizenship and spending powers.

Question 9 is based on the following fact situation.

The City of Middletown has undergone a massive redevelopment project aimed at remodeling and beautifying the downtown area. Recently the city council has passed an ordinance prohibiting the placing of any sign with dimensions larger than six feet on the exterior of any commercial building. Furthermore, the ordinance required that signs which were within the guidelines of the ordinance could only relate to advertising the business of the property's occupant. The intended purpose of the ordinance was to advance the municipality's interests in traffic safety and aesthetics.

Dirkson, who owned an office building in the newly developed section of town, placed a ten foot sign on the outside of his building endorsing his brother's political candidacy. The city council has ordered Dirkson to remove the sign from his building. But he has refused to take down the sign until after the election.

9. If Dirkson challenges the Middletown ordinance, the most likely result is that he will

   (A) prevail, because the ordinance violates his freedom of speech
   (B) prevail, because such a time, place and manner restriction on private property is discriminatory and overbroad
   (C) not prevail, because although commercial speech is protected by the First Amendment, it is subject to greater regulation than other forms of protected speech
   (D) not prevail, because the ordinance is rationally related to a legitimate state interest

Question 10 is based on the following fact situation.

For many years, persons engaged in real estate transactions in Utah have utilized "installment land contracts". The so-called "installment land contract" has been popular as a substitute for the mortgage or deed of trust. Under such a contract, the seller agrees to accept and the buyer agrees to pay the purchase price in installments over a stipulated period of time. The vendor retains legal title as security for the payment of the purchase price; the vendee has equitable title under the doctrine of equitable conversion. The most important characteristic of the "installment land contract", however, is the forfeiture clause which provides that if the vendee is in default for 30 days, the vendor may at his/her option declare a forfeiture of the contract in which case all payments made shall be forfeited as "liquidated" damages and the buyer shall become a tenant at will of the seller.

Over the years, many sellers of property under such "installment land contracts" have declared forfeitures in situations where the prospective buyers were delinquent in their payments, even when the buyer was late with a single payment after nearly all the other payments had been made. In order to remedy this inequitable situation, the legislature of Utah enacted a new law requiring any seller attempting to declare a forfeiture of an "installment land contract" to do so by instituting a formal foreclosure action in the courts. The new law also provided that prior to the commencement of such a foreclosure action, the seller under such an arrangement must give the buyer a sixty-day grace period to make up any delinquent installment payment with interest. The new law expressly applied both to "installment land contracts" entered into subsequent to its enactment and to "installment land contracts" already in existence at the time of its enactment.

10. Is this new Utah law likely to be held constitutional?

    (A) Yes, because it is a reasonable regulation of the procedure to be followed in such cases and does not substantially diminish the underlying obligations of the buyer.
    (B) Yes, because the authority to enact laws regulating real estate sales transactions occurring within the boundaries of individual states is reserved exclusively to the states by the Tenth Amendment.
    (C) No, because application of the law to "installment land contracts" entered into prior to its enactment is a violation of the obligation of contracts.
    (D) No, because application of the law to "installment land contracts" entered into before or after its enactment is a deprivation of a proprietary interest without due process of the law.

Question 11 is based on the following fact situation.

In late 2001, Congress passed an Act aimed at "countries assisting or furnishing aid or support to nations or movements engaged in hostilities with the United States." Section 5 of that Act authorized and directed the Treasury Department "to issue orders barring entry into the United States any category of goods the sale of which in the United States is likely to improve the economic or balance of payments posture of an assisting country." The Secretary of State was authorized by Section 6 to define "assisting countries." Pursuant to Section 5, the Treasury Department issued a regulation which provided in part that: "Imports of the following categories of goods from assisting countries are hereby prohibited:

... (c) Bulk shipments for resale within the United States of books, pamphlets, flags, decorations or other symbols, excepting, however, scientific, technical and literary works intended for scholarly purpose ..."

The State Department designated Rumelia, an Eastern European country, as an "assisting country," on the basis of its determination that medical supplies collected by public donation in Rumelia had been sent to Panamania, a country currently engaged in hostilities with the United States in Central America. As a consequence, the Treasury Department issued an order barring practically all products and goods from Rumelia into the United States.

Nationwide Flag and Banner Company, a St. Louis distributor of state and foreign flags, has had a lucrative contract with the Rumelia Department of Commerce for the importation and sale of Rumelia flags in the United States. However, on account of the Treasury Department's order, Rumelia is now barred from importing any of its flags into the United States.

11. In an appropriate federal court, Nationwide brings a suit against the Secretary of State and the Treasury Department to set aside the order barring Rumelia imports on the ground that it is inconsistent with the principles of our constitutional form of government. Which of the following is the most proper disposition of the Nationwide suit by the federal court?

    (A) Suit dismissed, because Nationwide does not have standing to bring this action.
    (B) Suit dismissed, because there is no adversity between Nationwide and the defendants.
    (C) Suit dismissed, because it presents a nonjusticiable political question.
    (D) Suit decided on its merits.

Constitutional Law

Question 12 is based on the following fact situation.

The state of North Durango enacted a statute prohibiting any motor vehicles traveling within the state to have window tinting or glass coating of any kind. The bill, known as the "Window Tint" Act, passed the state legislature at the urging of state and local law enforcement agencies who argued that tinted windows prevented them from observing interior car activity. Most citizens also supported the "Window Tint" Act, especially after a North Durango state trooper was gunned down and killed by an occupant in a window tinted limousine. The trooper was unable to see that his assailant was armed and dangerous when he approached the vehicle for a speeding infraction.

Luxury Limousine Company operates a limo service in the neighboring state of South Durango. Luxury has a fleet of 68 limos all of which have tinted windows. Each year Luxury makes thousands of trips into North Durango to transport passengers to Durango International Airport (situated ten miles from the South Durango border) and other destinations. Since all its limos are manufactured with tinted windows, Luxury will incur a great expense to specially order limos without tinting.

12. Luxury brings suit to challenge the constitutionality of the North Durango "Window Tint" Act. Assuming that Luxury has proper standing to assert such an action, which of the following is Luxury's strongest constitutional argument to invalidate the aforesaid statute?

    (A) Because window tinting is permitted on vehicles in neighboring states, this law denies Luxury the equal protection of laws whenever its limos operate within North Durango.
    (B) Because this law burdens interstate commerce by prohibiting all vehicles with window tinting from entering the state, this law violates the Commerce Clause.
    (C) Because window tinting on vehicles is legal in South Durango but illegal in North Durango, this law violates the contract clause by preventing Luxury from fulfilling its obligation to transport passengers into North Durango.
    (D) Because interstate travel is a fundamental right that may not be burdened by state law, it violates Luxury's substantive due process rights by arbitrarily and unreasonably regulating economic activity.

Question 13 is based on the following fact situation.

Kennedy was a candidate for the United States House of Representatives from the state of South Dakota. The state registrar of elections refused to put Kennedy's name on the ballot because the registrar believed that Kennedy was not a resident of South Dakota. The registrar contended that Article 1, Section 2 of the U.S. Constitution specifically required a candidate for the House of Representatives "be an Inhabitant of that State in which he shall be chosen". As a consequence, Kennedy filed suit in state court against the registrar of elections seeking to have her name placed on the ballot. The state court ruled in her favor and determined that Kennedy did in fact qualify as a resident of South Dakota. The registrar appealed the decision to the state Supreme Court which, in turn, affirmed the lower court ruling. Thereafter, Kennedy's name was placed on the ballot. After a hotly contested election in which Kennedy was depicted as a carpetbagger, she narrowly defeated the incumbent.

However, at the time that Kennedy was to be seated as a House member, the House of Representatives held hearings on her qualifications and eligibility. By a two-thirds vote, the House determined that Kennedy was not a resident of South Dakota at the time of her election and refused to seat her. Kennedy then brought suit in federal district court against the Speaker and other officers of the House, seeking back pay and an order that she be seated in the House of Representatives. The defendants demurred claiming lack of subject matter jurisdiction.

13. As such, which of the following is the strongest constitutional argument supporting defendant's demurrer?

   (A) There is no case or controversy between Kennedy and the officers of the House of Representatives.
   (B) The case presents a nonjusticiable political question.
   (C) The suit should have been brought as an original action in the United States Supreme Court.
   (D) Under Article III of the Constitution, the federal courts are not empowered to render advisory opinions.

Question 14 is based on the following fact situation.

There has been a great deal of news media coverage regarding the problem of underage teenage drinking. Many high school and college students have been purchasing fraudulent driver licenses with phony birthdates showing "proof" of being twenty-one years of age or older. As a consequence, many teenagers are able to purchase alcoholic beverages at liquor stores and at restaurants and bars. The situation is becoming especially alarming at many college campuses. A "Business World and Weekly Report" article reported that the majority of freshmen between the ages of eighteen and nineteen at many colleges (such as Cornell, University of Texas, and University of Colorado) had illegally purchased evidence of phony "proof."

With underage drinking reaching epidemic proportions, Congress passed a law establishing a federal commission to monitor and curtail alcoholic beverage sales to underage drinkers. To implement the program on a national scale, the bill required each state to pass legislation establishing a local "watchdog" agency to facilitate compliance with congressional intent.

14. The state of Alaska has filed suit challenging the constitutionality of the federal statute. The law is likely to be held

    (A) valid, because the sale of alcoholic beverages has a substantial impact on interstate commerce
    (B) valid, because the establishment of a state "watchdog" agency under the auspices of a federal regulatory scheme is consistent with the provisions of the 21st Amendment
    (C) invalid, because it violates the fundamental principles of state sovereignty embodied by the 11th Amendment
    (D) invalid, because the federal government may not compel state legislatures to enact and enforce a federal regulatory program

Questions 15–18 are based on the following fact situation.

The Women's Action Force of Steelham City, hereafter referred to as WAF, attempted for many months, unsuccessfully, to reach an agreement with the local professional men's club, the Downtown Club, to admit women to membership. On September 1, 2002, WAF leaders instituted a suit for a declaratory judgment in federal court to determine whether the Downtown Club was subject to the State's Anti-Discrimination Act.

On October 1, 2002, prior to the elections for city officials, four WAF members were sent to picket the City Hall offices of Mayor O'Reilly and District Attorney Mason, who were prominent members of the Downtown Club. Two members walked outside the front of the building where the Mayor's Office was located carrying signs which read: "Mayor O'Reilly is supposed to serve all the people but his lunch club is for men ONLY. So don't vote for O'Reilly." The other two pickets walked outside the rear of the building where D.A. Mason's Office was located, carrying similar signs, telling the public not to vote for Mason. This picketing was carried on from 9 A.M. to 5 P.M.

The same day, two more pickets were assigned to carry identical signs in front of "Blueberry Hill," the Mayor's official residence. Two pickets also carried duplicate signs in front of Mason's suburban home in Steelham Gardens during the early evening hours. The picketing at all sites was carried on peacefully without any disturbances. The relevant Steelham ordinances concerning picketing read as follows:

> "Section 201. No picketing shall be permitted inside of, or on any sidewalk or street immediately adjacent or continuous to, City Hall, without express permission of the Mayor. Applications for such permission shall be filed at least three days before such picketing is intended to begin and shall state the purpose, place and time of the proposed picketing.
>
> Section 202. It shall be unlawful for any person to engage in picketing before or about the residence of an individual. Nothing herein shall be deemed to prohibit the holding of a meeting or assembly on any premises used for the discussion of subjects of general public interest."

15. The federal district court will mostly likely avoid decision on the merits of the WAF suit for declaratory judgment because

    (A) the case lacks adequate ripeness
    (B) there is no case or controversy
    (C) the relief sought is essentially for an advisory opinion
    (D) WAF lacks standing

16. After a few days of picketing, Mayor O'Reilly seeks a temporary injunction in the state court to restrain further picketing of City Hall. The court will most probably

    (A) grant relief, since WAF failed to follow the procedure outlined in the ordinance
    (B) grant relief, unless the ordinance is declared unconstitutional
    (C) deny relief, since the picketing ordinance was unconstitutional on its face
    (D) deny relief, since the ordinance does not provide procedural due process

17. Assume that the court granted the temporary injunction against WAF's picketing of City Hall. In a subsequent action challenging the constitutionality of Sec. 201 of the Steelham Picketing Ordinance, the court will most likely rule that the section is

    (A) constitutional, since the ordinance is a valid exercise of the state's police power
    (B) constitutional, since the ordinance is within the Tenth Amendment's reserved power
    (C) unconstitutional, since the ordinance is void for vagueness and overbreadth
    (D) unconstitutional, since the ordinance violates petitioner's rights of freedom of speech

18. In an action by WAF to challenge the validity of Sec. 202 of the Steelham Picketing Ordinance, the court will most likely declare the section

    (A) constitutional, as within the area of compelling state interest
    (B) constitutional, as a valid exercise of a state's reserved powers under the Tenth Amendment
    (C) unconstitutional, as discriminatory on its face
    (D) unconstitutional, as vague and overbroad

Questions 19–21 are based on the following fact situation.

The State of Brighton imposes a graduated income tax upon net income calculated as under federal law. Section 22 of the Brighton Reform Act of 2002, which is to become effective on January 1, 2003, provides that "Any parent or guardian financially responsible for the education of his ward may claim a direct tax credit against his income tax liability equal to the amount of tuition of a child or children of high school age who does not attend a public high school." Other provisions define "tuition" very broadly but limit the credit to tuition paid to schools meeting the educational requirements as determined by the State Department of Public Instruction.

In addition, Section 40 of the Act provides that "Upon proper application, any non-public religious school may apply to the State Department of Public Instruction for salary supplements for teachers, as long as such teachers were restricted to the teaching of secular subjects." Further, Section 40 provides that "The money to finance the salary supplements is to come from the general appropriations fund of the Department of Public Instruction."

19. On December 1, 2002, the parents of two students, who attend a public high school in Brighton, sue for a declaratory judgment and injunction in federal court, claiming that Section 22 of the Brighton Reform Act of 2002 violates the Establishment Clause of the First Amendment. The federal court will most likely

    (A) hear the action on its merits
    (B) dismiss the action, since the plaintiffs lack standing
    (C) dismiss the action, since the issues are not ripe
    (D) dismiss the action, since there is no case or controversy

20. Assume that the federal court decides to hear the case on its merits. Which of the following is the State of Brighton's **LEAST** persuasive argument for sustaining the validity of Section 22?

    (A) Section 22 benefits the parents/guardians of all the children in private schools, religious and nonreligious.
    (B) The primary effect of Section 22 is not to advance or inhibit religion.
    (C) The administration of the Section by the State Department of Education does not foster excessive governmental entanglement with religion.
    (D) Section 22 is a valid exercise of state regulatory action in the field of education.

21. In an action brought by ten Brighton taxpayers, all avowed atheists, to challenge the constitutionality, of Section 40 of the Brighton Reform Act of 2002, the enactment will most likely be declared

    (A) unconstitutional, as violative of the First Amendment Establishment Clause
    (B) unconstitutional, as violative of the First Amendment Establishment Clause as applicable through the Fourteenth Amendment
    (C) constitutional, as non-violative of the First Amendment Establishment Clause
    (D) constitutional, as being within the area of compelling state interest

Question 22 is based on the following fact situation.

Fishman entered into a franchise contract with Samurai Sushi, Inc., to operate a Samurai Sushi fast-food restaurant in Carson City, Nevada. Samurai Sushi, Inc.'s national headquarters is located in San Pedro, California. After the Fishman-Samura Sushi contract was executed, Fishman leased a store in a shopping mall where he planned to open his sushi restaurant. Carson City public officials, however, refused to grant Fishman the necessary food vendor's license despite the fact that he can prove that his restaurant complies with all provisions of the municipal licensing ordinance. Section 1287 of the Carson City Food Vending Ordinance provides, in part, that "a food vendor's license shall be issued to any applicant who properly complies with all of the health requirements of this ordinance." After Fishman's application for a food vendor's license was rejected, he requested a hearing to establish his qualifications. Carson City officials refused this request and also declined to give any reason for his license denial.

22. Which of the following is the strongest constitutional argument that Fishman may use to challenge the refusal of Carson City officials to grant him a food vendor's license?

    (A) The Carson City action denies him procedural due process.
    (B) The Carson City action denies him substantive due process by arbitrarily regulating economic activity.
    (C) The Carson City action constitutes an undue burden on the potential interstate commerce between Fishman and his out-of-state franchisor.
    (D) The Carson City action impairs the obligation of Fishman's contract with the franchising company and his rental agreement with the shopping mall.

Question 23 is based on the following fact situation.

Congress has recently enacted a law requiring all males between the ages of 18-30 to take a physical examination each year. The results of the exam are sent to a government data information center located in Fairfax, Virginia. According to the statute, such information is made available to the public upon request.

Freeman, a 25-year-old Yale law school student, has herpes. He has recently sent resumes to many prestigious Wall Street law firms. Fearful that the information about his herpes condition will become public knowledge, he seeks a declaratory judgment that would forbid the government from requiring him to take a physical examination.

23. Which of the following is the best consitutional basis in support of the federal law?

    (A) Commerce clause
    (B) Necessary and proper clause
    (C) To raise and support an army and navy
    (D) To provide for the general welfare

Question 24 is based on the following fact situation.

The Santa Monica Civic Auditorium is owned by the city of Santa Monica. The auditorium is rented out to various organizations throughout the year. The auditorium, which has a seating capacity of 1,500, is customarily leased for such events as rock concerts, rodeos, the Ice Capades, sporting events, fashion shows, etc. In January, Bruce Springsteen held a week-long concert at the auditorium drawing full houses each night. Generally, the city leases the auditorium's facilities for a charge of $2,000 per day.

In February, the Hare Krishna religious sect applied to rent the auditorium for its annual Festival of Chariots celebration. However, the Santa Monica City Council voted 7 to 3 against permitting the Hare Krishnas from using the auditorium. When their rental application was denied, the Hare Krishnas threatened to take legal action against the City Council. They contended unfair discrimination inasmuch as Billy Graham and Reverend Ike leased the auditorium in previous months for their religious gatherings. Amid this controversy, the Santa Monica City Council passed an ordinance prohibiting the rental of the auditorium to any religious group. The City Council passed the ordinance in a "closed door" session, and did not permit any debate or hearings on the matter.

24. Is this newly enacted Santa Monica city ordinance likely to be held constitutional?

    (A) No, because the ordinance was passed by the City Council in a "closed door" session, it violates the due process rights of religious groups by not affording them an opportunity for a hearing.
    (B) No, because the ordinance discriminates against religious groups in violation of the free exercise clause of the First Amendment, as it is incorporated in the Fourteenth Amendment.
    (C) Yes, because the ordinance treats all religious groups equally.
    (D) Yes, because a city ordinance is not state action per se, and, therefore, it is not subject to the limitations of the Fourteenth Amendment.

Constitutional Law

Question 25 is based on the following fact situation.

The state of Golden has enacted a statute imposing a tax on the extraction of all platinum in Golden. The extraction of other minerals is not taxed by Golden. This is true even though there is considerable mining of silver, turquoise, sulfur and stone within the state. As a result, Underground Extraction Comp., Golden's largest platinum mining concern, has filed suit challenging the constitutionality of the Golden platinum tax statute.

25. Which of the following best states the burden of persuasion if Underground attacks the statute as violating the equal protection of the laws?

    (A) The state of Golden must convince the court that the classification in the statute is rationally related to the advancement of a legitimate state interest.
    (B) The state of Golden must convince the court that the classification in this statute is the least restrictive means by which to advance a compelling state interest.
    (C) Underground Extraction Comp. must convince the court that the classification in this statute is not necessary to advance a compelling state interest.
    (D) Underground Extraction Comp. must convince the court that the classification in this statute is not rationally related to the advancement of a legitimate state interest.

Question 26 is based on the following fact situation.

Mary Jo Crockett attended Baylor University in Waco, Texas. One afternoon she was approached by Keith Kodak, a photographer for Playboy magazine, who asked her if she would be interested in posing nude for an upcoming issue featuring "Girls of the Southwest Conference." Mary Jo, who was an aspiring model, agreed and posed for a number of nude pictures which subsequently appeared in the magazine.

Afterwards, Baylor University administrators and professors began to harass Mary Jo for what they considered to be her imprudent behavior. During class her instructors frequently referred to Mary Jo by such names as "Playmate" and "Stripper." Consequently, Mary Jo brought suit in federal court against Baylor University alleging harassment and seeking an injunction and damages. After this action was instituted, the university signed a stipulation agreeing not to harass Mary Jo in the future.

26. The federal court should now

    (A) hear the case
    (B) dismiss the action as moot
    (C) dismiss the action since the issues are no longer ripe
    (D) dismiss the action because there is no case or controversy

Questions 27–28 are based on the following fact situation.

Section 2022(a) of the Arizona Medical Licensing Code provides:

"For the purposes of this statute, only those persons, who have graduated from an optometry school located in the State of Arizona and accredited by the Arizona Board of Optometrists, shall be licensed to conduct the practice of optometry within the State."

In June 1995, Dr. Joe Bradley graduated from the Hastings School of Optometry, which was located in the state of California. The following month, Dr. Bradley was granted a license to practice optometry in California by the State Board of Optometrists. From July 1995 until June 2005, Dr. Bradley was engaged in the practice of optometry in the San Francisco bay area. During the summer of 2005, Dr. Bradley decided to relocate his practice in the neighboring state of Arizona.

In July 2005, Dr. Bradley redomiciled in Scottsdale, Arizona, where he opened a new office for the practice of optometry. When he initially opened his office in Scottsdale, Dr. Bradley was unaware of the Arizona licensing provision for optometrists. Since Dr. Bradley was a licensed California optometrist for ten years, he assumed that he could practice optometry in Arizona by reciprocity.

In September 2005, Dr. Bradley received notification from the Arizona Board of Optometrists that he was illegally practicing optometry and ordered him to immediately cease and desist from such practice.

27. If Dr. Bradley challenges the constitutionality of Section 2022(a) of the Arizona medical licensing statute as violating the Commerce Clause, which of the following is the **WEAKEST** defense?

    (A) The statute will help to assure that only the most qualified optometrists practice in the state.
    (B) The statute will help protect the optometrists of the state of Arizona from competition outside the state.
    (C) The statute will help to assure a continuously available number of practicing optometrists within the state.
    (D) The statute will help to assure that the practicing optometrists in Arizona are subject to standards of a regulatory body.

28. Suppose Dr. Bradley challenges the constitutionality of the medical licensing statute on grounds that it violates the Due Process Clause of the Fourteenth Amendment. Which of the following statements is most accurate?

    (A) Dr. Bradley has the burden of persuasion to show that Arizona does not have a compelling state interest in enacting such legislation.
    (B) Dr. Bradley has the burden of persuasion to show that the denial of a license to practice optometry violates his rights of due process.
    (C) Arizona has the burden of persuasion to show a compelling state interest in enacting such legislation.
    (D) Arizona has the burden of persuasion to show that the denial of a license to practice optometry does not violate petitioner's rights of due process.

Questions 29–30 are based on the following fact situation.

The State of New Mexico has recently enacted a statute requiring the following of all firms who do business with and for the state (defined generally as selling goods or providing services to the state, its agencies, or subdivisions):

"(A) Such businesses must purchase insurance only from insurance companies chartered in the state and thus subject to regulation by the state insurance commissioner;
(B) In hiring any unskilled laborers for employment in connection with state business, preference must be given to citizens of New Mexico;
(C) Nonresident aliens shall be prohibited from engaging in any state related business activities;
(D) All buildings constructed for the state must have roofs composed of adobe, which is composed of yellow silt or clay deposits found only in New Mexico."

The proposed statute's preamble recites that its provisions will assure:

"(A) responsible insurance coverage for all those who do business with the state;
(B) an increased standard of living for the citizens who comprise the State's labor force;
(C) the lowest possible expenditures by the state government; and
(D) a beautiful uniform aesthetic decor for all new state buildings."

29. In evaluating the constitutionality of this New Mexico statute under the Supremacy Clause, which of the following would be most directly relevant?

(A) The number of aliens presently residing in the state of New Mexico.
(B) The necessity for the enactment of this particular statute.
(C) The treaties and immigration laws of the United States.
(D) The overall unemployment rate in the United States.

30. If the New Mexico statute is attacked as violating the Commerce Clause, which of the following statements is most accurate?

(A) The statute is a valid exercise of the State's police power to legislate to protect the health, safety, morals and welfare of its citizens.
(B) The statute falls within the reserved powers of the Tenth Amendment.
(C) The statute should be invalidated if there are non-discriminatory reasonable alternatives available to serve legitimate local interests.
(D) The statute is a valid exercise of state action, only if the federal government has not previously "occupied the field" in this area.

Questions 31–32 are based on the following fact situation.

The state of Corona has recently enacted a statute prohibiting the sale of beer in glass bottles. In accordance with the new law, known as the "Bottleless Beer Bill," all beer consumed within the state must be sold in aluminum cans that are recyclable. There is a provision of the statute that does permit breweries to distribute beer to bars, taverns and restaurants in kegs for "on-site" consumption by patrons.

Before the passage of the "Bottleless Beer Bill," approximately 28% of all beer consumed in Corona was packaged in glass bottles. Of that total, 75% of the beer was bottled outside the state while 25% was bottled by companies within Corona. The legislature passed the bill at the strong urging of the aluminum can industry. It was estimated that Alcoa Aluminum Company alone spent over $5,000,000 in its lobbying campaign for the passage of the bill. Ironically, the new law even received strong support from environmentalists who believed that recyclable cans would help prevent littering and unsightly trash accumulation.

31. The strongest federal constitutional argument against the validity of the "Bottleless Beer Bill" is that it violates the

(A) equal protection clause of the Fourteenth Amendment by discriminating against beer bottlers
(B) privileges and immunities clause of the Fourteenth Amendment by preventing out-of-state beer bottlers from conducting their business in Corona
(C) commerce clause by violating the negative implications on interstate commerce
(D) contracts clause by impairing the ability of beer bottlers to honor existing contracts for the sale of bottled beer in Corona

32. Assume for the purposes of this question only that the Corona state supreme court adjudges the "Bottleless Beer Bill" to be unconstitutional on the ground that it violates the contracts clauses of both the federal and the state constitutions. The Corona Supreme Court so holds because, in the court's judgment, the statute retroactively impairs the ability of beer bottlers to honor their existing contracts for the sale of bottled beer in Corona. The state attorney general now seeks review of this decision in the United States Supreme Court. How should the United States Supreme Court rule on this case?

    (A) Refuse to review this case on the merits because there is an adequate and independent state ground for the decision rendered below.
    (B) Reverse the decision on the merits with respect to the state constitutional issue because the federal constitutional holding rendered below makes such a state constitutional decision unnecessary.
    (C) Affirm the decision on the merits with respect to the federal constitutional issue and abstain from reviewing the state constitutional issue.
    (D) Affirm the decision on the merits with respect to both the federal and state constitutional issues because the state constitution must substantially conform with the federal constitution on this issue.

Questions 33–34 are based on the following fact situation.

The state of Hermosa has recently released medical statistics showing that the number of new AIDS cases within the state has quadrupled from the preceding year. In 1986, Hermosa reported that 2,250 people were diagnosed as being stricken with the AIDS virus. However, in 1987 the state confirmed that over 9,000 new persons contracted the deadly virus. In an effort to improve the health care of AIDS patients in the state, the Hermosa state legislature has enacted a law providing public funds to assist hospitals.

According to the law, every hospital in the state would receive $5,000 annually for each AIDS patient who was admitted at that hospital, and whose period of hospitalization exceeded one week. Although this bill was initially opposed by several churches and other organizations, the Hermosa legislature re-drafted the bill in a compromise effort to appease the opposition. In its final re-draft, the bill provided that the $5,000 annual subsidy "would not be paid to any hospital performing abortions."

33. Which of the following is the strongest argument against the constitutionality of the Hermosa statute?

   (A) The statute violates the establishment clause of the First Amendment, as incorporated into the Fourteenth Amendment, by adopting the controversial views of particular churches on abortion.
   (B) The statute violates the Fourteenth Amendment by conditioning the availability of public funds upon the recipient's agreement to act in a way that makes more difficult the exercise by others of their fundamental constitutional rights.
   (C) The statute violates the equal protection clause of the Fourteenth Amendment by denying non-AIDS patients the same subsidy benefits as those received by AIDS patients.
   (D) The legitimate importance of the state interest that this statute seeks to advance is insufficient to justify the statute as a lawful exercise of state police power.

34. Which of the following is the strongest argument in support of the constitutionality of the Hermosa statute?

   (A) The Tenth Amendment reserves to the states plenary power over the allocation of their public funds.
   (B) Public subsidies in hospitals are privileges rather than rights and, therefore, are not entitlements protected by the due process clause of the Fourteenth Amendment.
   (C) The funding limitation in this statute does not directly prohibit or penalize the exercise of a fundamental right and is rationally related to the achievement of a legitimate state interest.
   (D) Since the AIDS epidemic is rapidly becoming a public health emergency, the statute promotes a compelling state interest in advancing the health, safety and welfare of its citizenry.

Question 35 is based on the following fact situation.

National Bus Company operates passenger buses between all the major cities from New York City and Miami. This service is authorized under a certificate of convenience and necessity issued by the Interstate Commerce Commission, pursuant with federal statute. The certificate does not, however, specify particular highways, streets, or location for the bus service. National's advertising stresses that it picks up and delivers passengers at the center of each city that it serves. National's management regards this as a particularly effective advertising point in competition with the airlines and the railroads, because short-haul traffic supplies a major part of the bus company's revenues.

The City Council of Baltimore, a major metropolis between Philadelphia and Washington, D.C., acting to relieve traffic congestion and air pollution, has recently enacted an ordinance that prohibits (a) the operation of all trucks and buses in a five square mile central business area (known as Center City) between the hours of 10:00 a.m. and 4:00 p.m. on weekdays, and (b) all on-street parking of passenger automobiles in Center City between the same weekday hours.

The Baltimore station of the National Bus Company is located in the heart of the Center City area. According to its transportation schedules, more than 75 National buses either enter or leave the Baltimore station between the hours of 10:00 a.m. and 4:00 p.m. each weekday.

35. If National Bus Company brings suit challenging the constitutionality of the Baltimore ordinance, the court will most likely declare the ordinance

    (A) constitutional, since it is within the City Council's police power to regulate transportation services in the Center City business district
    (B) constitutional, as a valid exercise of municipal regulation in the area of intra-state commerce
    (C) unconstitutional, as violative of the Commerce Clause if less restrictive alternatives are available
    (D) unconstitutional, since the ordinance is discriminatory per se

Question 36 is based on the following fact situation.

Rosemont City Ordinance 123 provides:

"*Section 1.* It shall be unlawful for any person to litter a public park.

Section 2. Violation of this ordinance shall be punished by a fine of not more than $100 or imprisonment for not more than 30 days."

On February 3, Carlos Santana organized a demonstration against "Contra Aid" to rebels in Central America. The rally took place in Rosemont Park, a city park, and attracted about 100 supporters. During the rally, Carlos delivered a speech to the people in attendance. At the conclusion of his speech, Carlos said, "I'm sick and tired of the garbage this Administration is getting away with in Central America. Here's what I think about their policy of contra aid …" At which point, Carlos walked over to a trash can and dumped its contents on the ground. As the crowd cheered wildly, Carlos shouted, "No more contra aid … let's stop this garbage now!" After littering the park, Carlos and his supporters left without picking up the trash.

36. As a matter of constitutional law, may Carlos be prosecuted under the aforementioned Rosemont city ordinance for littering the public park?

    (A) No, because littering the park in these circumstances could be construed as symbolic speech and, thus, it is protected from government regulation by the First and Fourteenth Amendments.
    (B) No, because the facts do not indicate that Carlos' actions presented a clear and present danger that was likely to produce or incite imminent lawless action, thereby necessitating an abridgment of his freedom of speech.
    (C) Yes, because the city ordinance advances an important and legitimate public interest and is not directed at the suppression of communication.
    (D) Yes, because littering the park is conduct, not speech, and therefore it may not be treated by the law as communication.

Question 37 is based on the following fact situation.

The Million Man March in Washington, D.C. called attention to the fact that many Blacks and other minorities are still disenfranchised from the electoral process. A congressional report revealed that in the South only 42% of Blacks eligible to vote were, in fact, registered. The report also indicated that certain southern states (such as Alabama and Tennessee) had residency laws restricting a person's right to vote. As a consequence, Congress passed the 2000 "Voting Rights Bill" that provided "any law denying Blacks and other minorities the right to vote shall be deemed unconstitutional."

Constitutional Law

37. This federal statute will most likely be upheld under which of the following constitutional provisions?

    (A) 13th Amendment
    (B) 14th Amendment
    (C) 15th Amendment
    (D) 20th Amendment

Question 38 is based on the following fact situation.

Carmen Cantillo is an illegal alien from Nicaragua. She and her three children live in San Diego. The San Diego City Council has enacted an ordinance requiring illegal aliens to pay a $100 "school fee" for each child enrolled in a San Diego public school. Citizens and legal aliens are not required to pay the "school fee".

The city council has enacted this law to raise funds to hire additional teachers who are bilingual. The city determined that over 15% of children attending public schools in San Diego were offspring of illegal aliens. Furthermore, the city conducted a study and found that the overwhelming majority of illegal aliens residing in San Diego did not pay any local property taxes. As a result, since the city provided educational benefits to the children of illegal aliens, the "school fee" furthered a significant governmental interest.

38. Carmen, who is indigent, is unable to pay the San Diego "school fee". The city will not allow Carmen's children to attend school unless the fee is paid. If Carmen seeks your legal advice regarding the constitutionality of the "school fee," you should advise her that the ordinance is

    (A) valid, if the city can demonstrate that the "school fee" is necessary to further a compelling governmental interest because elementary public education is a fundamental right
    (B) valid, if, and only if, the city can prove that the imposition of the "school fee" is substantially related to a legitimate governmental interest because illegal aliens, who have not been admitted for permanent residence in the United States, are a nonsuspect class
    (C) invalid, because even though public education is not a fundamental right and illegal aliens are not a suspect class, denying educational services to children of undocumented aliens is not substantially related to an important governmental interest
    (D) invalid, unless the city can demonstrate the cost of educating children not fluent in English imposed an undue burden on the public school system by requiring the school board to hire additional bilingual teachers

Question 39 is based on the following fact situation.

Route 66, a state highway, runs through the center of Maplewood's business district. As Route 66 passes through this business district, there is a stretch where the highway is too narrow to satisfy the safety standards for state roadways. Along this narrow stretch and on opposite sides of the street are located two taverns. Situated on the east side of the street is the Rendezvous Bar and Grill and directly across the street on the west side of the highway is the Hideout Lounge.

In order to comply with state highway regulations, the state highway department, acting pursuant to state statute, ordered the city of Maplewood to prohibit parking on one side of Route 66 within the business district. The Maplewood City Council convened a special meeting to determine whether parking should be prohibited on the east or west sides of the street. During the meeting the City Council was unable to resolve the issue on which side of the street to ban parking. Finally, Marge Schotte, City Council President, decided the only fair way to resolve the matter was by means of a coin flip. After the coin flip, the City Council prohibited parking at all times on the west side of the highway. On account of this decision, parking in front of the Hideout Lounge was permanently prohibited. This caused the Hideout Lounge to suffer a substantial decline in business because of the unavailability of on-street parking.

39. As a consequence, the owner of the Hideout Lounge brought suit against the Maplewood City Council alleging that the parking ban on his side of the street was unconstitutional. In all likelihood will the plaintiff be successful in this cause of action?

   (A) No, because as a governmental entity, the city of Maplewood enjoys immunity from such suits under the Eleventh Amendment.
   (B) No, because the action of the city of Maplewood was reasonable.
   (C) Yes, because since the owners of businesses on the west side of the highway are not being treated equally, the action of the city violated the equal protection clause of the Fourteenth Amendment.
   (D) Yes, because responsible government officials cannot conduct or formulate its decision-making process by means of coin flips.

Questions 40–41 are based on the following fact situation.

North Berlin, an industrial town with a population of 100,000, is located on the north side of the Germantown River. On the south side of the river is situated South Berlin, a rural community with a population of 40,000. For many years, various civic groups have urged that both communities merge into one township with a single governmental body. Independent studies have indicated that such a merger would result in an enormous tax savings to the residents of both municipalities by eliminating the duplication of services. On one previous occasion, proponents of the merger plan succeeded in having the proposal appear as an election referendum in each community. Although the merger referendum passed in North Berlin by a sizable margin, the voters of South Berlin rejected the measure, fearing the combined government would be dominated and controlled by its neighbor's larger representation.

Constitutional Law

In order to alleviate the concern of South Berlin voters regarding underrepresentation in a merged governmental system, the respective city councils of both municipalities appointed a steering committee to formulate a new proposal. Accordingly, the steering committee devised a merger scheme wherein the city council of Berlin, the united city, would consist of eight members. Within this proposed new system of government, each former municipality would be divided into four districts. With respect to North Berlin, each district would consist of 25,000 persons and each would have one elected city council member. By the same token, South Berlin would be divided into four elective districts with each containing 10,000 residents. One city council member would be elected from each of these districts as well. The mayor would be elected at large by a popular vote of all residents in the newly created eight districts.

Before this merger proposal was placed on the ballot, the state attorney general issued an advisory opinion stating that the measure did not, in her opinion, violate any statutory or constitutional provisions. Thereafter, the "Berlin Proposal," as It came to be known, was placed on the ballot and was overwhelmingly passed by the voters in both North Berlin and South Berlin. After the election but before the merger had officially been carried out, two taxpayers from North Berlin initiated suit to enjoin the unification, attacking the constitutionality of the disproportionate representative districts.

40. Which of the following represents the plaintiffs' strongest constitutional argument in support of their action?

    (A) The plaintiffs and other North Berlin residents have been denied the equal protection of the law.
    (B) The plaintiffs and other North Berlin residents have been denied the due process of the law.
    (C) The plaintiffs and other North Berlin residents have been denied the privileges and immunities of citizenship as guaranteed by Article IV, Section 2.
    (D) The merged city "Berlin Proposal" would not constitute a republican form of government.

41. Assume for the purposes of this question only that the plaintiffs' suit reaches the state supreme court, and that the court ruled the "Berlin Proposal" establishing a unified city entity was constitutional under both the state and the federal constitutions. The plaintiffs now file a motion seeking to have this case reviewed by the U.S. Supreme Court. The Court should

    (A) hear the federal issues involved, but decline to rule on the state issue
    (B) not hear the case, but have it remanded to federal district court
    (C) not hear the case, because it was decided on independent state grounds
    (D) rely on the advisory opinion rendered by the state attorney general and not hear the case on its merits

Question 42 is based on the following fact situation.

A federal grand jury in Washington, D.C. was convened to investigate the alleged bribery by the Libyan government of Jordan Holmes, special advisor to the President of the United States for Middle Eastern affairs. The grand jury was probing the Libyan government's efforts to obtain delivery of American made transport planes, which were embargoed by the State Department. The Justice Department was trying to ascertain whether the Libyan government had offered bribes to Holmes and other members of the Administration in order to secure delivery of the transport planes.

On March 4, 2003, Holmes testified before the grand jury that both he and the President had several conferences with Mohammed Kakuri, the Libyan ambassador to the United States, at the White House. He stated that during these meetings, they discussed problems in the Middle East in general. He, however, denied any involvement in the Libyan government's efforts to secure delivery of the transport planes.

Two weeks after Holmes testified, the grand jury returned an indictment, charging him and two other members of the Presidential staff with conspiracy to commit bribery and conspiracy to defraud the United States government. A special prosecutor was then appointed by the Justice Department to prepare the Government's case.

On April 15th, upon motion by the special prosecutor, a subpoena *duces tecum* was issued directing the President to produce the minutes of his meetings with Holmes and Ambassador Kakuri. The special prosecutor was able to determine the exact dates of the meetings because the White House daily logs and appointment records had been previously subpoenaed. On April 20th, the President released several edited transcripts of his conversations with Holmes and Kakuri. On the same day, the President's counsel filed a motion to quash the subpoena *duces tecum,* claiming an absolute executive privilege.

42. Which of the following is the most accurate statement with regard to the President's claim of executive privilege?

    (A) Under the separation of powers doctrine, the federal judiciary is without authority to review an assertion of executive privilege by the President.
    (B) The need for the confidentiality of high level communications will sustain an absolute unqualified Presidential privilege of immunity from judicial process on all occasions.
    (C) Article III does not vest the federal courts with power to resolve a nonjusticiable intra-branch dispute.
    (D) Article II does not vest the President with an absolute, unqualified privilege to withhold evidence from a criminal prosecution.

Question 43 is based on the following fact situation.

Congress recently passed the Federal Smog Control Act. Pursuant to this newly-enacted statute, Congress created the Smog Alert Agency, a nine member body, which was empowered to promulgate rules governing air quality standards for the nation. In accordance with the Smog Control Act, the President of the United States was authorized to appoint a majority of six members to the Agency. The other three positions were to be filled by the Senate.

Constitutional Law

The nine members were then duly appointed to the Agency, and all appointees were subsequently approved in confirmation hearings. Thereafter, the Smog Alert Agency issued the following regulations:

"(a) Requiring each motor vehicle operating in the United States to be equipped with a specified air/fuel control device;
(b) Requiring each gas or oil furnace located in the United States to be fitted with a specified device to reduce emissions;
(c) Requiring each State to establish and maintain a program under which each vehicle and each furnace shall be tested annually for compliance with federal emissions standards."

43. Which of the following arguments would provide the strongest constitutional grounds against the authority of the Federal Smog Control Act?

    (A) The President does not have the constitutional power to appoint a majority of members to an administrative agency.
    (B) Congress does not have the executive authority to appoint members to an administrative agency.
    (C) An administrative agency does not have the constitutional authority to promulgate regulations that unduly burden interstate commerce.
    (D) An administrative agency does not have the constitutional authority to require states to supervise federal regulatory guidelines such as those enumerated in subsection (c).

Question 44 is based on the following fact situation.

Voters in New Orleans passed a referendum legalizing gambling in the French Quarter section of the city. The law established a Gambling Commission (consisting of five individuals) that was in charge of licensing and overseeing the activities of the casinos. The members of the Gambling Commission were to be appointed by the Mayor. Pursuant to his statutory power, the Mayor appointed four private citizens and a clergy member to the Commission.

44. There is a constitutional challenge to the appointment of the clergy member as violating the Establishment Clause of the First Amendment. The Mayor's action is

    (A) unconstitutional, because the appointment of a clergy member to the Commission fosters excessive governmental entanglement with religion
    (B) unconstitutional on its face, if members of the commission are vested with enforcement powers
    (C) constitutional, because the primary effect of appointing only one religious member to the commission does not per se advance or inhibit religion
    (D) constitutional, because commission membership is an appointive privilege and not an elective right

Question 45 is based on the following fact situation.

The Commonwealth of Islandia has enacted an abortion statute in an attempt to reconcile the conflicting interests involved when a woman chooses to terminate a pregnancy by abortion. The Islandia statute provided that during the first trimester of pregnancy, a woman's right to choose to terminate the pregnancy was paramount and could not be restricted in any manner. After the first trimester, the right of a woman to obtain an abortion was limited to cases where it was demonstrated by a physician that an abortion was necessary to protect the life or health of the woman seeking the abortion.

45. In all likelihood this abortion statute is

(A) constitutional, because the Islandia statute strikes a proper balance between the fundamental right of a woman to choose to terminate a pregnancy by abortion and the due process right to life of the unborn child
(B) constitutional, because the Islandia statute is substantially related to the important state interest in protecting the health and life of the mother
(C) unconstitutional, because the Islandia statute imposes an undue burden on the right to obtain an abortion
(D) unconstitutional, because it is irrational to impose virtually no restrictions on the right to obtain an abortion in the first trimester while imposing significant restrictions on the right to obtain an abortion thereafter

Question 46 is based on the following fact situation.

Congress has recently enacted a federal law which prohibits racial discrimination in the sale, transfer or rental of real estate, either privately or publicly. Which of the following constitutional provisions would provide the best rationale for the enactment of this federal statute?

(A) Under Article I Congress has the power to enact laws that are "necessary and proper" to the general welfare.
(B) The enforcement provision of Section 2 of the 13th Amendment.
(C) The enforcement provision of Section 5 of the 14th Amendment.
(D) The due process clause of the 5th Amendment.

Questions 47–49 are based on the following fact situation.

Carl Caucus, a staff assistant for the Senate of the state of Scam, was convicted in federal court in 1975 of taking bribes from Arab sheiks for the purpose of influencing an upcoming vote on a waterworks bill. He was sentenced to probation. Caucus had served on the Senate staff since 1945, and in 1965, he became fully qualified for his pension upon retirement, under the terms of an agreement between the Scam Board of Pensions and Retirement and the Scam Senate Staff Union. On November 16, 1973, Caucus retired and immediately started receiving monthly state pension checks.

On July 8, 1978, the governor of Scam signed into law the Public Employee Pension Forfeiture Act, which provided in part:

"Section 8. Any member of the Senate staff ... who is convicted of ... bribery ... shall not be entitled to receive any retirement or other benefit or payment of any kind from the state ... Such conviction shall be considered a breach of the staff member's employment contract ...

Section 12. The provisions of this Act shall be retroactive to December 31, 1941.

Section 14. This Act shall take effect immediately."

On September 12, 1978, Caucus received a letter from the Board of Pensions and Retirement which stated, "Pursuant to the Public Employee Forfeiture Act, the Board is immediately discontinuing pension benefit payments to you on account of your 1975 bribery conviction."

Caucus contacted his attorney, F. Lee Belli, who challenged the discontinuance of benefits on the grounds that the new law was unconstitutional.

47. To counter one of Belli's possible arguments regarding the unconstitutionality of Section 8 of the Public Employee Pension Forfeiture Act, the state's best rebuttal would be:

    (A) Caucus was afforded an opportunity to express his views about the new legislation at public hearings, prior to the enactment of the statute.
    (B) Deprivation of pension benefits is not cruel and unusual punishment.
    (C) A letter sent through ordinary mail is sufficient notice to satisfy due process for discontinuation of pension benefits.
    (D) It is implicit that one of the conditions of the state's contract of employment with a Senate staff member is that he shall not engage in bribery.

48. In order to reinstate Caucus's pension on the grounds that the statute is unconstitutional, Belli might successfully allege that:

    (A) Caucus was retroactively punished.
    (B) The Public Employee Pension Forfeiture Act is an *ex post facto* law
    (C) The Supremacy Clause invalidates the state law, because there is federal legislation regulating pension and profit sharing plans.
    (D) The Act has a chilling effect on legislators' rights to freely discuss pending bills with members of their staffs.

49. Assume that the state's highest court holds the statute constitutional. Caucus might still be able to eventually have his pension reinstated if:

    (A) he exercises his constitutional right to discretionary review in the U.S. Supreme Court.
    (B) he receives a Presidential Pardon for his bribery offense.
    (C) he can show that he was convicted before the effective date of the Public Employee Pension Forfeiture Act.
    (D) all of the above.

Question 50 is based on the following fact situation.

Within the last two years, the number of cases coming before the United States Supreme Court has quadrupled. Because of this increased work load, the Court has complained that it is unable to properly review all of its cases. As a consequence, a Congressional committee was formed to conduct a study on improving the functioning and operation of the Court. Based on the committee's recommendations, Congress enacted a statute dividing the Court into two panels. One panel would be assigned to handle criminal cases exclusively; while the other panel would handle all non-criminal matters. Each panel would be composed of four associate justices and a Chief Justice. According to the new law, the decisions of each panel would be final and not reviewable by any other court or judiciary.

50. Which of the following is the strongest argument against the constitutionality of this federal statute?

    (A) The statute contravenes the requirement in the Constitution that there be one Supreme Court.
    (B) The statute is unconstitutional because it does not fall within the enumerated powers of Congress and is not necessary and proper for the effectuation of those powers.
    (C) Based on the doctrine of judicial supremacy, Congress does not have authority to legislate with respect to the jurisdiction of the Supreme Court.
    (D) Based on the separate sovereignty doctrine, Congress does not have authority to interfere with the procedural machinery of the Supreme Court.

Questions 51–52 are based on the following fact situation.

In 2006, the President of the United States appointed a delegation to enter into negotiations with representatives of the Canadian government to study the problem of preventing the extinction of certain species of seals in the North Pacific waters bounding on Alaska and the Canadian provinces. The delegation's goal was twofold: to study the problem and to formulate regulations in a bilateral agreement which would protect the endangered species and provide for a permanent commission that would continually monitor enforcement of the proposed regulations. After compiling their findings and drafting the necessary regulations, the U.S President and the Canadian Prime Minister entered into a treaty to form a permanent commission to oversee the problem and to grant it the necessary enforcement powers.

51. The validity of this treaty would most likely be upheld under which of the following principles?

    (A) the presidential power to conduct foreign affairs
    (B) an ancillary power of the President under his treaty making power
    (C) the treaty-making power but only if the treaty is ratified by two-thirds of the Senate
    (D) the treaty-making power but only if the treaty is ratified by a majority in Congress

52. Assume for the purposes of this question only that after the treaty goes into effect, the State Legislature of Alaska enacts a statute which provides that "any licensed seal-hunter in the State of Alaska and its surrounding environs, may increase their monthly catch of seals from ten to fifteen in each of the specified months of the authorized seal-hunting season from the first day of October until the last day of February." The enactment of the aforementioned statute would most likely be declared

    (A) constitutional, because the regulation of hunting is within the area of state action
    (B) constitutional, as the enactment falls within the Tenth Amendment's reserved powers
    (C) unconstitutional, under the Commerce Clause
    (D) unconstitutional, because all treaties "which shall be made under the authority of the United States are the Supreme Law of the land"

Constitutional Law

Question 53 is based on the following fact situation.

During a three month period, the city of Peoria was stunned by a series of mysterious deaths which claimed the lives of twenty people. Although all the victims had apparently died from poisoning, the police were in a quandary as to who was responsible for the killings. There was finally a breakthrough in the investigation when a police toxicologist determined that all the victims had died after eating poisoned apples which had been purchased at the Peoria Produce Market. The apples had all been contaminated with the pesticide dichloro-diphenyl-trichloro (commonly known as DDT). The police then received a letter from a person who claimed responsibility for the poisonings. The letter, which was signed the "Pesticide Poisoner," stated that the killings were in retaliation for the city's new policy of prosecuting toxic polluters.

Acting upon an anonymous tip, the police then arrested Armand Hammerstein, owner of Pest Control, a company engaged in the manufacture of pesticides, and charged him with twenty counts of murder. Thereafter, the Peoria Press, the city's largest newspaper, ran a series of articles on the killings and referred to Hammerstein as the "Peoria Pesticide Poisoner." After the preliminary hearing, the state trial judge issued an ex parte injunction against the Peoria Press prohibiting it from "publishing any news during the trial that might be prejudicial to Hammerstein." The newspaper appealed.

53. In light of the United States Supreme Court cases to date, the state appellate court should

    (A) dissolve the injunction, because a news story about a matter of public interest is absolutely privileged
    (B) dissolve the injunction, because it is an impermissible prior restraint on the freedom of the press
    (C) uphold the injunction, because the inference of guilt in the name "Peoria Pesticide Poisoner" would deny the defendant his constitutional right of a fair trial
    (D) uphold the injunction, because reference to the defendant by the name "Peoria Pesticide Poisoner" would be inflammatory and prejudicial

Question 54 is based on the following fact situation.

Capano was charged with murder. The killing took place on February 1. At the time the crime occurred, this jurisdiction required a unanimous verdict of all twelve jury members for a conviction on a capital offense. On November 1, the state legislature enacted a new law requiring a majority vote of seven of twelve jurors to convict on a capital offense. Capano's trial began on December 1. He was subsequently convicted of murder by an eight to four vote. Following the trial, Capano's attorney filed a motion to set aside the verdict.

54. Which of the following would provide the **BEST** constitutional grounds to overturn the verdict?

    (A) The Ex Post Facto Clause.
    (B) The Contracts Clause.
    (C) The Due Process Clause of the Fourteenth Amendment.
    (D) The Sixth Amendment right to a fair trial.

Question 55 is based on the following fact situation.

The Pentagon has recently released a civil defense plan in the event of nuclear war. According to the Pentagon's study, certain "essential" citizens would be evacuated once it was determined that a nuclear war was imminent. "Essential" citizens would include scientists, carpenters and the young. On the contrary, the Pentagon study recommended that certain "non-essential" citizens such as the elderly, the infirm and persons in penal institutions not be evacuated since their (future) contributions would be less important in the rebuilding of the country (following the devastation of a nuclear war).

Adams, an employee of the Pentagon's Civil Defense Unit, was instructed to conduct a public opinion survey regarding the controversial plan. Pentagon officials directed Adams to interview citizens in a door-to-door canvass to determine public opinion for the civil defense plan. After Adams conducted his door-to-door interview canvassing, he was prosecuted for not obtaining prior consent.

55. Adams's strongest argument is that the prosecution

    (A) violates his right to free speech
    (B) violates the intergovernmental immunity of a federal employee
    (C) deprives him of his employment interest without due process
    (D) impairs the obligation of his employment contract

Question 56 is based on the following fact situation.

State Red is concerned with the increase in teenage use of cigarettes, chewing tobacco, cigars and other tobacco products. In an effort to decrease exposure to these items which pose harmful health risks, the state legislature has enacted a statute to restrict various methods of advertising by tobacco manufacturers. One of the provisions of the law states that "advertising of tobacco prices is not permitted except by placement of a sticker on the package or box itself." Chesterfield Tobacco Company, a major distributor of such products in State Red, claims the advertising restriction violates its constitutional rights protected by the First and Fourteenth Amendments.

56. If Chesterfield Tobacco Company files suit challenging the validity of the State Red statute, the court should rule the statute

    (A) constitutional, because the state law is rationally related to the health and safety of Red citizens
    (B) constitutional, because the restriction on commercial speech directly advances a substantial government interest
    (C) unconstitutional, because the regulation on commercial speech is not necessary to further an important government interest
    (D) unconstitutional, because the state could achieve its objective by a less restrictive means

Constitutional Law

Questions 57–58 are based on the following fact situation.

Fuji Sales, Inc., an American franchise, operates as an importer and distributor of bicycles manufactured by Fujuma Inc. in Osaka, Japan and maintains several warehouses throughout the West Coast area for the wholesale distribution of the bicycles. A warehouse located in Salem County, Oregon handles the distribution of bicycles for the Oregon and Washington State areas. The bikes and bike tires are shipped separately to the Salem County warehouse. The tires are mingled, stacked and stored in the warehouse along with various other tires. The bicycles, on the other hand, arrive completely assembled in their shipping crates and remain on the loading docks. Salem County imposes an *ad valorem* property tax on the bikes and tires.

57. Salem County's *ad valorem* tax may properly be assessed against the

    (A) tires only
    (B) bicycles only
    (C) tires and bicycles
    (D) none of the above

58. The power of Salem County to impose an *ad valorem* tax on the Japanese bicycles and/or tires would most likely be sustained under

    (A) the Commerce Clause
    (B) the reserved power of the States as granted under the Tenth Amendment
    (C) the Necessary and Proper Clause
    (D) the Import and Export Clause

Questions 59–62 are based on the following fact situation.

Merrill Pharmaceutical Company manufactured a new vaginal contraceptive sponge that was marketed under the trade-name, FEEL-FREE. However, a study by the Federal Food and Drug Administration revealed that FEEL-FREE might prove harmful to users. As a result, Congress enacted legislation prohibiting the shipment and sale of FEEL-FREE across state lines.

59. This law is probably

    (A) constitutional, because Congress has the power to provide for the general welfare
    (B) constitutional, because Congress has the power to regulate interstate commerce
    (C) unconstitutional, because it deprives the manufacturer of FEEL-FREE a property right without just compensation
    (D) unconstitutional, because it interferes with the right of privacy of contraceptive users

60. The state of Vermont has a statute which regulates the shipment and sale of FEEL-FREE within its territory. In light of the federal legislation prohibiting the shipment and sale of FEEL-FREE across state lines, the Vermont statute is probably

    (A) constitutional, because it is within the state's police power
    (B) constitutional, because the Tenth Amendment reserves to the states exclusive power to regulate economic transactions that are wholly intrastate
    (C) unconstitutional, because it affects the regulation of interstate commerce
    (D) unconstitutional, because the federal law pre-empts any conflicting state legislation regarding the sale and shipment of FEEL-FREE

61. Assume for the purposes of this question only that Congress now imposes a tax of 14 cents on each FEEL-FREE contraceptive sponge sold in the United States. This tax is

   (A) unconstitutional, unless the FEEL-FREE sponges are sold in interstate commerce
   (B) unconstitutional, because it interferes with the sovereign right of state governments to engage in intrastate commerce
   (C) constitutional, because the Supremacy Clause validates laws enacted by Congress
   (D) constitutional, because it is within the power of Congress to raise revenue

62. Assume for the purposes of this question only that President Bush issues an executive order prohibiting the shipment and sale of FEEL-FREE — as well as all other contraceptive sponges — within the United States. Under this executive order, federal agents are empowered to prosecute all interstate shippers and sellers of contraceptive sponges. The President claims that he is acting upon a recommendation of the Surgeon-General who has conclusive evidence that contraceptive sponges cause cervical cancer in" laboratory monkeys. This executive order is

   (A) valid, because the President has the authority to insure that laws are faithfully executed
   (B) valid, because the President has the authority to impose economic regulations unless overruled by Congress
   (C) invalid, because it is an unauthorized extension of executive power
   (D) invalid, because the President does not have the power to regulate interstate commerce

Question 63–65 are based on the following fact situation.

Passaic, New Jersey, imposes a municipal excise tax of $200 per year on commercial photographic studios of that city. It also imposes an excise tax of $100 per year on every itinerant commercial photographer for the privilege of using the streets and sidewalks; a credit is allowed against this latter tax for any excise tax paid to the city by the photographer or his employer in respect to the maintenance of a photographic studio in Passaic.

The Carspecken Galleries, located in the neighboring State of New York, has been sending two itinerant photographers into Passaic. Their practice is to snap a picture of a pedestrian, ask him to order a finished photograph and collect a payment of $2.00. The film is sent to the New York studio, which processes it and mails a print to the customer, who may then order additional or enlarged copies by mail. New York does not impose a tax on photographic studios.

63. In an action by Picasso Studios, a Passaic, New Jersey, photographic studio, challenging the constitutionality of the $200 per year excise tax, the court will most likely declare the tax

   (A) constitutional, as a non-discriminatory license tax
   (B) constitutional, as within the powers of the state to tax the instruments of interstate commerce
   (C) unconstitutional, as an undue burden on interstate commerce
   (D) unconstitutional, as a discriminatory tax on the privilege of doing business within the state

Constitutional Law

64. Carspecken Galleries challenges the constitutionality of the $100 per year excise tax which is imposed upon its itinerant photographers in Passaic. The court will most likely declare this tax

    (A) constitutional, as a valid *ad valorem* tax on interstate commerce
    (B) constitutional, since the tax was levied not on the photographic business as a whole but on the local activity of taking pictures
    (C) unconstitutional, since a state or municipality may not impose a license tax on drummers (order takers) for goods or services to be performed in another state
    (D) unconstitutional, as a discriminatory privilege tax

65. Assume for the purposes of this question only that the State of New Jersey imposes a tax on non-resident photographers, who operate photographic studios in New Jersey, at a rate of two percent of their New Jersey derived income above $12,000. This so-called "N.J. Photographers Income Tax" exempts taxable income earned by New Jersey photographers outside of the State. Moreover, resident-photographers of New Jersey are not taxed on their in-state earned income. Photographer Phillips, who operates a photographic studio in New Jersey, but is a resident of New York, challenges the constitutionality of this tax. Which of the following provisions would furnish the most applicable basis for this constitutional challenge?

    (A) Equal Protection Clause of the Fourteenth Amendment
    (B) Due Process Clause of the Fourteenth Amendment
    (C) the Commerce Clause
    (D) the Privileges and Immunities Clause of Article IV

Question 66 is based on the following fact situation.

State Green has a statute that prohibits "anyone over 60 years of age to run for public office." Shirley Sullivan has been a state senator for three terms and wishes to seek re-election. Shirley, who is 61, brings suit challenging the constitutionality of the State Green statute.

66. Which of the following best states the burden of persuasion?

    (A) Since a fundamental right is involved, the state must show the regulation is necessary to vindicate a compelling government interest.
    (B) Since no fundamental right is involved, the petitioner must show the age restriction is not rationally related to a legitimate government interest.
    (C) The state must show the age regulation substantially furthers an important government objective and does not impair the fundamental right to vote.
    (D) The petitioner must show the statute violates due process by depriving her of the right to be a candidate.

Question 67 is based on the following fact situation.

The state of Tasmania has enacted a party affiliation statute prohibiting a person from being an independent candidate in a general election if she or he had either (1) registered with a political party during the year prior to the immediately preceding primary; or (2) voted in that primary. Tasmania adopted the so-called "disaffiliation" statute in order to have intraparty feuds resolved in primary elections rather than in the general election. Moreover, Melba Moore, the Tasmania Elections Director, strongly supported the law and argued that it was necessary to avoid voter confusion and to insure that the general election winner received a majority.

Harry Hink, who was a registered Democrat in 2001, now wishes to run as an independent candidate in the November, 2002 general election. However, Ms. Moore ruled that Hink's candidacy violated the state's "disaffiliation" statute and barred Hink from appearing on the ballot.

67. If Hink files suit in federal district court challenging the constitutionality of the Tasmania election statute, which of the following best states the burden of persuasion?

    (A) The state of Tasmania must demonstrate that the law is necessary to further an important state interest.
    (B) The state of Tasmania must demonstrate that the law is necessary to further a compelling state interest.
    (C) Hink must demonstrate that the law is not rationally related to any legitimate state interest.
    (D) Hink must demonstrate that the state has less restrictive alternative means available for independent candidates to get a ballot position.

Question 68 is based on the following fact situation.

Fidel Fidellio was charged with the crime of rape. In accordance with section 4.3 of the Constitution of the State of Badlands, Judge Goodfield denied him bail. Section 4.3 provides: "For the crimes of rape, sexual assault on a child and sexual assault, no person who stands accused thereof shall be entitled to bail prior to a trial in the courts of this state."

Fidellio was brought to trial and found guilty. After being sentenced to five to ten years in prison, Fidellio appealed his conviction to the Badlands Supreme Court. The grounds for his appeal was an argument that he was denied his right to counsel at the time of his arrest.

While his appeal was pending, Fidellio filed a civil rights action in federal court against Judge Goodfield. Fidellio claimed that Judge Goodfield violated his rights under the excessive bail clause of the Eighth Amendment to the U.S. Constitution.

68. The federal court should refuse to hear the case, because

    (A) the issues presented are no longer "live"
    (B) Fidellio lacks a legally cognizable interest in the outcome
    (C) the case is moot
    (D) the issue of bail is capable of repetition, yet evading review

Question 69 is based on the following fact situation.

In 1986 when Rock Hudson disclosed that he was suffering from AIDS, most Americans were unfamiliar with the deadly disease. Since most of the early victims were homosexual men and IV drug users, mainstream America was rather apathetic and uneducated about the epidemic.

Since 1986 over 250,000 Americans have died from AIDS. Moreover, it is estimated that over 2,000,000 people in the United States are infected with the HIV virus. The Center for Disease Control (CDC) states that 100,000 new victims contract the HIV virus in the United States each year.

Constitutional Law

On account of these alarming statistics, the American Foundation of AIDS Research (hereafter referred to as Am FAR) has embarked on a $2,000,000 advertising campaign highlighting the dangers of unsafe sex and urging the use of condoms. As part of the Am FAR campaign, large billboards have been painted with pictures of brightly colored condoms with captions stating "IF IT DON'T FIT—YOU MUST BE AN IDIOT!" Additionally, as part of its AIDS awareness campaign, Am FAR has sent unsolicited mailings to over 1,000,000 American families. In each envelope, Am FAR has enclosed a condom with a letter explaining the risks of unprotected sex.

After Am FAR started sending condoms in the mail, thousands of Americans became incensed and objected to this type of unsolicited advertising. A group of people calling themselves "Skinheads Against Rubbernecks" started a nationwide campaign against the use of condoms. This new organization also started a strong lobbying movement to have Congress pass legislation prohibiting the distribution of condoms in the U.S. mail system.

69. Assume for the purposes of this question only that the "Skinheads Against Rubbernecks" lobbying effort was successful and Congress passed a law prohibiting "any unsolicited advertising for condoms to be distributed through the U.S. postal system." Am FAR has challenged the constitutionality of this federal statute. The best argument **AGAINST** the constitutionality of this law is which of the following?

    (A) The statute is invalid because it violates the First Amendment protection of commercial free speech.
    (B) The statute is invalid because it unduly burdens interstate commerce.
    (C) The statute is invalid because it violates the Fifth Amendment right of privacy.
    (D) The statute is invalid because it violates the equal protection clause of the Fourteenth Amendment.

Question 70 is based on the following fact situation.

In recent years there has been much publicity regarding juries approving excessively high multi-million dollar damage awards in personal injury actions across the United States. In one highly publicized case a customer at McDonald's was awarded $3,500,000 in damages claiming the coffee (she purchased at McDonald's) was excessively hot, causing her to suffer first and second degree burns when it spilled on her legs.

As a result, Congress passed the Tort Liability Reform Act (TLRA) that limited recovery in personal injury actions filed in state court(s) to $400,000 and punitive action recovery to a maximum of $750,000.

Ishii was injured in an automobile accident when a car driven by Nguyen drove through a red light and struck his vehicle. Ishii was paralyzed from the accident and became a paraplegic. Ishii brought a personal injury action against Nguyen in state court. The jury returned a verdict on Ishii's behalf and awarded him $1,000,000 in damages.

After the jury verdict, Nguyen filed an appeal challenging the amount of the award, claiming it was excessive and violated the federal guidelines set forth in the Tort Liability Reform Act.

70. Assume that Ishii has filed suit challenging the constitutionality of the Tort Liability Reform Act. The TLRA should be ruled

    (A) unconstitutional, because Congress cannot enact legislation involving local matters, such as automobile accidents, unless it involves interstate commerce
    (B) unconstitutional, because a limitation on damage awards in tort actions would violate the equal protection clause of the 14th Amendment as applicable to the states by operation of the 5th Amendment
    (C) constitutional, because under Article III Congress has plenary power to regulate the jurisdiction and scope of judicial review of federal and lower state courts
    (D) constitutional, because under the supremacy clause when there is a conflict between federal law and state law, the federal law "preempts" and takes precedence over the conflicting state law

Question 71 is based on the following fact situation.

Litigation arose in the courts of the state of Seneca, when the Seneca Secretary of Commerce attempted to stop Calvin Clean from sending his new advertising brochures through the mail. Under the Secretary's interpretation, the new brochures contained obscene photographs and sexually suggestive language. The Secretary was acting under authority given to him by section 1123(b) of the Seneca Trade Statute, which provided:

"Whenever the Secretary of Commerce shall determine that a commercial mailing to residents of the state of Seneca is inappropriate for minors, the Secretary shall have the authority to prohibit such mailing."

The case reached the highest court in Seneca, the Seneca Supreme Court, which held that the statute was unconstitutional, being in violation of both the Commerce Clause and the Supremacy Clause of the United States Constitution.

71. If the United States Supreme Court reviews this case, it will reach that court:

    (A) by appeal
    (B) by certiorari
    (C) only if five justices vote to review the case
    (D) despite the doctrine of adequate and independent state grounds

Question 72 is based on the following fact situation.

Sid Sleezy owns and operates The Peeping Tom, an adult bookstore, in the state of Organa. The Organa state legislature has recently enacted an obscenity statute prohibiting "the selling or offering for sale of any obscene printed or video materials." Following numerous complaints from a local citizens' group, the police entered Sleezy's bookstore, examined materials on the shelves and purchased magazines that depicted actual pictures of sexual intercourse and oral sex between heterosexual partners. Sleezy was subsequently arrested and charged with violating the Organa obscenity law. At his trial, Sleezy's defense was that the sale of the materials complained of was constitutionally protected speech.

Constitutional Law

72. Which of the following, if established, would be most helpful to Sleezy's defense:

    (A) The particular materials involved depicted normal, not deviant, sexual conduct.
    (B) The particular materials involved consisted of serious scientific studies of human sexual urges.
    (C) The police did not have a search warrant when they entered the bookstore to purchase the particular materials involved in this obscenity prosecution.
    (D) 85% of the citizens of Organa believe that the sale of sexually explicit material does not contribute to antisocial sexual behavior.

Question 73 is based on the following fact situation.

Congress enacts a statute which makes Pennsylvania Avenue a one-way street. Congress has enacted the statute solely for the purpose of enabling members of Congress to travel back and forth to the Capital without being tied up in heavy traffic each day. Before Congress enacted this law, the Washington D.C. City Council had previously passed an ordinance designating Pennsylvania Avenue as a two-lane street.

73. Which of the following is the most accurate statement regarding the constitutionality of the federal statute designating Pennsylvania Avenue as a one-way street?

    (A) It is valid because Congress has exclusive power over the District of Columbia.
    (B) It is valid because it is a proper exercise of Congress's enumerated property power.
    (C) It is invalid because the Washington D.C. City Council has exclusive power over the public thoroughfares within the District of Columbia.
    (D) It is invalid because it is a discriminatory burden on interstate commerce.

Question 74 is based on the following fact situation.

The Housing Code of the City of Westport limits the occupancy of all dwelling units in the city to members of a single family. Section 2104.8 of the Code provides that a "family" means a number of individuals related to the nominal head of the household or to the latter's spouse living as a single housekeeping unit in a single dwelling unit, but is limited to the following:

(A) husband or wife of the nominal head of the household;
(B) married or unmarried children of the nominal head of the household or the latter's spouse, provided, however, that such married or unmarried children have no children of their own residing with them;
(C) father or mother of the nominal head of the household or of the latter's spouse.

Beatrice Spaulding, a resident of Westport, lives in her home together with her son Bob and his two children Bob Jr. and Willy.

In February, 2006, Beatrice received a notice of violation from the City which stated that both Bob Jr. and Willy were illegal occupants of her home and that she must comply with the Housing Code. After failing to remove her two grandchildren, the City brings criminal charges against Beatrice.

74. In an action by Beatrice challenging the constitutionality of the Housing Code provision, the court will most likely declare the provision

    (A) constitutional, on the grounds that the housing provision bears a rational relationship to permissible state objectives
    (B) constitutional, under the state police power
    (C) unconstitutional, as violative of the Due Process Clause of the Fourteenth Amendment
    (D) unconstitutional, as having no substantial relation to the public health, safety, morals and general welfare of the state

Questions 75–76 are based on the following fact situation.

The Ames state legislature has proposed a bill setting up a state postal service. Under the proposal, the Ames Postal Service would be established as a separate state agency under the direction of a state Postmaster-General who would be appointed by the Governor. The postal service would be responsible for the "overnight" or "express" delivery of official governmental mailings within the state. The bill further provides that all Ames state government employees may utilize the "overnight" postal service at no charge for sending mailings to persons or corporations within the state.

Assume that the proposed legislation does not conflict with Article 1, Section 8, Clause 7 relating to the power of Congress "to establish post offices and post roads." Assume also that no other state has established such a postal service to date. Moreover, assume there is uncontradicted evidence that the establishment of such an independent state postal agency will diminish the revenues of the United States Postal Service.

75. Which of the following, if established, is the strongest argument in support of the proposed legislation?

    (A) Under the 10th Amendment a state has exclusive authority to regulate transactions that are wholly intrastate.
    (B) Since the proposed bill is not inconsistent with congressional postal power, it is valid under the Supremacy Clause.
    (C) State employees may be exempt from paying for mailing charges under intergovernmental immunity provided Congress has enacted a similar exemption for federal governmental employees.
    (D) There is a legitimate state interest in ensuring that governmental mailings are delivered expeditiously.

76. Which of the following is the strongest constitutional argument against the proposed legislation?

    (A) It constitutes a denial of equal protection of the laws, because employees of the state of Ames receive personal benefits that are not enjoyed by employees of other states.
    (B) The negative implications that flow from the delegation to Congress of the power to establish a post office prohibit such a state postal service.
    (C) It denies citizens of Ames who are not state government employees a privilege and immunity of state citizenship.
    (D) It interferes with the sovereign autonomy of the United States Postal Service to operate as an independent federal agency.

Questions 77–78 are based on the following fact situation.

Jefferson Davies, a resident of Foley, Alabama, announced his candidacy for state representative. Davies, however, failed to obtain the necessary number of authenticating signatures to have his name placed on the ballot.

77. Davies filed a complaint in federal district court alleging the unconstitutionality of the authenticating requirement. Which of the following, if established, is the state's strongest argument for sustaining the validity of the authenticating requirement?

   (A) Davies' petition contained a large number of false signatures.
   (B) A similar authenticating statute was held to be constitutional in Georgia the previous year.
   (C) The authenticating requirement was necessary to further a compelling state interest.
   (D) Two other candidates had successfully petitioned to have their names included on the ballot.

78. On the substantive constitutional issue regarding the validity of the authenticating requirement, the most probable judicial resolution will be to

   (A) hold the authenticating requirement unconstitutional as violative of the Due Process Clause of the Fourteenth Amendment
   (B) hold the authenticating requirement unconstitutional as violative of the Equal Protection Clause of the Fourteenth Amendment
   (C) dismiss the cause of action because state election procedures are a sovereign state function
   (D) assign the burden of proving the validity of the authenticating requirement to the state

Questions 79–80 are based on the following fact situation.

Red Simon, an avowed Communist, was elected First Vice-President of the National Amalgamated Mill Workers Union. Senator Cagey, in his investigation of Communist infiltration on the national labor unions, found a provision in the Landrum-Griffin Act which makes it a crime for a member of the Communist Party to act as an official of a labor union. After a subsequent legislative hearing, Red is dismissed from his position by the National Union's Executive Committee.

79. Which of the following most accurately summarizes the applicable rule of constitutional law regarding the aforementioned provision of the Landrum-Griffin Act:

   (A) the statutory provision is a form of unconstitutional prior restraint on a person's First Amendment right of free association
   (B) making it a crime for a Communist to hold a union office is a suspect classification which violates the Equal Protection Clause
   (C) the statutory prohibition is a reasonable method of discrimination since the benefit to the public outweighs the injury or restrictions which would be inflicted upon the person
   (D) the statutory provision in the act is a form of legislative punishment violative of the Constitution as a bill of attainder

80. Assume for the purposes of this question only that during the legislative hearing, Senator Cagey made certain derogatory statements about Red Simon's affiliation with the Communist Party. In determining whether Simon has a valid cause of action against Sen. Cagey for defamation, which of the following most accurately summarizes the applicable rule of law?

    (A) Congressional committees do not have the authority to violate a person's Fifth Amendment privilege against self-incrimination.
    (B) A Congressman shall not be questioned in any other place for any speech or debate made by him during a congressional hearing.
    (C) The constitutional requirement for actual malice must be proved by the party defamed in order to recover in a defamation suit.
    (D) It is not a denial of due process or of First Amendment rights for a congressional investigative committee member to make such utterances.

Question 81 is based on the following fact situation.

Montana, with an area of more than 147,000 square miles, is the fourth largest state. Only Alaska, Texas and California in that order are larger. But its population is relatively small; in 2002 it was approximately 753,000. Of the fifty states, Montana consistently has ranked forty-second or lower in population since statehood.

Montana maintains significant population of big game, including elk, deer, and antelope. Its elk population is one of the largest in the United States. Elk are prized by big-game hunters who come from near and far to pursue the animals for sport. The quest for big game has grown in popularity. During the ten year period from 1990 to 2000, licenses issued by Montana increased by approximately 67% for residents and by approximately 53% for non-residents.

For the 2001 hunting season, a Montana resident could purchase a license solely for elk for $4.00. The non-resident, however, in order to hunt elk, was required to purchase a combination license at a cost of $151.00; this entitled him to take one elk and two deer.

For the 2002 season, the Montana resident could purchase a license solely for elk for $9.00. The non-resident, in order to hunt elk, was required to purchase a combination license at a cost of $225.00; this entitled him to take one elk, one deer and one black bear. A non-resident, however, could obtain a license restricted to deer for $51.00. A resident was not required to buy any combination of licenses but if he did, the cost to him of all the privileges granted by the non-resident combination license was $30.00.

Owing to its successful management program for elk, Montana has not been compelled to limit the overall number of hunters by means of drawings or lotteries as have other states. Elk are not hunted commercially in Montana. Non-resident hunters seek the animal for its trophy value; the trophy is the distinctive set of antlers. Whereas the interest of resident hunters more often may be in the meat, among non-resident hunters, big-game hunting is clearly a sport in Montana.

81. Moose Dupont and Bear Bryant, residents of Michigan, bring suit against the Montana Fish and Game Commission. They assert in their complaint that the disparities, as between residents and non-residents, in the state hunting license system is unconstitutional. Montana's hunting license system should be found.

    (A) constitutional, since it is within the police power of a state to regulate a recreational, non-commercial activity
    (B) constitutional, as within the area of compelling state interest
    (C) unconstitutional, as violative of the Privileges and Immunities Clause of Article IV, Section II
    (D) unconstitutional, as it violates the Equal Protection Clause of the Fourteenth Amendment

Constitutional Law

Question 82 is based on the following fact situation.

The State of Oxton imposes a tax on non-residents' Oxton derived income above $1,700 at a three percent rate, except that if the non-resident's State of residence would impose a lesser tax, had the income been earned in that State, the Oxton tax would be reduced to that amount. This so-called "Commuters Income Tax" exempts taxable income earned by Oxton residents outside of the State. Moreover, residents of Oxton were not taxed on their in-state earned income.

Commuter Jones, who works in Oxton but is a resident of a neighboring state, challenges the constitutionality of this Oxton statute.

82. Which of the following provisions would furnish the most applicable basis for this constitutional challenge?

    (A) the Equal Protection Clause of the Fourteenth Amendment
    (B) the Fourteenth Amendment Due Process Clause
    (C) the Privileges and Immunities Clause of Article IV
    (D) the Commerce Clause

Questions 83–84 are based on the following fact situation.

Recreational Systems, Inc., under the authority of a statute of the State of Greenora, sued to have condemned 1000 acres of forested land owned by the Great Lakes Timber Co., which it planned to develop for use as a state recreational area and state gamelands. After a hearing, the state court ordered possession of the land surrendered to Recreational Systems, prior to determination of compensation, upon deposit in court of a sum deemed adequate to cover damages which might be awarded. Great Lakes Timber Co., immediately commenced an action to enjoin the court ordered sale of their property.

83. Indicate which of the following would be the best ground for upholding the state court's order?

    (A) The power of eminent domain may only be delegated directly to a private enterprise for a public related use or activity.
    (B) The power of eminent domain may only be delegated to a public authority through a legislative determination.
    (C) The injured party has not proved such irreparable injury to use as amounts to a "taking."
    (D) The Fifth Amendment power of eminent domain incorporated by the Fourteenth Amendment as applicable to the States does not require that payment be made prior to condemnation of the property.

84. Assume for the purposes of this question only that Great Lakes Timber Co., was not given any notice of the condemnation proceedings by the appropriate State authorities. Great Lakes Timber Co.'s best argument for challenging the validity of the condemnation proceedings would be:

    (A) violation of procedural due process
    (B) violation of substantive due process
    (C) unlawful delegation of legislative power because the legislature of Greenora had no authority to delegate power to a private enterprise for eminent domain
    (D) condemnee is entitled to a judicial or administrative proceeding in order that the amount of compensation may be determined prior to any "taking"

Questions 85–86 are based on the following fact situation.

The Missouri Constitution reserves to the people of each municipality in the State the power of referendum with respect to all questions that the municipality is authorized to control by legislation. Charles Johnson, a real estate developer, applied for a zoning change to permit construction of a convalescent home on land he owned in Lincoln City. While the application was pending, the city charter was amended by popular vote so as to require that any changes in land use agreed to by the Lincoln City Council be approved by a 55% vote in a referendum. The City Planning Commission and the City Council both approved the proposed zoning change. However, the Commission rejected Johnson's subsequent application for "recreational area" approval for the proposed home on the ground that the Council's rezoning action had not been submitted to a referendum.

85. In an action brought in state court seeking a judgment declaring the city charter amendment invalid, the court will most likely declare the amendment

   (A) unconstitutional, as violation of Johnson's due process rights
   (B) unconstitutional, as an unlawful delegation of legislative power to a regulatory body
   (C) constitutional, as a valid exercise of the city's police power
   (D) constitutional, as a valid exercise of a power reserved by the people to themselves

86. Assume that while the action was pending in the state court, the proposed zoning change was defeated in a referendum. Which would be the most applicable rule of constitutional law with respect to the referendum procedure when applied to a rezoning ordinance?

   (A) The referendum procedure as a basic instrument of the democratic process does not violate the Due Process Clause of the 14th Amendment.
   (B) The referendum procedure is arbitrary and capricious and thus should be held invalid as an unlawful delegation of legislative power.
   (C) The referendum procedure is violative of the Due Process Clause of the 14th Amendment.
   (D) The referendum procedure in this context is invalid as against public policy.

Question 87 is based on the following fact situation.

The town of Deer Park is less than one square mile in size and located on the exclusive north shore of Lake Michigan. As a result of the increasing northward movement of the population from Chicago, the Deer Park City Council enacted a zoning ordinance in 2004 restricting present and future land use in the town to single family dwellings, except in the downtown commercial shopping area, and except for a small area in which multi-family dwellings not over 40 feet in height were permitted. In addition, all new construction or exterior modifications of existing buildings required prior approval of an aesthetic control board. The zoning ordinance defined the term "family" in the context of "single family dwellings" to mean only one or more persons related by marriage, blood or adoption, thereby excluding unrelated unmarried persons from residing in a single residence unit. The enabling legislation contained the following provision:

Constitutional Law

"This enactment is necessary to preserve the physical and social homogeneity of this community, and preserve and protect the quality of life of its citizens."

Luther owns a single family residence with five bedrooms in Deer Park. Prior to the enactment of the zoning ordinance, Luther leased the premises on a month-to-month basis to Robert and Vernia (who were boyfriend and girlfriend) and three other male law students. The five individuals are all unmarried and attend the nearby John Mitchell Law School. Luther now brings suit to enjoin enforcement of the ordinance against himself.

87. Which of the following is the most accurate statement regarding the constitutionality of the zoning ordinance provision which prohibits unrelated unmarried persons from residing in a single family residence?

    (A) The zoning ordinance provision would be declared unconstitutional as violative for the Due Process Clause of the Fourteenth Amendment.
    (B) The zoning ordinance would be declared unconstitutional as violative of the Equal Protection Clause of the Fourteenth Amendment.
    (C) The zoning ordinance provision would be declared unconstitutional as violative of Luther's rights under the Contract Clause.
    (D) The zoning ordinance provision would be upheld as constitutional under the state's police power.

Question 88 is based on the following fact situation.

The state of York has a statute requiring all candidates for Lieutenant-Governor to file a petition with the signatures of 5,000 registered voters in order to have his or her name placed on the ballot. Flo Dwyer, a candidate for Lieutenant-Governor, did not receive the authorized number of signatures and did not have her name placed on the ballot.

88. If Dwyer brings an appropriate action challenging the constitutionality of the voter petition requirement, the best argument, if established, in support of the statute is that

    (A) it is constitutional under the Fifteenth Amendment
    (B) it is necessary to further a compelling state interest
    (C) Dwyer's petition contained 2,000 false signatures
    (D) only one other candidate successfully petitioned to have his name placed on the ballot

Question 89 is based on the following fact situation.

A consumer watchdog group presented petitions to the State X legislature bearing signatures of over 10,000 State X residents complaining about the recent increases in the cost of cable television. Cableco, a provider of cable television services, successfully persuaded the State X legislature to grant them an exclusive right to install cable television lines in all multiple family dwellings in State X in exchange for Cableco's promise to freeze cable television rates for the next four years. Oscar is an owner of several large multi-family apartment buildings in State X.

Oscar brought an action in federal district court challenging the constitutionality of the State X legislation claiming that the space in Oscar's building that was used by Cableco when they subsequently installed cable television lines in one of his apartment buildings amounted to a taking without compensation. In this action, Oscar will be awarded

- (A) no relief, because easements for utility lines are presumed to be beneficial to the servient estate
- (B) no relief, because the legislation is merely a regulation of the use of property and not a taking
- (C) no relief, because Cableco is not a government entity
- (D) damages for the value of property used by Cableco

Question 90 is based on the following fact situation.

90. In which instance would a state, under the enabling clause of the Fourteenth Amendment, be most able to regulate?

    - (A) A private individual from discriminating against a Black.
    - (B) A private individual from discriminating against a Mexican.
    - (C) A state official from discriminating against an Asian.
    - (D) A federal official from discriminating against a Black.

Question 91 is based on the following fact situation.

Jefferson Stuart, president of the senior class at Admiral Farragut High School in Biloxi, Mississippi, on his own initiative instituted among the students the practice of invoking divine blessing at the start of the daily luncheon served in the high school cafeteria. Although no teacher or school official either encouraged or discouraged the practice, all but two teachers, when present, joined in the invocation. Sam Smedley and his parents protested to the school superintendent and the Biloxi Board of Education, but they refused to intervene on the grounds that the matter was entirely up to the students. Moreover, the Biloxi School Board officials pointed out that the students who led the recital always sat at a table in the rear of the cafeteria and that no one was required to participate in the blessing.

91. In an action by Sam Smedley's parents to enjoin Jefferson Stuart from conducting the daily luncheon invocation at Admiral Farragut High School, the court will most likely

    - (A) grant relief, since the invocation violates the Establishment Clause of the First Amendment
    - (B) grant relief, since the primary effect of the invocation is to advance religious beliefs
    - (C) deny relief, since the lunch hour is not part of the educational process
    - (D) deny relief, since the noncompulsory nature of the invocation would not be violative of the Establishment Clause

Constitutional Law

Question 92 is based on the following fact situation.

In 2002 the state of New Haven enacted a statute which authorized the payment of state funds to any private institution of higher learning within the state that meets certain minimum criteria and refrains from awarding "only seminarian or theological degrees." The aid is in the form of annual subsidies to qualified institutions. The grants are non-categorical but may not, under a provision added in 2003, "be utilized by the institutions for sectarian purposes." The State Department of Higher Education determines the eligibility of applicant institutions. Eight New Haven taxpayers, all avowed atheists, bring suit in federal court to enjoin the payments of subsidies under the statute to all church-affiliated institutions in the state.

92. The federal district court will most likely:

(A) dismiss the action for lack of standing
(B) uphold the validity of the statute as non-violative of the Establishment Clause
(C) invalidate the statute as violative of the Establishment Clause
(D) uphold the validity of the statute as a valid exercise of the state's power to subsidize education

Questions 93–95 are based on the following fact situation.

The city of Doral has adopted the following ordinance which is to become effective on March 1, 1978. Doral City Ordinance 172 provides:

"*Section 1,* It shall be unlawful for any person, group, or organization to hold a meeting of fifty persons or more in any city park without first securing a city permit;

Section 2, The application shall specify the day and hours for which the permit is sought. The fee shall be $10 per hour, with a maximum fee of $50;

Section 3, Permits shall be issued on a first come basis; provided that the Chief of Police shall deny any application if, after hearing the applicant, it is his considered judgment that (a) the meeting would create serious traffic congestion, or (b) interfere with public enjoyment of the park, or (c) speakers at the meeting would advocate the commission of crime."

Bohan Imin, an Iranian foreign exchange student, planned to hold an anti-Shah protest demonstration at Independence Park in Doral on April 2, 1978. Although Bohan's previous anti-Shah protest rallies attracted fewer than twenty-five demonstrators, he decided to apply for a permit pursuant to Doral City ordinance 172. After meeting with Bohan, the Doral Chief of Police denied his permit application because he believed that the demonstration would incite the protestors and threaten imminent violence or serious disorder.

On April 2nd, Bohan and his fellow Iranian sympathizers staged their anti-Shah protest at Independence Park. The rally attracted only about twenty protestors and was conducted peacefully. As Bohan was making his final remarks to the gathering, the Doral police arrived at the park and arrested Bohan and his fellow demonstrators charging them with violating Doral City ordinance 172.

93. Which of the following would be the most accurate statement with regard to the arrest of Bohan and the other demonstrators?

    (A) The police were justified in arresting Bohan, since he and his fellow demonstrators violated the ordinance by staging the rally.
    (B) The police were justified in halting the rally and arresting the demonstrators, because of the threat of imminent physical disturbance.
    (C) The police were not justified in arresting Bohan and the demonstrators, since they did not violate the ordinance.
    (D) Since Bohan failed to obtain a rally permit, the group was not warranted to stage their protest in defiance of the permit denial.

94. In a subsequent action by Bohan in state court challenging the constitutionality of Sections 1 and 2 of Doral City ordinance 172, the court will most likely rule these sections

    (A) constitutional, since a state may regulate the communicative impact of speech related conduct
    (B) constitutional, since the aforementioned sections are within the ambit of the state's police power
    (C) unconstitutional, as vague and overbroad
    (D) unconstitutional, as discriminatory on their face

95. If Bohan now brings suit to challenge the constitutionality of Section 3 of the Doral ordinance, his best argument would be that

    (A) the section is void for vagueness and overbreadth
    (B) the section is discriminatory on its face
    (C) the section permits the police chief to exercise unbridled discretion in approving or disapproving permits
    (D) the section does not fall within the area of compelling state interest

Question 96 is based on the following fact situation.

The state of Ames is the only state that imposes a tax on the extraction of pitchblende. This black colored mineral consists of massive uraninite and contains radium which is the chief ore-mineral source of uranium. Minute quantities of plutonium are also found in pitchblende. This is particularly significant because plutonium undergoes slow disintegration with the emission of a helium nucleus to form uranium 235, and that is fissionable with slow neutrons to yield atomic energy. As such, pitchblende is vital to the economy of the entire country.

Congress has recently enacted a law forbidding any state from imposing a tax on the extraction of pitchblende. Because pitchblende is not mined in any state other than Ames, this federal legislation affects only the state of Ames. Thus, in practice this federal law only limits the taxing power of Ames.

Constitutional Law

96. In light of the Constitution and this federal law, the Ames extraction tax on pitchblende is most likely

    (A) invalid, because when Congress exercises its plenary power over interstate commerce, the Supremacy Clause voids inconsistent state action
    (B) invalid, because Congress may use its general welfare power to prohibit state legislation that it deems harmful to the nation as a whole
    (C) valid, because Congress does not have the authority to interfere with the taxing policies of a state
    (D) valid, because Congress may not enact a law that places one state on an unequal footing with other states

Question 97–98 are based on the following fact situation.

The American-Indian Party was founded and chartered in the state of South Dakota in 1980 "to promote the political power of Indian Americans." Members pledged themselves to vote only for candidates nominated by the party. At first, membership was open to any voter who pledged himself to those tenets, but after the defeats in the 1988 elections, the Party expelled all non- Indian members upon the ground that experience showed that only Indians could be trusted to honor the obligation to vote only for the Party's nominees. Membership is currently confined to Indians.

In every election since 1990, the Party's nominees have easily won election in the Sixth Congressional District, an area encompassing a large number of outlying Indian reservations. In 2000 the Executive Committee proposes that the Party choose its own Power" candidate for governor of South Dakota in the November 2002 election. It will put its slate for United States representatives, governor and United States Senator before Party members for mail ballot in August 2002, along with any rival candidates who qualify for the poll.

97. Will Herzog, a Caucasian, was expelled from membership in the American-Indian Party following the 1988 elections. Which of the following constitutional provisions would furnish Will best ground for challenging his exclusion from the Party?

    (A) Due Process Clause of the Fourteenth Amendment.
    (B) Right of Assembly as guaranteed by the First Amendment.
    (C) Equal Protection Clause of the Fourteenth Amendment.
    (D) The voting provisions of the Twenty-fourth Amendment.

98. In an action by Caucasian and Black citizens in the Sixth Congressional District to enjoin the American-Indian Party from conducting the August 2002 mail ballot primary, the federal court will most likely

    (A) grant relief, since the primary would be proscribed by the Thirteenth Amendment
    (B) grant relief, since the primary would be proscribed by the Fifteenth Amendment
    (C) deny relief, since the Party's primary would be "private action" and not subject to the Fourteenth and Fifteenth Amendments
    (D) deny relief, since a "pre-primary" election is not within the scope of federal election control

Question 99 is based on the following fact situation.

The Election Code of the State of New Caladonia, provides that "any political organization whose candidate received 20% or more of the vote at the most recent gubernatorial or presidential election is a 'political party'; other political organizations are construed as political bodies." Political parties conduct primaries and the winning candidates in each office may have their names placed on the ballot. However, nominees of "political bodies," or any independent candidate may only have their names placed on the ballot if they file a nominating petition signed by not less than 7% of those eligible to vote at the last election for the offices which they are seeking. The time for circulating the petition is 180 days, which is also the deadline governing party candidates in party primaries.

Joe Slow, an independent candidate, who desires to be listed on the ballot for the office of governor, challenges the constitutionality of this election law.

99. The court will most likely declare this statute

   (A) unconstitutional, as a violation of the First and Fourteenth Amendment rights of free speech
   (B) unconstitutional, as a violation of Fourteenth Amendment due process
   (C) unconstitutional, as violative of the Fifteenth Amendment's voting provisions
   (D) constitutional, because the election code is nonviolative of the Equal Protection Clause

Question 100 is based on the following fact situation.

Section 2105(a) of the New Carolina Labor Code provided that "no employer in the State shall knowingly employ an alien who is not lawfully residing in the United States if such employment would have an adverse effect on lawful residents' right to work." A group of immigrant farm workers belonging to the Farm worker's Union were continually refused employment contracts by the labor contractors in the Sierra Valley. Instead, the labor contractors had employed many alien workers since they would toil longer hours for less wages. The immigrant farm workers now bring suit in state court pursuant to the above-mentioned statutory provision.

100. Indicate which of the following determinations would most likely result as a consequence of the immigrant farm workers' lawsuit?

   (A) The court would declare the statute unconstitutional as violative of the Equal Protection Clause of the Fourteenth Amendment.
   (B) The court would declare the statute constitutional as within the realm of rights reserved to the States by the Tenth Amendment.
   (C) The court would declare the statute unconstitutional since the regulation of immigration is pre-empted under the Immigration and Nationality Act.
   (D) The court would declare the statute constitutional since the States are not pre-empted in the area of economic regulation of illegal aliens.

Questions 101–103 are based on the following fact situation.

In the secluded Parrish of Perezville, where prejudice festers and discrimination flourishes, there is a lovely lake which the Parrish has developed and maintained for recreational purposes. Although it is not the only lake in Perezville it is the largest and most scenic and it attracts visitors from miles around. One of its biggest assets is the excellent fishing and boating which is available to the public at large.

Three years ago, in order to enhance the recreational aspects of the lake, the Parrish leased a sizable portion of the lake and surrounding parkland to a company, owned by the most prominent family in Perezville, namely Perezville's Discrima-Boating, Inc. The lease required Discrima-Boating, Inc., to construct and operate a first-rate yachthouse and club, complete with bar, restaurant and private Marina, and to pay the parrish 10% of its net profits as rent. Discrima-Boating, Inc., set up by-laws, which were reviewed and approved by the Parrish at the time the lease was negotiated. According to the by-laws, the yacht-club, complete with its restaurant and bar, would be open to "members only," and the membership committee is empowered to set up strict membership "standards" as well as the cost of membership fees and dues.

Upon completion of the facilities, the State Liquor Control Board granted Discrima-Boating, Inc., a license to sell alcoholic beverages in its restaurant and bar. The membership committee announced that the membership fee is $5000.00 and the monthly dues are $75.00 per month. Furthermore, the membership committee had a policy of only approving membership applications for White-Anglo-Saxon-Men, while disapproving and denying all applications of Women, Blacks and other minorities.

101. A woman resident of Perezville brings suit against Discrima-Boating, Inc., claiming that her membership application was denied only because she is a woman, and that their policy of excluding women as a group, denies her equal protection rights. Which of the following is the most accurate statement?

    (A) Plaintiff will lose, because classifications based on sex have not yet been held to violate the Equal Protection Clause.
    (B) Plaintiff will prevail, unless denial of membership to women can be justified by some "compelling interest," since such discrimination is "suspect" and requires the strictest equal protection test.
    (C) Plaintiff will lose, providing other similar facilities are available to women, because the availability of such will preclude a finding of "state action."
    (D) Plaintiff will prevail, unless Discrima-Boating, Inc., can prove some important basis for the exclusion of women.

102. A Black resident of Perezville, upon denial of membership, brings an action against Discrima-Boating, Inc., seeking injunctive relief to compel his admission, claiming that denial of membership to Blacks violates his right to equal protection. Which of the following statements is most accurate?

    (A) Discrima-Boating, Inc. will prevail, because its denial of membership to Blacks lacks the requisite "state action."
    (B) Plaintiff will win, because even though Discrima-Boating, Inc. is a privately owned corporation, the state has affirmatively encouraged or facilitated its discriminating acts.
    (C) Discrima-Boating, Inc. will win because plaintiff lacks standing to assert the rights of discrimination against Blacks as a group.
    (D) Plaintiff will win, unless denial of membership to Blacks can be justified by some "rational basis."

103. Much of the population in Perezville cannot afford the membership fee and monthly dues. A resident who cannot afford to pay the membership fees, brings an action against Discrima-Boating, Inc., claiming that the high membership fees operate to discriminate against the poor in violation of the constitutional right to equal protection.

    (A) Discrima-Boating, Inc. will win, because de facto discrimination against the poor has not been held to violate equal protection.
    (B) Discrima-Boating, Inc. will win because yacht-club privileges are not an important or basic enough deprivation, for those unable to pay for them, to be held to violate equal protection.
    (C) Plaintiff will win, because all public rights cannot be limited to those who can afford them.
    (D) Plaintiff will win, because discrimination against poor people, violates the Equal Protection Clause of the 14th Amendment.

Question 104 is based on the following fact situation.

Jesus Alou is an indigent suffering from a chronic asthmatic and bronchial illness. In early July of 2003, Alou redomiciled from Albuquerque, New Mexico to Brisbee, County of Maricopa, Arizona. On July 10, 2003, Alou suffered a severe respiratory attack and was sent by his attending physician to the Clearview Hospital, a nonprofit private community hospital. Pursuant to an Arizona statute governing medical care for indigents, Clearview notified the Maricopa County Board of Supervisors that it had in its hospital an indigent who might qualify for county care and requested that Alou be transferred to the County's public hospital facility. In accordance with the approved procedures, Clearview claimed reimbursement from the County in the amount of $1,069, for the care and services it had provided Alou.

Under the relevant Arizona statute:

"Individual county governments are charged with the mandatory duty of providing necessary hospital and medical care for their indigent sick. In order to qualify for such hospital and medical care, an indigent shall be resident of the county for the preceding twelve months in order to be eligible for free nonemergency medical care."

104. As a consequence, Maricopa County refused to admit Alou to its public hospital or to reimburse Clearview because Alou had not been a resident of the County for the preceding year. In an action in federal court against the County of Maricopa challenging the constitutionality of the residency requirement for providing free medical care for indigents, the court will most likely declare the statute

    (A) constitutional, since the statute promotes a compelling state interest
    (B) constitutional, since the statute is a proper exercise of state action
    (C) constitutional, since the statute is within the state's police power to regulate the health, safety and welfare of its citizens
    (D) unconstitutional, as violative of the Equal Protection Clause of the Fourteenth Amendment

Question 105 is based on the following fact situation.

The California state fair is annually held in Modesta on a large tract of state owned property. In recent years, many outside organizations have entered the fairgrounds and distributed literature and paraphernalia to the many thousands of patrons visiting the fair. State fair officials did not endorse any of these organizations but permitted them to disseminate their materials throughout the fairgrounds without charge. Lately, however, many families attending the fair have complained about being harassed by canvassers from these various organizations.

In an effort to protect the safety and welfare of the persons visiting the fair, the California state legislature enacted a law prohibiting anyone from selling or distributing materials at the state fair. This new statute, which was referred to as the "Fairgrounds Bill," provided, however, that groups could pay a $50 license fee and distribute their literature from enclosed booths. These booths would be set up along the entrance to the fairgrounds and rented to anyone wishing to sell or distribute materials or soliciting money during the fair.

The first year the "Fairgrounds Bill" went into effect, approximately forty groups rented booth space. Among the various organizations paying the $50 license fee were: Federation for Marijuana Legalization, Hare Krisnas, Pro-Life Group, MADD, Polluters for Coastline Development, Sushi Preservation League, Gary Coleman Gubernatorial Election Committee, Farm Aid Coalition and Gay Rights Activists. One organization, the Ozontologists, a group of scientists opposed to the use of aerosol spray cans, requested permission to distribute literature at the fairgrounds. The Ozontologists claimed they simply wanted to warn people of the perils created by the disintegration of the ozone layer from the dispersion of fluorocarbons into the atmosphere. State fair officials offered to lease the Ozontologists a booth at the $50 fee, but refused to permit solicitation activities outside the booth enclosures. The Ozontologists were unwilling to pay the $50 license fee and instituted suit in state court seeking a court order permitting them to distribute literature anywhere in the fairgrounds area.

105. Which of the following is the strongest argument in support of the constitutionality of "The Fairgrounds Bill"?

(A) The statute applies to the limited area of the state owned fairgrounds, and does not discriminate among the various organizations by way of their political, religious or commercial viewpoints.
(B) The statute applies to representatives of popular organizations, as well as to representatives of unpopular organizations, and is a democratic expression of the will of the people because it was adopted by the state legislature.
(C) The statute is necessary to protect the safety and welfare of persons using a state facility, and does not discriminate among diverse viewpoints since there is an alternative means by which these organizations can reach their audience.
(D) The statute protects the patrons of a public facility against unwanted invasions of their privacy by restricting the solicitation activities of those organizations that the patrons do not support.

Question 106 is based on the following fact situation.

Pierre, who is lawfully in the United States as a permanent resident alien, applied for a position as a state trooper in the state of Evergreen. A trooper in Evergreen is a member of the State Police Force, a law enforcement body which exercises broad police authority throughout the state. The position of state trooper is filled on the basis of competitive examinations taken by all of the applicants. After Pierre applied for a state trooper position, the state authorities refused him permission to take the qualifying examination. The state authorities based their refusal on an Evergreen statute which provided:

"No person shall become a member of the Evergreen State Police Force unless he/she shall be a citizen of the United States."

Thus, under this provision as a prerequisite to becoming a member of the Evergreen State Police Force, an alien must relinquish his/her foreign citizenship and become an American citizen. In an opinion (upholding the validity of the Evergreen statute), the Evergreen state Attorney General noted that since "Police officers fall within the category of important non-elective officials who participate directly in the execution of broad public policy, only citizens of the United States should be qualified to apply for such positions."

At the time Pierre applied for a position as a state trooper, he was a citizen of France and not currently eligible for American citizenship. As a result of a federal statute, Congress has imposed a five-year residency requirement for the attainment of citizenship. Under this federal law, an alien must reside in this country for a period of five years as a prerequisite before applying for U.S. citizenship. At this time, Pierre had only lawfully been residing in the United States for two years and thus would not be eligible to apply for naturalization until three years later.

106. If Pierre brings suit in federal court challenging the constitutionality of the Evergreen statute limiting the membership of its State Police Force to citizens of the United States, the court will most likely declare the statute:

(A) constitutional, since the statute is within the state's plenary power to regulate the health, safety and welfare of its citizens
(B) constitutional, since citizenship bears a rational relationship to the special demands of the police function
(C) unconstitutional, as a violation of the Equal Protection Clause of the Fourteenth Amendment
(D) unconstitutional, as a violation of the Due Process Clause of the Fourteenth Amendment

Questions 107–108 are based on the following fact situation.

Congress has recently passed a law legalizing marijuana. The law, signed by the President, imposes a tax of $1 on each pack of marijuana cigarettes sold in the United States. The statute provides that this tax is to be paid by the purchaser of each pack into a special segregated fund in the United States Treasury to be known as the "Weed Tax Fund."

In an inseverable portion of that same law, the entire proceeds of the Weed Tax Fund are appropriated on a continuing basis for direct payments to the Civil War Art Museum located in Gettysburg, Pennsylvania. The public museum, founded in 1986, is dedicated to the collection of pictures, artifacts, weapons and other historical memorabilia of the Civil War era.

107. Which of the following most clearly has standing to attack the constitutionality of this appropriation of the Weed Tax Fund monies to the Civil War Art Museum?

(A) A state other than Pennsylvania in which several other public museums are located that are not subsidized by this law.
(B) A non-profit organization of Vietnam Veterans that claims it can demonstrate a greater need for the funds than can the museum.
(C) A purchaser of marijuana cigarettes who is required to pay the tax.
(D) An association of medical doctors that alleges that the legalization of marijuana will result in a public health hazard.

108. As a matter of constitutional law, which of the following statements concerning the continuing federal appropriation to the Civil War Art Museum is most accurate?

(A) It is constitutional because Congress could reasonably believe that such a subsidy to this particular museum will benefit the cultural life of the nation as a whole.
(B) It is constitutional only if Congress can demonstrate that such a subsidy is rationally related to a legitimate public interest.
(C) It is unconstitutional because it is not apportioned among the several states on an equitable basis.
(D) It is unconstitutional because it advances the welfare only of those persons who are interested in the Civil War.

Questions 109–110 are based on the following fact situation.

The state of Providence has recently enacted a statute wherein aliens are forbidden from owning more than 10 acres of land within the state. Mork, a resident alien, has entered into a contract with Mindy to buy 50 acres of land located in Providence.

109. Assume for the purposes of this question only that the statute empowers the state attorney general to bring an ejectment action against any alien who owns more than 10 acres of land. If Mork brings an action in federal court to enjoin the state attorney general from enforcing the statute against him, Mork's best argument is

(A) The statute violates the Privileges and Immunities Clause of the 14th Amendment.
(B) The statute violates the Contract Clause.
(C) The statute violates the Commerce Clause in that it interferes with land ownership.
(D) The statute violates the Equal Protection Clause of the 14th Amendment.

110. Assume for the purposes of this question only that both Mork and Mindy join in a declaratory judgment action to test the validity of the Providence statute in federal court. The court should rule that:

I. Mindy does not have standing.
II. Either Mork or Mindy has standing, but not both.
III. The burden of proof is on Mork to show that there is no compelling state interest to support the statute.
IV. Providence has the burden of proof to show that there is a compelling state interest to support the statute.

(A) IV only.
(B) I and III.
(C) III only.
(D) II and IV.

Question 111 is based on the following fact situation.

The state of Arizona has had a tremendous influx of retired people in recent years. There has been considerable concern among state health officials who foresee that many of the senior citizens will become victims of price gouging on certain medical supplies and services. In an attempt to curb such fraudulent sales practices, the state legislature has enacted a law prohibiting the sale of hearing aids by non-otorhinolaryngologists (or ear, nose and throat specialists). The measure provides, however, that all non-otorhinolaryngologist sellers who are presently engaged in the business of selling hearing aids will not be affected.

111. Assume for the purposes of this question only that after the statute goes into effect, Jiminez, a non-otorhinolaryngologist, moves to Arizona and wants to open a business selling hearing aids. After being advised that the Arizona law prohibits him from doing so, Jiminez brings suit challenging the constitutionality of the statute. The most likely result is that the Arizona law will be declared

    (A) constitutional, because there is a rational basis for distinguishing between non-otorhinolaryngologists who are not so engaged
    (B) constitutional, because a state has the power to regulate any phase of local business, even though such regulations may have some effect on interstate commerce, provided that Congress has not enacted legislation regarding the subject matter
    (C) unconstitutional, because it denies non-otorhinolaryngologists who are not presently engaged in the business of selling hearing aids the equal protection of the law in violation of the Fourteenth Amendment
    (D) unconstitutional, because it violates the Commerce Clause since Congress has plenary power to regulate any activity which has any appreciable effect on interstate commerce

Questions 112–113 are based on the following fact situation.

Over the last several years, the economy of the state of Grambling has substantially changed. Grambling's economy used to be based solely on heavy industry. In 1971, however, the Grambling legislature approved legalized gambling within the state. As a consequence, many casinos and new hotels were built and the state's economy boomed. These moves were often induced by the granting by the state of special tax benefits for the construction of new casinos and hotels under Chapter 122 of the Grambling Statutes.

Recently, however, neighboring states have legalized gambling and offered greater tax incentives to the gaming industry. As a result, many of the casino and hotel owners have begun to leave Grambling for elsewhere. The unemployment and social welfare benefits Grambling has had to pay have substantially increased, burdening the remaining casinos, and also making it difficult for Grambling to lower its taxes to remain competitive with other states.

On account of this predicament, the Grambling legislature passed, and the governor duly signed an emergency "Slot Tax" bill into law. According to the statute, the state imposed a one cent tax on the playing of any slot machine in any gambling casino. Since virtually all the slot machines required a payment of either a dime, quarter or dollar, the imposition of this tax required a major costly adaption on each slot machine to allow for the deposit of the additional one cent tax. Although many casino owners have complained about the "Slot Tax," their only alternative is to absorb the tax themselves and lose one cent per game. As a consequence of the "Slot Tax," fewer slot machines are purchased in Grambling by the casino owners. No manufacturer of slot machines is located in the state of Grambling.

112. Which of the following constitutional provisions provides the strongest ground to attack the validity of the Grambling "Slot Tax" bill?

    (A) The Commerce Clause.
    (B) The Equal Protection Clause of the Fourteenth Amendment.
    (C) The Due Process Clause of the Fourteenth Amendment.
    (D) The Privileges and Immunities Clause of Article IV, Section 2.

Constitutional Law

113. Which of the following is most likely to have standing to bring suit challenging the constitutionality of the Grambling "Slot Tax" bill in an appropriate federal court?

    (A) A manufacturer of slot machines who is attempting to sell them to a casino owner in Grambling.
    (B) A Grambling resident who frequently plays slot machines at the casinos.
    (C) A national gambling association whose members travel to Grambling to play slot machines at the casinos.
    (D) The director of the Grambling C.Y.O. (Christian Youth Organization) who wants to provide slot machines which only play for free at C.Y.O. recreation centers within the state.

Question 114 is based on the following fact situation.

The Board of Regents of the State University of South Bay has adopted the following rule concerning residency requirements: "A student will be considered a legal resident of South Bay for the purpose of registering at the State University if such person is over the age of twenty-one and has established a legal residence in the State for at least one year next preceding the last day of registration for credit."

John Baxter, aged 23, moved to the State of South Bay in November 2000. He enrolled at the State University on August 15, 2001. Since he did not fulfill the university residency requirement, John was required to pay $1800 tuition each semester, which was $400 more than the tuition of South Bay resident-students.

114. In an action by Baxter challenging the constitutionality of the provision governing the determination of residency for the purpose of fixing a fee differential for out-of-state students in public college, the court will most likely declare the provision

    (A) unconstitutional, as a violation of the Equal Protection Clause of the Fourteenth Amendment
    (B) unconstitutional, as a violation of the Privileges and Immunities Clause of Article IV, Section II
    (C) constitutional, only if the fee differential promotes a compelling state interest
    (D) constitutional, without triggering strict scrutiny

Question 115 is based on the following fact situation.

During a violent electrical storm one night, a bolt of lightning struck the Germantown High School building and set it ablaze. The high school was severely damaged and needed to be rebuilt. As a consequence, the Germantown City Council held an emergency meeting to determine what measures should be taken to locate an appropriate alternative facility in which to conduct classes. Thereupon, the city council passed the following resolution: "During restoration of the high school building, classes shall be conducted at the most suitable facility which submits the lowest bid. In determining a 'suitable' facility, the city council shall consider such factors as its location and available classroom space."

118

Several bids were submitted. The lowest bid was submitted by the Greek Orthodox Church (hereafter referred to as Church). Church was located on the same block as the high school and contained sufficient seating capacity for all students. In addition, there were a sufficient number of separate rooms to allow different classes to meet at the same time. The Germantown City Council voted unanimously to accept Church's offer. Furthermore, Church agreed to remove all religious symbols and paraphernalia from the "classrooms" utilized by the students. Only the main chapel was exempt, so that it could remain open for prayer. No high school classes or activities were to be held in the main chapel.

115. Plaintiff, a parent of one of the Germantown High School students, is upset at this arrangement. On his son's behalf, Plaintiff has filed suit in federal district court to challenge the constitutionality of permitting public school classes to be held in a church. In Plaintiff's action, judgment for whom?

    (A) Germantown City Council, because the classroom arrangement does not inhibit nor advance religion.
    (B) Germantown City Council, because Church was the lowest bidder in accordance with the emergency ordinance.
    (C) Plaintiff, because the present arrangement for conducting classes in a church-owned facility constitutes excessive entanglement with religion.
    (D) Plaintiff, absent proof by Germantown City Council that the emergency measure was necessary to further a compelling state interest.

Question 116 is based on the following fact situation.

Brian Spector owned a record store on the corner of 14th Street and Rock Avenue in the downtown business area of the city of Wilton. The Rolling Stones were scheduled to perform at the Wilton Civic Center on September 15th, and Spector featured the Rolling Stones' records in a special sale for the two weeks prior to the concert. On September 2, in order to promote his sale, Spector installed loud speakers on the outside of his store window so that he could play Rolling Stones' records for passers-by to hear. It was Spector's hope that when they heard the records, the passers-by would turn into record customers and buy the Rolling Stones' records.

On September 8, a Code Enforcement Official of the city of Wilton cited Spector for violating Wilton Ordinance 72.499, which provides that:

> "An owner of property located within the city limits of Wilton shall not permit to be used on his property any device which causes sounds, other than clock chimes, to be heard upon the street or sidewalk. Violation of this ordinance shall subject the property owner to a fine of $50.00 for each occurrence."

116. If Spector is successful in challenging this ordinance in court, the court would most likely reason that:

    (A) The ordinance violates equal protection, because some sounds are permitted, while others are not.
    (B) The ordinance violates Spector's rights of freedom of speech, because there is not valid interest to support the ordinance.
    (C) The ordinance violates Spector's rights of freedom of speech, because a municipality may not regulate the use of sound amplification equipment.
    (D) The ordinance violates Spector's rights under the First and Fourteenth Amendments, because it is vague in defining unpermitted sounds.

Constitutional Law

Question 117 is based on the following fact situation.

Simon Simpleton, outraged by the recent Church decision to clear Galileo of charges of heresy, decided to present a lecture, open to the public disproving "The Theories of Galileo." A state S statute provides that: "State S Universities can permit the use of their lecture halls to the public for worthwhile programs of public benefit, upon approval of the School Board."

The appropriate School Board refused to make a university lecture hall available to Simon on the ground that the proposed lecture was not of "worthwhile benefit to the public."

As a result, Simpleton brought suit in a State S court against the School Board and requested injunctive relief requiring the Board to allow him the use of the lecture hall. The trial court denied relief and dismissed the suit. The judgment was affirmed by the State S Appellate Court, and is now before the United States Supreme Court.

117. In analyzing the State S statute, which of the following statements is applicable, and should be asserted in support of Simpleton's position:

I. The statute is overly broad, since it may necessarily result in the exclusion of protected speech as well as unprotected speech.
II. The statute, as applied to Simpleton, violates his First Amendment rights, since Simpleton's proposed speech does not involve the type of speech that the First Amendment will not protect.
III. Indirect speech regulations are only permissible if necessary to serve compelling state interests.
IV. The action of the School Board can be looked upon as a prior restraint on speech.

(A) I and II
(B) II and III
(C) I, III and IV
(D) I, II, III and IV

Question 118 is based on the following fact situation.

Malibu is a small picturesque Southern California beachtown. For the past twenty years, Malibu has been a popular location for surfboarding (a sport in which a person stands, kneels, or lies prone on a surfboard and rides the crest of a breaking wave). Malibu residents have recently complained that the surfers are creating a public nuisance by littering the beaches, harassing sun bathers and injuring swimmers with their surfboards. As a consequence, the Malibu Town Council adopted an ordinance prohibiting all surfing on its beaches. The newly enacted ordinance further prohibited the sale of surfboards within the township's limits.

118. Hobie, a Florida surfboard manufacturer, had planned to sell a new line of fiberglass surfboards in Malibu in the upcoming year. This is now precluded by the recently adopted measure. If Hobie seeks to enjoin application of the Malibu ordinance, which of the following is the WEAKEST defense for the township

    (A) there is no case or controversy
    (B) Hobie's case is moot
    (C) Hobie lacks standing
    (D) the case is not ripe

Questions 119–120 are based on the following fact situation.

Cuba Now, a group advocating the resumption of United States diplomatic relations with Cuba, planned to hold a rally at Midtown Park in downtown Center City in the State of West Bank at noon on May 1, 2002. The group secured a rally permit in accordance with a local ordinance. Several members of the group including DeeDee Quick, a political science professor at the State University of West Bank and one of the group's leaders, were scheduled to give speeches. Other members of the group were assigned to walk among the crowd to solicit signatures for a petition which the group planned to present to the President of the United States.

A large crowd gathered in Midtown Park at the appointed date and time, anxiously waiting for the speeches to begin. As DeeDee, the first speaker, began addressing the gathering, the WTC television news team started filming her presentation, which was to be shown on the local news that evening.

After DeeDee finished her speech, a few members of the crowd began hissing and booing and shouting, "Down with Cuba Now. They're a bunch of Commies." The police soon arrived and attempted to break-up the rally. Several members of Cuba Now, including DeeDee, were arrested for inciting a riot.

On the six o'clock news that evening the film of the rally was shown during the broadcast. Bud Mouthy, the WTC news anchorman, then made the following commentary: "It's a shame that public funds are spent to pay the salaries of such Commie-radical State University professors, who are the force behind Cuba Now. In my opinion, these Castro sympathizers should be deported to Cuba."

119. Which of the following would be the most accurate statement with regard to the police halting the Cuba Now rally?

    (A) The police were justified, since the rally threatened imminent violence and serious disorder.
    (B) The police were justified in order to protect the Cuba Now leaders.
    (C) The police violated Cuba Now's First Amendment rights of assembly.
    (D) Since Cuba Now obtained the rally permit, the police were not permitted to interfere with the staging of the rally.

120. If DeeDee asserts a claim based on invasion of privacy against WTC and Bud Mouthy for his television commentary, the most likely result is that DeeDee will

    (A) not prevail, since Mouthy's criticism was not directed at DeeDee personally
    (B) not prevail, since the broadcast was privileged as being in the public interest
    (C) prevail, since DeeDee, as a private individual, was placed in a "false light"
    (D) prevail, since Mouthy's comments were made with actual malice

Constitutional Law

Question 121 is based on the following fact situation.

As a legislative aide to U.S. Senator Roe V. Wade of the Commonwealth of New Plymouth, you are called upon to provide an analysis of the constitutionality of a bill pending congressional approval. The bill, euphemistically referred to as The Trojan Tax, imposes a 15% percent tax upon the gross annual receipts from the sales of all birth control devices (including but not limited to condoms, birth control pills, contraceptive sponges and cream). The bill, drafted by Senator Jefferson Helms from the state of Fertilia, has the strong support of conservative and pro-life organizations. The stated purpose of the proposed measure is twofold: (1) it is conducive to revenue raising and (2) it would spur population growth across the country.

121. In your learned opinion, the proposed tax is probably

  (A) constitutional, because the fact that the tax applies to all sales of every type of birth control device invalidates any possible objection to the tax on the ground that it violates the equal protection clause of the Fourteenth Amendment
  (B) constitutional, because the fact that controversial policy motives may have induced the enactment of an otherwise reasonable measure calculated to raise revenue does not *ipso facto* invalidate the tax
  (C) unconstitutional, because in inseverable aggregates the domestic purchases and sales of birth control devices affect interstate and foreign commerce
  (D) unconstitutional, because the tax burdens the fundamental right to privacy of users of birth control devices without establishing a compelling national interest for doing so

Questions 122–124 are based on the following fact situation.

Monroe University, located in Monroeville and financially supported by the State of Mizzou, was the scene of campus protests against the neutron bomb. On April 19, 2000, a group of students led by Bennie Spock painted purple a statue of President Monroe, the University's founder, in protest to the University's federally subsidized neutron bomb experimental studies. Spock, 20 years of age, was a first-year student from the neighboring State of Bijou and began classes in September 1999, also establishing residency in Mizzou at that time.

Spock had been the recipient of $5000 annual grant from Mizzou to finance his education. However, the aid was withdrawn because of a Mizzou statute which provided: "Any student attending Monroe University who engages in disruptive campus activities will not be eligible for State aid."

Bennie was married to Winnie, also a student at Monroe. However, in light of his involvement in defacing Monroe's statue and the loss of his State aid, Winnie left Bennie in June 2000. At that time, Bennie received a tax bill from Monroeville for $150. This tax was imposed uniformly by Monroeville on all individuals over nineteen years of age with the exception that full-time female college students were exempted. The tax notice stated that Winnie, twenty-two years of age, qualified for the exemption, and there was no bill enclosed for her.

On July 4th, Bennie moved in with his new girlfriend Wendy and began making arrangements to secure a divorce from Winnie. However, Bennie was not able to obtain a divorce since he had not fulfilled the twelve month residency requirement as imposed by the Mizzou Divorce Law.

122. In an action by Bennie against the State of Mizzou challenging the constitutionality of the Mizzou statute regarding "disruptive campus activities" in order to regain his $5000 annual grant, the court will most likely declare the statute

    (A) constitutional, as the statute promotes a compelling state interest
    (B) constitutional, since the statute is a proper exercise of state action designed to regulate the activities of state university students
    (C) unconstitutional, for vagueness and overbreadth
    (D) unconstitutional, as discriminatory on its face

123. Which of the following most accurately summarizes the correct rule of constitutional law regarding the Monroeville tax exemption for full-time female college students over the age of nineteen?

    (A) the tax exemption would be invalidated as a denial of due process
    (B) the tax exemption would be invalidated as violative of the Equal Protection Clause
    (C) the tax measure would be upheld as within the area of substantive due process
    (D) the tax measure would be upheld as within the power of a municipality to tax different classes of persons unequally

124. In an action by Bennie challenging the constitutionality of the residency requirement of the Mizzou Divorce Law, the court will most likely declare the provision

    (A) constitutional, as the requirement promotes a compelling state interest
    (B) constitutional, as within the area of state action
    (C) unconstitutional, as a violation of the Equal Protection Clause
    (D) unconstitutional, as a violation of the Privileges and Immunities Clause of Article IV, Section II

Question 125 is based on the following fact situation.

Christiana Mall is a shopping center complex located outside St. Joseph in the state of Mizzou. It is privately owned by Christiana Mall, Inc., which leases retail store space to private retailers. On January 21, 2001, a group of black students from the local high school began to distribute pamphlets commemorating Martin Luther King Day in the enclosed Mall area of the shopping complex. The Christiana management requested that the black students cease distributing the pamphlets or leave the premises. When they refused, the St. Joseph police were summoned to disperse the students. Upon the arrival of the police, the students were removed from the premises.

Two weeks later, a group of students from Mizzou Law School requested permission to distribute pamphlets advertising their upcoming Law Day ceremony. The Christiana Mall management permitted six white girls to distribute these pamphlets at the shopping center.

125. Subsequently, the black students brought suit in federal court seeking an injunction which would order the Christiana Mall management to allow them to distribute the pamphlets within the Mall. The black students will

    (A) prevail, because pamphleteering is a speech related activity which is protected by the First and Fourteenth Amendments
    (B) prevail, in the absence of an anti-pamphleteering statute
    (C) not prevail, because pamphleteering on private property is not a constitutionally protected activity
    (D) not prevail, because pamphleteering may be prohibited as a public nuisance which invades the privacy interest of persons not wishing such communicative contact

Constitutional Law

Questions 126–127 are based on the following fact situation.

The Florida Legislature has recently enacted the following statutes:

"Statute 1220. Whoever shall curse or revile or use obscene or opprobrious language toward or in reference to a police officer performing his duties shall be guilty of a misdemeanor.

Statute 1221. it shall be unlawful for an individual to publicly mutilate, trample upon, deface or treat contemptuously the flag of the United States. Whoever shall violate this statute shall be guilty of a misdemeanor."

Mohammad Atta, a Palestinian exchange student at the University of South Florida, organized an anti-Zionist protest demonstration on campus. The rally was attended by a group of fifty Palestinian students who paraded with Pro-Arafat placards and shouted anti-Bush and anti-Israeli slogans.

To show his contempt for the United States, Mohammad sewed the American Flag to the rear of his jeans. When Officer O'Malley saw the flag sown on Mohammad's jeans, he approached Mohammad and told him to remove the flag or he would be placed under arrest. Mohammad became angered and shouted at O'Malley, "Listen, you bastard, I'll wear this rag anywhere I damn please." Mohammad was subsequently placed under arrest and charged with violating Statutes 1220 and 1221.

126. Mohammad subsequently brings suit in Florida state court challenging the constitutionality of Statute 1220. The strongest constitutional argument for Mohammad is that

   (A) the statute is void for vagueness under the Fourteenth Amendment Due Process Clause
   (B) the statute is invalid because it violates petitioner's freedom of speech under the First and Fourteenth Amendments
   (C) the statute is an abridgment of freedom of speech under the First Amendment because less restrictive means are available for achieving the same purpose
   (D) the statute is overbroad and consequently invalid under the First and Fourteenth Amendments

127. If Mohammad is subsequently prosecuted under Statute 1221 for his flag-misuse, he

   (A) should be convicted
   (B) should not be convicted, since the lack of ascertainable standards for defining "treat contemptuously" violates the Equal Protection Clause of the Fourteenth Amendment
   (C) should not be convicted, since the statutory language is void for vagueness under the First and Fourteenth Amendments
   (D) should not be convicted, since the statute has a "chilling effect" on non-verbal forms of speech and therefore is invalid under the First and Fourteenth Amendments

Question 128 is based on the following fact situation.

The Delmarva state legislature recently enacted a bill legalizing standardbred harness racing. The statute authorized parimutuel betting at certain track locations within the state. A seven member Delmarva Racing Commission was established and empowered to supervise and regulate the sport's activities. Under an inseparable provision of the bill, the Commission was authorized to suspend the racing license of any trainer whose horse tested positive for illegal drugs. The bill permitted the Commission to make the suspension without any prior hearing. However, suspended trainers were entitled to a prompt post-suspension hearing and decision on any issues in dispute.

The Delmarva racing season was inaugurated at Brandywine Racetrack. The featured race at Brandywine was the Dupont Futurity, a $1,000,000 harness race for two-year-old Delmarva bred trotters. The race was won by a horse named Biden Time. After the awards presentation, the horse underwent a standard drug test and traces of cocaine were found in the horse's urine sample. Immediately thereafter, the horse was disqualified and the Commission suspended Ceasar Rodney, Biden Time's trainer, without a prior hearing.

128. Without seeking a post-suspension hearing as provided by statute, Rodney brings suit in federal district court challenging the constitutionality of the Delmarva harness racing law. The statute is probably

(A) constitutional, because being granted a racing license is a privilege not a right
(B) constitutional, because the state's interest in suspending the license of horse trainers suspected of illegal drugging is sufficiently important to permit the suspension of any prior hearing
(C) unconstitutional, because the suspension provision unreasonably interferes with a trainer's right to contract with horse owners and seek gainful employment
(D) unconstitutional, because the suspension provision violates due process by not affording a prior hearing

Questions 129–130 are based on the following fact situation.

Governor Hammersmith of the State of Columbianna and Milton Wertz, leader of the majority Progressive Party, presented proposed legislation to the State Senate which would reorganize the State Police Bureau. The bill created a great deal of controversy both within and outside of the state government. Several leaders of the Labor Party, which composed the minority party in the Senate, decided to oppose the legislation. Senator Red Turner, a member of the Labor Party, disagreed with his party's opposition to the bill and publicly announced his support for the legislation.

The Labor Party leaders called a party caucus to discuss and determine their legislative strategy for floor debate on the bill. When Red appeared at the door to the caucus room, he was denied admission because of his anti-party stance. Senator Swifty Logan, the Labor Party Whip, also informed Red that he would be removed from all of his committee assignments.

During the caucus, the party members discussed other means of disciplining Red for his party insubordination. Swifty suggested that they issue a press release in which the Party would publicly castigate Red for his actions. He also said that "Red is a cutthroat politician, who is only looking out for where his next buck will come from."

As floor debate began on the bill, a group of wives of the State Policemen began a demonstration and sit-in in the hallway adjacent to the Senate Chambers in the State Capitol building. The wives only engaged in orderly activities aimed at defeating the legislation. The Governor, however, annoyed by all of the publicity caused by the sit-in, asked the wives to disperse. When they refused, he ordered their arrest under the authority of a state statute which provided that: "Whoever pickets or parades in or within 50 feet of a state building with the intent of interfering with the administration of official business shall be guilty of a criminal offense."

129. Which of the following constitutional provisions would furnish Senator Turner's best grounds for challenging his exclusion from the Labor Party caucus?

(A) Equal Protection Clause of the Fourteenth Amendment
(B) Right of assembly as guaranteed by the First Amendment
(C) Speech and Debate Clause
(D) Due Process Clause of the Fourteenth Amendment

130. In determining whether Senator Turner has a valid cause of action against Senator Swifty Logan for his remarks made during the caucus, which of the following most accurately summarizes the applicable rule of law?

(A) Turner must prove actual malice in order to recover for defamation.
(B) Any remarks made during the caucus were privileged.
(C) Swifty's remarks violated Turner's First Amendment right of privacy by placing him in the "false light."
(D) Swifty's remarks constitute a "fair and substantial" relation to "important governmental objectives."

Questions 131–132 are based on the following fact situation.

Congress, under intense lobbying pressure from the Moral Majority and the Right to Life organizations, has enacted the Contraceptive Closure Act prohibiting the sale of contraceptive devices to married persons. The act further prohibits the use of contraceptive devices by married persons. Congress claimed that the statute was passed because it might help deter illicit sexual relationships.

131. The law is probably

(A) constitutional, as a regulation of interstate commerce
(B) constitutional, as a measure promoting the general welfare
(C) unconstitutional, because the law deprives the manufacturers of contraceptives of their property interest without just compensation
(D) unconstitutional, as violating the right of privacy of contraceptive users

132. Assume for the purposes of this question only that the state of New Hampshire enacts an analogous statute prohibiting the sale of contraceptive devices to married persons. Similarly, the state statute prohibits the use of contraceptive devices by married persons. Dr. Doe, a New Hampshire physician, brings suit in federal court challenging the constitutionality of the state contraceptive statute. Dr. Doe attacks the validity of the statute on the grounds that it prevents him from giving his professional advice concerning the use of contraceptives to three patients (all of whom are married) whose condition of health might be endangered by child bearing. The plaintiff is likely

(A) to have standing
(B) to have standing *jus tertii*
(C) not to have standing
(D) not to have standing *jus tertii*

Question 133 is based on the following fact situation.

On November 18, 2005, Multistate Legal Studies, Inc. (hereafter referred to as Multistate) sent an advertisement regarding its PMBR Multistate Bar Review course to The Culver City Gazette. In an accompanying letter, Pamela Stevens, Multistate's West Coast Regional Director, instructed the newspaper to publish the ad in the "Legal Education Section" of its December 1, 2005 edition. The following ad was received by Horace Sensor, the newspaper's advertising editor, on November 19th from Multistate:

The next day Sensor telephoned Ms. Stevens and told her that he would not permit the newspaper to run the PMBR ad. When Ms. Stevens asked for an explanation, Sensor replied, "My daughter, Daphne, took your bar review course and failed her California bar exam for the sixth time. Because of your incompetent instructors, she's now pumping gas at the Mobil Station on the corner of Centinela and Washington. She's so discouraged, she might not take her bar exam again. That's why I'm prohibiting *The Gazette* from publishing your ad." Sensor then forwarded a letter to Ms. Stevens reiterating his newspaper's refusal to have the ad published.

133. In an appropriate action, Multistate Legal Studies, Inc. brings suit against Mr. Sensor and *The Culver City Gazette* seeking an order which would require the newspaper to publish the PMBR advertisement. Judgment for whom?

(A) Advertiser, because such advertising is protected by the 1st Amendment under the "commercial speech" doctrine.
(B) Advertiser, because there is a constitutional right of advertising under the 1st and 14th Amendments.
(C) Newspaper, because Congress is empowered to prohibit truthful advertising, even where it urges the purchase of a legal, validly offered item.
(D) Newspaper, because there is no constitutional right of advertising under the 1st and 14th Amendments.

Question 134 is based on the following fact situation.

John J. Stone was serving a life sentence in an Iowa prison as a result of his conviction of murder of a child who had trespassed onto Stone's farmland. Stone came from a family of farmers, dating back to at least 1750. His family believed that all nourishment comes from the ground and that one's soul will be saved only if his diet consists totally of natural, farm-grown food. Stone followed that belief and ate only fresh fruits and vegetables."

When Stone entered the prison on March 7, 2001, state prison officials agreed to grant his wishes and served Stone only fresh fruits and vegetables for his meals. After six months, deciding that catering to his special diet was overly burdensome and administratively unworkable, the officials decided to stop giving Stone special treatment and began to serve him the same food as served to the rest of the prison population. Although nothing physically prohibited Stone from eating and surviving on the general prison population's diet, Stone refused to eat the food that was not in conformity with his special diet. *NOTE:* In 2000 the state legislature of Iowa enacted and the governor signed into law a statute entitled "The Prisoner's Rights Act of 2000," which included a requirement that prison officials accommodate prisoners' religious beliefs.

134. Stone's best constitutional argument to support his claim of right to a fresh fruit and vegetable diet is based on:

(A) the First Amendment
(B) the Eighth Amendment's prohibition against cruel and unusual punishment, as applied to the states
(C) the Prisoner's Rights Act of 2000
(D) the First and Fourteenth Amendments

Question 135 is based on the following fact situation.

In *Branzburg v. Hayes,* 409 U.S. 665 (1972), the United States Supreme Court by a 5 to 4 majority rejected a reporter's claim that, as the flow of information available to the press would be impeded if newsmen were compelled to release the names of confidential sources for use in a government investigation, the First Amendment must be held to embrace a privilege to constitutionally refuse to divulge such information in order to protect the reporter's channels to the community.

In the wake of *Branzburg,* however, several states have enacted "state shield" laws which provide a varying range of protection for newsmen. Now, Congress—under intense lobbying pressure from the press—proposes to enact legislation forbidding any state from requiring journalists to reveal the sources of their news articles in civil suits.

135. Which of the following is the strongest constitutional argument in support of this proposed law?

    (A) Congress has the authority under the Commerce Clause to regulate the flow of news.
    (B) Acts of Congress are the supreme law of the land and take precedence over any conflicting state laws.
    (C) Congress is essentially reaffirming the free speech guarantees of the First and Fourteenth Amendments.
    (D) Under Article 1, Section 8, Congress has the authority to secure to authors and inventors the exclusive right to their respective writings and discoveries.

Question 136 is based on the following fact situation.

Joey Holmes is the owner-proprietor of the Green Door Motel located in the state of Ames. The motel advertises the showing of pornographic, or "adult", movies in the privacy of each room. The motel has a strict policy permitting adults only to occupy the rooms. The state of Ames has recently enacted a statute that prohibits the showing of any obscene film in an area open to the public.

136. Holmes is prosecuted for violating the statute by showing pornographic movies in the motel rooms. On appeal, Holmes' conviction probably will be

    (A) sustained, because a state can use its police power to prohibit the showing of pornography in public areas
    (B) sustained, because a state may use local standards in determining whether a movie has redeeming literary, artistic, political or scientific merit
    (C) overturned, on the grounds that his prosecution violates the right of consenting adults to view such films in private
    (D) overturned, because the First and Fourteenth Amendments prohibit the suppression of sexually oriented materials on the basis of their allegedly obscene contents

Question 137 is based on the following fact situation.

Each year the state of Virginia provides a number of non-interest bearing loans and/or scholarships to candidates for the degree of LL.B or J.D. at the University of Virginia School of Law. The applicable state statute limits eligibility to citizens of the United States and aliens seeking U.S. citizenship. Hector Martinez, a candidate for a J.D. degree at the University of Virginia School of Law, applied for one of the non-interest bearing loans. Since Mr. Martinez was a Guatemalan alien who did not intend to seek U.S. citizenship, he was refused the loan for ineligibility under the state statute.

137. In a suit by Mr. Martinez challenging the constitutionality of the Virginia statute, he will

(A) win, because the statute is violative of the Privileges and Immunities Clause of the Fourteenth Amendment
(B) win because classifications by a state that are based on alienage are inherently suspect and subject to close judicial scrutiny
(C) lose, because the statute promotes a compelling state interest
(D) lose, because alienage classifications are not per se unconstitutional under the Fourteenth Amendment

Question 138 is based on the following fact situation.

The state of Chippewa has a statute generally prohibiting the installation and use of radar detection devices in any motor vehicle operating on the roadways within the state. This prohibition was enacted to prevent motorists from evading radar or speed checkpoints on county and state highways. The neighboring state of Dakota has no such regulation in effect. By the same token, Congress has taken no action on the matter.

138. McGovern, a resident of the state of Dakota, has installed a radar detection device in his automobile. While driving to visit his mother, a resident of Chippewa, McGovern is arrested and charged with violating the aforementioned Chippewa statute. McGovern files a complaint challenging the constitutionality of the Chippewa statute. As applied to McGovern, the Chippewa prohibition against the use of radar detection devices is likely to be held

(A) constitutional, because it protects a legitimate state interest
(B) constitutional, because the Commerce Clause does not invalidate a state regulation relating to interstate commerce unless Congress takes express action to do so
(C) unconstitutional, because the Chippewa statute fails to give credit to the law of a neighboring state
(D) unconstitutional, because it unduly burdens interstate commerce

Question 139 is based on the following fact situation.

139. Which of the following constitutional provisions are *not* applicable to corporations?

I. The Privileges and Immunities Clause of the Fourteenth Amendment.
II. The Comity Clause—the interstate Privileges and Immunities Clause—of Article IV.
III. The Fifth Amendment prohibition against compulsory self-incrimination.
IV. The Equal Protection Clause of the Fourteenth Amendment.

(A) I and II
(B) II, III and IV
(C) I, II and III
(D) I, II, III and IV

Question 140 is based on the following fact situation.

The state of Missoula has recently enacted a statute that provides:

> "No person or company may be awarded any state construction contract unless said person or company agrees to hire only citizens of the state of Missoula in the performance of the contract."

The primary purpose of the statute is to help alleviate Missoula's high rate of unemployment.

140. Which of the following, if established, is the strongest argument in support of the statute if it is attacked as violating the Commerce Clause?

 (A) The statute will help racial minorities living in Missoula obtain gainful employment.
 (B) The state of Missoula has the highest unemployment rate in the country.
 (C) If Missoula uses its own taxpayer funds to purchase construction materials, it is responsible for creating demand for the required labor.
 (D) The statute was overwhelmingly adopted by the voters of the state.

Question 141 is based on the following fact situation.

In light of the current oil glut, many oil producing states have experienced extreme economic hardship. Due to the precipitous drop in oil prices, many oil companies have been forced to cut back on oil production and lay off many workers. As a result, unemployment has reached all-time high levels in such states as Texas, Oklahoma and Louisiana. In order to alleviate this potentially catastrophic situation, the Oklahoma legislature recently enacted a statute requiring that 10% of all oil produced within the state be purchased by the state and reserved for use by Oklahoma residents. The purpose of the statute was twofold. First, it was intended to stimulate the oil industry within the state by encouraging more production and exploration. Second, the statute was designed to create an oil reserve so that Oklahoma residents and industries would not suffer unduly from future oil shortages.

141. Is this Oklahoma statute constitutional?

 (A) Yes, if Congress has not expressly forbidden states to reserve local resources for local use.
 (B) Yes, because the Oklahoma statute requires that the oil be used for the general welfare of the people in emergency situations.
 (C) No, because a state may not protect its residents from out-of-state competition for its natural resources without the express permission of Congress.
 (D) No, because application of the statute denies non-oil producing companies to equal protection of the law in violation of the Fourteenth Amendment.

Questions 142–144 are based on the following fact situation.

The state of Brandywine built a racetrack that was specially designed and constructed for thoroughbred horse-racing. State bonds were issued to finance the construction of the racetrack. The bond agreement provided that for the first five years the racetrack was in operation at least $2 from each admission charge would be used to repay the bond debt. The bond agreement further stipulated that if the proceeds from the admission charges during the first five years were not sufficient to repay the bondholders, then at least $1 from each admission charge for the next five years would be applied to make the necessary bond payments.

142. After the racetrack was built and in operation for two years, the Brandywine state legislature passed a bill requiring the racetrack to admit all senior citizens over the age of 65 for the discounted admission fee of 50 cents. This law is probably

    (A) constitutional, because it is a justifiable exercise of the state's police power
    (B) unconstitutional, because it denies citizens under the age of 65 the equal protection of the law
    (C) unconstitutional, because it impairs the obligation of the bondholders' contract
    (D) unconstitutional, because it is an ex post facto law

143. Assume for the purposes of this question only that three years after the racetrack had been in operation, a subsequent session of the Brandywine state legislature passed a bill entirely prohibiting horse-racing at the racetrack because four jockeys were killed in racing mishaps. This statute is probably

    (A) constitutional, because it is a justifiable exercise of the state's police power
    (B) constitutional, because of the clear and present danger of horse-racing in the state
    (C) unconstitutional, because it impairs the obligation of the bondholders' contract
    (D) unconstitutional, because it violates the due process rights of the owners of the racehorses

144. Assume for the purposes of this question only that the Brandywine state legislature passes a statute prohibiting all horse-racing at privately owned racetracks in the state. Is this law likely to be held constitutional if most racehorses were from out-of-state?

    (A) Yes, because the act was expressly authorized by the Brandywine state legislature.
    (B) Yes, but only if the local interest in safety outweighs the burden of interstate commerce.
    (C) No, because out-of-state racehorses are part of interstate commerce.
    (D) No, because the statute violates the due process rights of the owners of the racehorses.

Question 145 is based on the following fact situation.

Herb Score, seventeen years of age, was a junior at Jeb Stuart High School in Memphis. Herb was suspended for five days by school officials after he came to school wearing a beard (which he had grown during "Spring break"). The school had a rule prohibiting any student from growing a beard or mustache while attending classes. The rule required an automatic five day suspension in such cases. Herb, who was aware of the rule prohibiting beards and mustaches, requested a trial-type hearing before the suspension was imposed.

145. If the Memphis School Board denies Herb's request for a trial type hearing, which of the following statements is most accurate?

    (A) The suspension violated Herb's due process rights because it deprived him of his entitlement to an education.
    (B) The denial of a trial-type hearing violated Herb's due process rights because the suspension was arbitrarily imposed.
    (C) The denial of a trial-type hearing did not violate Herb's due process rights because under the circumstances he had no right to a hearing.
    (D) There was no violation of Herb's due process rights because his conduct could be deemed so injurious to school discipline that it warranted suspension prior to a hearing.

Question 146 is based on the following fact situation.

David Dirkson was an eleventh grade student at Oliver High School in Townson City in the State of Goldsboro. On January 15, 2006, David was charged by the school administration with violating certain sections of the Disciplinary Code of the Townson City School District. Specifically, he was charged with being disrespectful to a teacher by using profanity and with using abusive language to a fellow student.

On January 16th, Harold Hopson, the principal, sent David's parents a letter notifying them of David's three day suspension for his above-mentioned charges. The suspension was to take effect on February 1st. Hopson also included a copy of the Disciplinary Code in the letter. On January 19th, David and his mother met with Hopson in his office to discuss the matter and David admitted that he used abusive language to a student.

On January 22nd, David's parents received a letter informing them that David's teacher had upheld the school administration's decision to suspend David. They then were notified of a hearing on the recommended suspension to be held at the School Board's office. David's parents did not attend this hearing, but were advised that the School Board had upheld David's suspension, effective February 1st.

146. Which of the following most accurately summarizes the applicable rule of constitutional law with respect to David's suspension?

    (A) David's suspension deprived him of "liberty" and "property" without due process as guaranteed by the Fourteenth Amendment.
    (B) David's conduct was protected under the First Amendment guarantee of freedom of speech.
    (C) David's suspension did not constitute a denial of due process.
    (D) The Disciplinary Code violated David's right to a compulsory school education.

Constitutional Law

Question 147 is based on the following fact situation.

The state Blue legislature passed a law requiring state universities to have male and female students live in separate dormitory facilities. The so-called "Dorm Segregation Act" was passed in order to curtail the increasing number of co-ed pregnancies on college campuses.

Jolene and Chuck are sophomores at State University of Blue (SUB). They are engaged to marry and wish to share a dormitory room together. Citing the "Dorm Segregation Act", university housing officials refuse to allow Jolene and Chuck to live together in a campus dormitory facility.

147. Jolene and Chuck bring an appropriate action to challenge the constitutionality of the "Dorm Segregation Act." Which of the following correctly states the applicable burden of persuasion?

    (A) Since the law deals with the fundamental right of privacy, the state must show that it furthers a compelling state interest.
    (B) Since the law deals with the freedom of association, the state must show that it furthers a compelling state interest.
    (C) Since the law involves gender discrimination, the state must prove that the law is substantially related to an important state interest.
    (D) Since the law does not affect a fundamental right nor involve gender discrimination, the burden is on the plaintiffs to show that it is not rationally related to a legitimate governmental interest.

Question 148 is based on the following fact situation.

Bicardi Butta was the prime minister of Chevnoski, a country situated in eastern Asia. Butta, the leader of the Christian Party, was assassinated by a group of right wing Islamic terrorists. Butta's death triggered a civil war between rival Muslim and Christian factions within the country. To prevent United States' involvement in Chevnoski's political crisis, Congress passed an appropriations bill prohibiting any funding for U.S. military operations in Chevnoski.

The appropriations bill was passed over a presidential veto. Thereafter, President Clinton issued an executive order directing U.S. Navy and Army troops to Chevnoski to restore order.

148. Is this executive order constitutional?

    (A) Yes, because the President as commander-in-chief of the armed forces has the power to authorize such military expeditions.
    (B) Yes, because the President has inherent power to regulate foreign affairs as long as there is no formal declaration of war.
    (C) No, because the President cannot usurp Congress's spending power by taking action that supersedes a congressional appropriations bill.
    (D) No, because the executive order was neither authorized by federal statute nor ratified by the Senate.

Question 149 is based on the following fact situation.

Dwight Dickman, a recent graduate of University of Virginia School of Law, took and passed the Maryland Bar Examination. Before the swearing-in ceremony, however, Dwight received a letter from the Committee of Bar Examiners indicating that his admission would be delayed until a character fitness investigation had been completed. The Committee also requested information as to whether Dwight had ever been arrested, convicted or placed on probation for a criminal offense. Dwight had been arrested as a juvenile for possession of marijuana. He was placed in a special drug education program for first time juvenile offenders and was told that the arrest would be expunged. Since Dwight believed that he had been totally exonerated of criminal liability, he didn't report the arrest on his bar application form.

However, the Maryland Committee of Bar Examiners had received an anonymous letter making reference to Dwight's juvenile arrest and suggesting that he was not morally fit to be admitted as an attorney. In addition, the letter provided detailed information about the facts related to the offense. As a result, the Committee hired Ernest Riles, a special investigator, to look into the matter. As part of Ernest's inquiry, he went to the clerk of the juvenile court where the offense occurred and demanded access to the records concerning Dwight. The clerk refused and cited a state statute that required all court and police records relating to juveniles be sealed. After all other attempts to gain access to the records proved futile, the Committee of Bar Examiners filed suit in federal district court demanding access to the relevant documents.

149. The court should rule that, as applied to this case, the state statute regarding the sealing of juvenile records is

(A) constitutional, because juveniles are entitled to the equal protection of the laws
(B) constitutional, because the state has a strong and legitimate interest in rehabilitating juvenile offenders and this is furthered by protecting them from embarrassment in later life through revelation of juvenile offenses
(C) unconstitutional, because the Committee of Bar Examiners, as a quasi-judicial agency, is entitled to have access to all relevant public documents
(D) unconstitutional, because it hinders the interests of justice by preventing the Committee of Bar Examiners from determining the fitness of candidates to practice law

Question 150 is based on the following fact situation.

Notre Dame University is located in the city of South Bend, Indiana. For many years, residents have complained to local officials about the boisterous noise and senseless shouting among students before and after Notre Dame football games. In response to these complaints, the South Bend City Council enacted an "anti-noise" ordinance prohibiting the singing and chanting of songs from 1:00 p.m. to 1:00 a.m. by two or more persons, if such noise is audible off the premises where the singing takes place. The ordinance expressly exempted from its purview the singing or chanting of religious songs.

After the ordinance was enacted and went into effect, Notre Dame played an important football game against University of Southern California for the national championship. The game, which was played in South Bend, was won by the Irish. Following the game, a large group of Notre Dame students were walking down Main Street on their way to a victory celebration. They began loudly chanting, "We're number 1 … we're number 1." One of the residents who lived on Main Street was greatly disturbed by the noise. As a result, he reported the incident to the police who were immediately summoned to the scene. The students who engaged in the chanting were arrested and charged with violating the South Bend "anti-noise" ordinance.

150. The students who were prosecuted now bring suit challenging the constitutionality of the South Bend ordinance. Which of the following would constitute their WEAKEST argument against enforcement of the "anti-noise" statute?

    (A) The ordinance deprives persons of their freedom of expression in violation of the First and Fourteenth Amendments.
    (B) The ordinance deprives persons of their liberty without due process of law because the ordinance is not related to any legitimate community interest.
    (C) The statutory language of the ordinance is vague and overbroad since it attempts to encompass all forms of singing.
    (D) The ordinance deprives the persons of the equal protection of the laws by impermissibly distinguishing between religiously inspired singing and all forms of singing.

EXPLANATORY ANSWERS

1. **(D)** While the President has the power both to issue executive orders and to remove purely executive officers appointed by him without being subject to any Congressional limitation, the scope of these powers must not contravene federal constitutional limitations, such as the First Amendment rights of freedom of speech and association. The executive order banning all executive employees from having conversations with members of the press unless prior permission has been obtained from an administrative supervisor clearly violates the First Amendment as an overbroad prior restraint limiting otherwise protected speech. The executive order is therefore unconstitutional. Choice (D) is correct.

2. **(B)** The Constitution gives the President broad authority with respect to *foreign affairs.* Article II, Section 2 explicitly enumerates a number of powers given him in this area (e.g., commander-in-chief power, treaty-making power and the right to appoint ambassadors). However, *the President's power over foreign affairs is not plenary or absolute.* Rather, the President and Congress have concurrent powers over foreign affairs. To be sure, Congress is given war power authority and treaties must be ratified by two-thirds of the Senate. In this regard, choice (A) is not the best answer for two reasons. First, it is doubtful that the President would have authority as commander-in-chief to mobilize non-military federal employees in this manner. Second, the President's authority to direct foreign affairs is not "unfettered" or absolute. Therefore, choice (B) would be a better answer since the President as Chief Executive probably would have authority to direct executive employees to engage in such an international relief effort (especially given the fact that Border Patrol guards are stationed at the Mexican border).

3. **(C)** Since Congress has the power to regulate interstate commerce under Article 1, Section 8, choice (C) is the best answer. Alternative (B) is incorrect because the facts do not state that the United States and Russia are at war. Similarly, you may *not* assume that the airline takeover was a wartime or war related act.

4. **(B)** Article IV, Section 3, clause 2 gives Congress power "to dispose of and make all needful rules and regulations respecting" lands of the United States. Therefore, since the District of Columbia is under federal jurisdiction, choice (B) is the best answer.

5. **(D)** Article II, Section 2 specifies that the President shall appoint "with the advice and consent of the Senate" all "Ambassadors, other public Ministers and Consuls, Judges of the Supreme Court, and all other Officers of the United States." Note that although Congress may appoint officials to exercise such investigative power as it might delegate to one of its own committees, *it may not appoint members or an agency or commission with administrative powers.* Such persons are deemed "officers of the United States" and must be appointed pursuant to Article II, Section 2. *Buckley v. Valeo,* 424 U.S. 1 (1976).

6. **(D)** The Supreme Court has said that the core of Article III's requirement for cases and controversies is found in the rule that *standing is limited to those who allege that they personally have suffered or imminently will suffer an injury.* In *City of Los Angeles v. Lyons,* 461 U.S. 95 (1983), the Court stated *"the plaintiff must show that he has sustained or is immediately in danger of sustaining some direct injury as a result of the challenged action."* With respect to standing in environmental cases, the Supreme Court has handed down two conflicting rulings. In *Sierra Club v.*

Constitutional Law

Morton, 405 U.S. 727 (1972), the Sierra Club sought to prevent construction of a ski resort in Mineral Valley in California. The Court ruled that the Sierra Club lacked standing because *there was **no allegation that any of the Sierra Club's members ever had used Mineral Valley***. By contrast, in *United States v. Students Challenging Regulatory Agency Procedures*, 412 U.S. 669 (1973), the Court upheld the standing of a group of George Washington law students alleging that an administrative rate hike would decrease recycling which would lead to more use of natural resources and increased pollution. The students maintained that their enjoyment of the forests, streams, and mountains in the Washington D.C. area would be lessened as a result. The Court **upheld the group's standing because the plaintiffs actually used the environmental area for hikes, biking and other recreational purposes**. In this hypo, there is no showing that Professor Kingfish is making any personal use of the coral reef area. Therefore, he would lack standing on environmental grounds.

7. **(C)** A bill of attainder is any form of legislative punishment of a named group or individual without judicial trial. Under Article I, Section 9,10, federal and state governments are prohibited from enacting bills of attainder. The Cahuenga Statute revoking the state insurance license of Iris Fox is a sufficient form of legislative "punishment" to constitute an impermissible bill of attainder. Choice (C) is correct.

8. **(D)** In light of the decision in *Mathews v. Diaz,* 426 U.S. 67 (1976), choice (D) is the best answer. In *Mathews*, the Court applied "relaxed scrutiny" in upholding the validity of a federal statute that conditioned an alien's eligibility for participation in a federal medical insurance program on the satisfaction of a durational residency requirement, but imposed no similar burden on citizens. The Court was at pains to emphasize that Congress, as an aspect of its **broad power over immigration and naturalization,** enjoys rights to distinguish among aliens that are not shared by the states. Although (C) is a correct statement of law, it does not provide any rationale supporting or justifying the federal government's treatment of aliens.

9. **(B)** In *Metromedia, Inc. v. San Diego,* 453 U.S. 490 (1981), the Court struck down a San Diego ordinance which, *inter alia,* prohibited all billboards containing non-commercial messages, except for those messages falling within certain defined categories (e.g., temporary political campaign signs, signs carrying news items or telling the time or temperature, etc.). The Court objected to this handling of non-commercial speech, on the grounds that "the city may not choose the appropriate subjects for public discourse"; the city was required to either allow ***all, or no,*** non-commercial messages. Here the Middletown ordinance would have been valid if it were limited to restricting the size of billboards. But since the ordinance also attempted to impose **non-content-neutral regulations** (by requiring that signs only relate to advertising the business of the owner-occupant), it will be struck down under the strict (and usually fatal) scrutiny test.

10. **(A)** Although nowhere mentioned in the Constitution, the concept of police power has developed closely with that of the dormant commerce power to enable a state to regulate health and safety interests and to enact economic and social welfare measures. As a general rule, "where the state regulates even-handedly to effectuate a legitimate local public interest, and its effects on interstate commerce are

only incidental, it will be upheld unless the burden imposed on such commerce is clearly excessive in relation to the putative local benefits." *Pike v. Bruce Church, Inc.* 397 U.S. 137 (1970). The Utah law requiring sellers under "installment land contracts" to institute foreclosure actions to relieve the harsh effect of forfeiture by allowing the buyer a 60-day reinstatement period serves a legitimate purpose and leaves unchanged the initial monetary obligations of both parties. Therefore, it will be upheld. Choice (A) is correct. In order to protect the health, safety, and welfare of its citizens, a state may enact legislation which impairs contracts under certain conditions. The action of the Utah legislature may be reasonably viewed as a **permissible police power modification** of the "installment land contract" because no prior underlying contractual obligation has been impaired, since the buyer must still pay in full the original bargained-for purchase price. In general, note that private parties who enter into contracts may not stop the legislature from exercising its proper police power for the public good. Nowak, p. 376. Choice (B) is incorrect because the authority to enact laws regulating intrastate real estate sales transactions is not reserved exclusively to the states under the 10th Amendment. Such transactions have a cumulative impact on interstate commerce and are subject to the federal commerce power. The court has refused to use the 10th Amendment to reserve subject areas of commerce for state regulation.

11. **(C)** The doctrine of political questions precludes federal judicial review of nonjusticiable issues, i.e., matters not capable of judicial resolution due to inherent separation of powers limitations. The leading case of *Baker v. Carr* 369 U.S. 186 (1962) established a test to identify such nonjusticiable issues. For example, where a textually demonstrable commitment to a coordinate political branch of government has been made, or where there is a lack of judicially manageable standards to resolve the issue, or where judicial resolution would create the potential for embarrassment from multifarious pronouncements by various branches of government, then the judiciary will decline resolution of such nonjusticiable political questions. Choice (C) is correct because foreign affairs is a nonjusticiable political question over which federal courts will not exercise jurisdiction.

12. **(B)** Under Article I, Section 8, Congress shall have the power "To regulate Commerce with foreign Nations, and among the several States, and with the Indian Tribes." This plenary federal commerce power is held concurrently with the states, which may freely govern matters which do not require uniform national regulation. For a state regulation affecting interstate commerce to pass judicial scrutiny, the statute must be found **reasonable** and **non-discriminatory** upon **balancing** the benefit to the state against the burden imposed on interstate commerce such that **no less restrictive alternative means** of regulation is available. Where a state statute imposes a discriminatory burden on out-of-state interests its validity is seriously in question. The North Durango "Window Tint" Act effectively prevents Luxury Limousine Company from doing business in its state. Luxury's strongest constitutional argument to invalidate the statute would be the Commerce Clause challenge presented in answer choice (B). Choice (A) is incorrect because **all** motor vehicles in North Durango are treated equally under the law. Choice (D) is incorrect because strong support is given in the facts to demonstrate that the purpose for enacting the "Window Tint" Act was neither arbitrary nor unreasonable.

Constitutional Law

13. **(B)** This Constitutional Law question focuses on the specific case of *Powell v. McCormack,* 395 U.S. 486 (1969) but there is an important "twist." In Powell, the House of Representatives refused to seat him (after he had been elected) due to the fact that he had wrongfully diverted House funds for his own personal use. In brief, the Court held that the House did not have authority to *exclude* him since he met all the requirements for membership expressly prescribed in Art. I, Section 2 (namely, age, citizenship and residency). Thus, the Court held that Powell's claim did not present a political question. In this example, however the *issue is* whether Kennedy fulfilled the "residency" requirements set forth in Art. I, Section 2. Since the House has the *unreviewable power* to determine the "residency" (as well as "age" and "citizenship") qualifications for its members, the case presents a nonjusticiable political question. Note that choice (A) is incorrect because due to the fact that Powell demanded *back pay* (as Kennedy has done), the Court held that "a prayer for specific relief prevented a finding of mootness and demonstrated that there was in fact a 'case or controversy'." See *Powell,* pg. 497.

14. **(D)** The landmark case of *New York v. United States*, 505 U.S. 144 (1992) clearly limited Congress's right to interfere with a state's ability to make and apply laws through legislative, judicial, and administrative functions. Based on principles of state sovereignty under the Tenth Amendment, **Congress may not simply commandeer the legislative processes of the States by directly compelling them to enact and enforce a federal regulatory program**. The Court explained that allowing Congress to commandeer state governments would undermine government accountability because Congress could make a decision but the states would take the political heat and be held responsible for a decision that was not theirs. Therefore, if a federal law compels state legislative or regulatory activity, the statute is unconstitutional even if there is a compelling need for the federal action. **Chemerinsky**, p. 233. Under its commerce power, Congress could clearly pass legislation to establish a federal commission to monitor and curtail alcoholic beverage sales to underage drinkers. However, a Tenth Amendment violation arises when implementation of the bill requires each state to pass legislation to establish a local "watchdog" agency to facilitate compliance with congressional intent. Congress cannot compel state regulatory activity. The federal statute will be held invalid under the Tenth Amendment. Choice (D) is the correct answer.

15. **(C)** When a federal constitutional claim is premised on an unsettled question of state law, the federal court should "stay its hand" (abstain temporarily), so as to give state courts a chance to settle underlying state law questions. In the present case, WAF initially should have brought suit in state court (thereby exhausting all state remedies) before seeking federal judicial review. Clearly, WAF is presently "harmed" by the Downtown Club's exclusionary membership policy. Therefore, choice (A) is incorrect. Choice (B) is wrong since an actual "case and controversy" is presented by the Downtown Club's exclusion of women members.

16. **(C)** A frequently tested Constitutional Law area deals with licensing statutes. As a general rule, whenever an ordinance is "void on its face," the defendant need not apply for a permit. In this situation, he is entitled to deliver his speech and can successfully defend any subsequent prosecution. An ordinance may be deemed to be facially invalid for the following three reasons: (1) "vagueness," (2) "overbreadth,"

Explanatory Answers

(3) "unfettered discretion" in the licensing official. On the other hand, students should be aware that when an ordinance is *valid* on its face (although a permit may be arbitrarily denied), the applicant must seek judicial relief *before* engaging in his speech. See *Poulos v. New Hampshire*, 345 U.S. 395 (1953).

17. **(D)** In *Cox v. Louisiana*, 379 U.S. 537, the U.S. Supreme Court held that an analogous ordinance prohibiting "parades or demonstrations along any street except in accordance with a permit issued by the police chief" was clearly unconstitutional. The Court reasoned that it would be an arbitrary exercise of state police power to enable a public official to determine which expressions of view will be permitted and which will not. Allowing unfettered discretion in local officials in the regulation of the use of streets is an unwarranted abridgement of one's freedom of speech and assembly as secured by the First Amendment, and applied to the States by the Fourteenth Amendment. Be advised that choice (C) is not the best answer because the statute is neither overbroad nor vague. Rather it is invalid because it gives the Mayor the "unfettered discretion" to approve or disapprove permit applications.

18. **(A)** In *City of Wauwatosa v. King*, 182 NW2d 530 (1971), the Wisconsin Supreme Court upheld a local ordinance prohibiting "picketing before or about the residence or dwelling of any individual." The Court held that it is a proper serving of a proper state interest for a state or community to seek to protect the privacy and tranquility of the homes of its residents.

19. **(C)** Since the Brighton Reform Act will not become effective until January 1, 2003, the court will dismiss this action for lack of ripeness. In this regard it is crucial that a person asking the court to hold a statute unconstitutional must be able to show, not only that the statute is invalid, but that "he has sustained or is immediately in danger of sustaining some direct injury" as a result of its enforcement. Here, the parents must wait until after the Reform Act has gone into effect before initiating suit.

20. **(D)** Choice (D) is the LEAST accurate choice since the U.S. Supreme Court has invalidated (under the Establishment Clause of the First Amendment) parental tuition reimbursements or tax benefits for persons with children in parochial schools even as part of a broader program for all private school children. See *Committee for Public Education v. Nyquist*, 392 U.S. 236 (1973). Choices (A), (B) and (C) are correct applications of the law.

21. **(B)** In *Lemon v. Kurtzman*, 403 U.S. 602, the United States Supreme Court held unconstitutional a statute which provided for payment of salary supplements to parochial school teachers who taught solely secular subjects. The Court concluded that the degree of government surveillance necessary to insure that the supplements would be restricted to teachers of secular subjects would entangle the government excessively.

22. **(A)** Procedural due process ***guarantees a fair decision-making process*** before the government takes some action directly impairing an individual's life, liberty, or property interests under the Fifth and Fourteenth Amendments. Where such a deprivation occurs which is serious in nature, the procedural safeguards of notice and opportunity to be heard (i.e., hearing) are available.

Constitutional Law

23. **(C)** Here, choice (C) is the best answer. Under Article I, Section 8, clauses 11 and 12, Congress has wide war power authority. Certainly, the draft and selective service systems have been repeatedly upheld as a proper exercise of Congress' war powers. Based on the decision in *United States v. O'Brien,* 391 U.S. 367 (1968), individuals may be constitutionally required to register and submit to examinations reasonably required by the selective service system to facilitate the conscription of manpower for military service.

24. **(B)** During the 1940's and 1950's, the Supreme Court invalidated a number of laws which restricted religious practices primarily on the basis that they interfered with the free speech protection of the First Amendment. These decisions overturned statutes regulating the dissemination of religious views because they interfered with both the freedom of speech and religion. In sum, the Court struck down licensing systems for demonstrations or meetings which gave government officials discretion to deny licenses on the basis of the content of speech, while upholding ones which had permit requirements based on nondiscriminatory "time, place or manner" factors. In these cases the fact that religious meetings were suppressed under discretionary statutes indicated a violation of free exercise rights, but the statutes were invalid in total as they conflicted with the free speech clause. By analogy, the Santa Monica ordinance would be unconstitutional because it unfairly burdens the freedom of religion (as well as speech). Here, the Santa Monica ordinance does not further a "compelling state interest" as less restrictive means are available.

25. **(D)** A very highly tested area of Constitutional Law deals with the standards of review used by the courts in equal protection challenges, and specifically, **what is the burden of persuasion** in each situation. In this question, the state of Golden has imposed a statute taxing the extraction of platinum. The tax discriminates against Underground, the state's largest platinum mining company, raising an equal protection challenge since Golden is not taxing the extraction of any other mineral. The standard of review that the court will use in this case will be the traditional ***rational-basis test***. The rational basis test, which is used for classifications relating to non-suspect (or quasi-suspect) classes and to non-fundamental rights, includes the following: ***classifications based on poverty, wealth, age, public housing, and welfare benefits***. See Nowak, **Constitutional Law** pp. 620–623. Under the rational basis test, *the burden is on the plaintiff to prove that the challenged measure is not rationally related to a legitimate state interest*. Choice (D) is therefore correct. Note that it is extremely difficult for the plaintiff to prevail under the "mere rationality," or rational basis, test because ***any legitimate interest*** which is reasonably furthered by enactment of the challenged measure will be purportedly valid.

26. **(A)** The doctrine of standing requires that a person asserting the violation of a constitutional (or statutory) right must show a direct and immediate personal injury due to the challenged action. Note that choice (B) is incorrect since it is irrelevant whether the university signed a stipulation agreeing ***not to harass Mary Jo in the future***. The facts clearly indicate that the plaintiff suffered personal injury (humiliation and damage to reputation) which can be traced to the challenged action. As a result, the federal court will likely hear the case because a genuine controversy" is presented.

Explanatory Answers

27. **(B)** The WEAKEST defense to Dr. Bradley's constitutional challenge of the statute under the Commerce Clause is that the statute will help protect optometrists in the state from out-of-state competitors. State regulations, such as the medical licensing statute, that appear primarily to favor local economic interest as against outside competition are generally found to be unconstitutional as unreasonable burdens on interstate commerce. However, if the regulation is perceived as within a legitimate health and safety measure that cannot readily be achieved by less drastic means, the Court will uphold even a regulation that is discriminatory. While a state may legislate to protect the health of its citizens, the statutory purpose regarding the licensing provision could be achieved by "reasonable nondiscriminatory alternatives, adequate to conserve the legitimate interests of the local optometrists." Therefore, the statute could be challenged as a discriminatory burden on interstate commerce. Students should refer to *Dean Milk Co. v. Madison,* 340 U.S. 349 (1951), where the Supreme Court invalidated a local health ordinance under the "unreasonable burdens" rule.

28. **(B)** Since Dr. Bradley is challenging the constitutionality of the medical licensing statute, he has the burden of persuasion to show that the denial of the license violates his rights of due process. Upon such a showing, the burden then shifts to the state to prove that it has a compelling state interest in enacting such legislation. In *re Ruffalo,* 390 U.S. 544 (1968), the Supreme Court held that if the government terminates an individual's ability to engage in a profession, it must grant that individual a procedure to determine his fitness to be a member of the profession. Thus, an individual must be afforded a fair hearing, before a government agency may revoke his license to practice a profession such as optometry in this case.

29. **(C)** Under the Supremacy Clause of Article IV, Section II, **federal treaties are the supreme law of the land and supersede any state statutes which are in conflict therewith.** Since Congress is vested with the primary authority to regulate immigration and aliens, under Article I, any state legislation which affects aliens is thus likely to be pre-empted (depending, however, in part on the activity regulated). Students should note that the Supreme Court has upheld a state law, forbidding employment of illegal aliens under the state's police power, since it did not interfere with the exclusive federal power over aliens.

30. **(C)** If the New Mexico statute is challenged on Commerce Clause grounds, the court would apply the unreasonable burdens rule (also referred to as the least restrictive means test). State regulations, even in areas generally described as local, cannot be accepted if they impose an unreasonable burden on interstate commerce. In order to determine the reasonableness of the burden, the Court will balance the nature and extent of the burden which the state regulation would impose on interstate commerce against the purposes of the state regulation. Subsection (d) of the statute would place a discriminatory burden on producers of other building materials, both within and outside of the state.

31. **(C)** Although the federal commerce power is **plenary,** the states may also regulate commerce among themselves, subject to implications flowing from the Supremacy Clause. State regulation of interstate commerce must be reasonable and nondiscriminatory, and the states may not interfere with the free flow of interstate commerce by favoring local interests or burdening out-of-state competition. The

Corona statute which prohibits the sale of beer in glass bottles will effectively curtail out-of-state production of 21% (75% of 28%) of all the beer consumed in Corona. Not only is it arguable that this large proportion is **discriminatory** against out-of-state bottlers, but **unreasonable** as well, since the urging of the aluminum can industry was the basis on which the state legislature passed the bill. Based on these facts, the strongest argument against the validity of the Corona statute would be that it violates the Commerce Clause and the negative implications flowing from it. Choice (C) is correct. Commerce Clause is a broader and stronger source of power than Contracts Clause, choice (D). Note that choice (A), Equal Protection Clause, is not as strong an argument because even though the statute does arguably discriminate against out-of-state bottlers, the standard of review the Court would use to determine its validity would be the rational basis test, under which the state could prevail upon a showing of any rational basis for enacting the bill.

32. **(A)** The Supreme Court may properly deny review of any matter which rests upon an adequate and independent state ground, since resolution of the "state" issue by the state court might preclude the need for federal review. As a general rule, the Supreme Court, upon reviewing a decision of a state court, only reviews the federal questions and not the state law questions. Nowak, **Constitutional Law,** p. 85. Since the Corona "Bottleless Beer Bill" was found by the state court to be unconstitutional as violative of the contracts clause of the **state** constitution, the Supreme Court would avoid review of the case on the merits because a separate and sufficient state law basis for unconstitutionality exists. Choice (A) is correct in stating this conclusion under the doctrine of adequate and independent state grounds. Choice (B) is incorrect as a misstatement of this doctrine, since the Supreme Court will decline to hear the case, not reverse the decision. Likewise, choices (C) and (D) reach the wrong conclusions because the Supreme Court will refuse review altogether as long as any adequate state ground for state court review exists.

33. **(B)** This fact pattern is extremely representative of both the difficulty of Constitutional Law questions on the bar and of the closeness between long, and often similar, answer choices. The substantive guarantees of due process under the 14th Amendment require that legislation, to be constitutional, have a rational relationship to a legitimate end of government. In the area of fundamental rights, such as privacy (and including abortion), governmental power is limited to the extent that individuals may be afforded freedom of choice in matters relating to their personal life. The Hermosa statute limits the availability of funds for AIDS patients only to hospitals refusing to perform abortions. While the statute does not preclude individuals from having abortions performed, it does make more difficult the exercise of that right. Since legislation restricting fundamental rights is viewed under the strict scrutiny standard of review, the **state** then has a heavy burden to show that the measure is necessary to further a compelling interest. Choice (B) is the strongest argument presented and is therefore correct.

34. **(C)** Choice (A) is incorrect since *the 10th Amendment reserved powers do not authorize plenary power to the states regarding allocation of public funds*. Choice (B) is incorrect since the Court would generally examine the purpose and circumstances underlying the authorization of public subsidies before mechanically applying the rights-privilege rationale. Choices (C) and (D) are both very persuasive. To determine which one is stronger, consider that the primary purpose of the statute itself

Explanatory Answers

is to provide public funding to hospitals for AIDS victims, not to directly restrict abortion. This purpose promotes a legitimate interest which, under equal protection analysis, would be reviewed using the rational basis standard, as stated in choice (C). Since choice (C) presents a federal constitutional basis of analysis, whereas choice (D) addresses merely a source of state power (i.e. police power), choice (C) is preferred and therefore the correct answer.

35. **(C)** In all likelihood, the Baltimore ordinance prohibiting the operation of all trucks and buses within its Center City business area between 10:00 a.m. and 4:00 p.m. would be violative of the Commerce Clause if less restrictive alternatives are available.

36. **(C)** When the government regulates speech *in a traditional public forum*, it may only base its restriction on the *content* of the speech being regulated 1) if that content falls within a category of speech which the Court has found unprotected by the First Amendment, or 2) if the government can demonstrate a compelling interest in suppressing the speech. However, the government may employ a time, place, or manner regulation to regulate speech in a traditional public forum (streets, parks) so long as the regulation promotes an important interest unrelated to the suppression of a particular message and does not unnecessarily restrict the ability to communicate the message. Nowak, **Constitutional Law** pp. 975–6. In this question, the test maker is trying to trick students into thinking the Rosemont city ordinance regulates a protected First Amendment area. In fact, the littering ordinance regulates neither speech-related conduct nor speech-related content. The regulation promotes a legitimate objective by advancing a health and safety interest under the state's police power, and the ordinance passes First Amendment scrutiny since it is not directed at the suppression of communication. Choice (C) is correct.

37. **(C)** *The Fifteenth Amendment is a limitation prohibiting the states and the federal government from denying any citizen the right to vote on account of race or color.* Note, too, that the Fifteenth Amendment has an "enabling clause" that allows Congress to enact legislation protecting against discrimination affecting the right to vote. Choice (A) is incorrect because the Thirteenth Amendment provides that slavery shall not exist in the United States. Choice (B) is wrong because *the Fourteenth Amendment prohibits states* from depriving any person of life, liberty or property without due process and equal protection of the laws.

38. **(C)** In *Plyler v. Doe,* 457 U.S. 202 (1982), the Supreme Court held that illegal alien children are entitled to free public education. In *Plyler,* the Court struck down a Texas statute which (1) denied local school district funds for education of illegal alien children and (2) allowed school districts to deny free public education to these children. The majority of Justices determined that the Equal Protection Clause of the 14th Amendment was intended to cover any person physically within a state's border regardless of the legality of his/her presence. Students should also be aware that the Court rejected the notion that *illegal aliens* be treated as a "suspect" class. Instead, *the Court applied "intermediate-level" scrutiny* based on the following two factors: (1) the importance of public education and (2) the powerless nature of the group. Thus, choice (C) is correct.

39. **(B)** In dealing with the area of state economic regulation enacted so as to affect the health or safety of the citizenry, the Court will not strike down the state legislation if the benefit to health and safety outweighs the burden imposed on interstate commerce. The challenged legislation must pass a commerce clause test of "reasonableness" that is stricter than that used for due process and equal protection cases. Nowak, p. 271. Following the holding in *South Carolina v. Barnwell* 303 U.S.177 (1938) where the Court upheld a width restriction on trucks using South Carolina state highways due to the safety concern arising from the state's narrow roads—the city of Maplewood's parking ban on one side of the highway due to the narrowness of Route 66 as it passes through the business district, promotes a safety interest that is reasonable and it will be upheld.

40. **(A)** State control over the right to vote is not expressly limited by the federal constitution. However, any inequality in allocating the right to vote based on using electoral districts established on criteria other than street population dilutes the "one man, one vote" principle and will be subject to strict scrutiny review by the Court. In *Reynolds* v. Sims, 377 U.S. 533 (1964), Justice Warren formulated the one person, one vote rule: "If a State should provide that the votes of citizens in one part of the State should be given two times, or five times, or 10 times the weight of votes of citizens in another part of the State, it could hardly be contended that the right to vote of those residing in the disfavored areas had not been effectively diluted. The Equal Protection Clause requires that the seats in both houses of a bicameral state legislature must be apportioned on a population basis." Nowak, **Constitutional Law**, p. 754.

41. **(A)** If *a state court holds a state law valid under both state and federal constitutional provisions*, then the Supreme Court *may* exercise review. Specifically, if the Court *disagreed* with the state court's review of the *federal constitution,* the state decision would have to be reversed regardless of the interpretation of the state law. Therefore, the doctrine of adequate state grounds would not apply, and the Court would hear the federal issues presented. In this question, if the state court improperly interpreted federal law—namely the Equal Protection issue arising from the diluted reapportionment scheme under the "Berlin Proposal"—then the Supreme Court would hear the case and reverse the state court's decision. Choice (A) is thus correct.

42. **(D)** *Article II does not vest the President with an absolute, unqualified executive privilege as against a subpoena essential to enforcement of criminal statutes.* To vest the President with such powers would upset the separation of powers doctrine and gravely impair the role of the courts under Article III. The Supreme Court, in *United States v. Nixon,* 418 U.S. 683 (1974), held that the courts have the power of judicial review and are the final arbiter of a claim of executive privilege. Moreover, the court concluded that the executive privilege may not be asserted as to subpoenaed materials sought for use in a criminal trial, since the Constitution requires the courts to adhere to the due process of law.

43. **(B)** The power of the president to appoint and remove officers of the United States stems in part from express provisions of the Constitution and in part from the implications of express grants of power. Article II, Section 2, Clause 2, establishes in the president the power to appoint officers of the United States; it also provides

Explanatory Answers

that Congress may vest the appointment of inferior officers in either the president alone, in the courts, or in the heads of departments. At no time, however, may the legislative branch exercise executive authority by retaining the power to appoint those who will execute its laws. Thus, in *Buckley v. Valeo*, 424 U.S. 1 (1976), the U.S. Supreme Court held that Congress had violated Article II in providing the President pro tem of the Senate and the Speaker of the House were to appoint a majority of the voting members of the Federal Election Commission.

44. **(C)** Another issue commonly tested on the MBE deals with **whether religious members are precluded from holding government offices**. In *McDaniel v. Paty*, 435 U.S. 618 (1978), the Supreme Court declared unconstitutional a state law that prevented "Minister(s) of the Gospel, or priest(s) of any denomination whatever from serving as delegates to the state constitutional convention." Interestingly enough, the disqualification of clergy members from legislative office existed in England and was followed by seven of the original states. The Supreme Court, however, found that this history was **not decisive** and invalidated the state law. The majority of Justices ruled that **the free exercise of religion allowed members of the clergy to hold government office**. Based on the holding in *McDaniel*, the appointment of a member of the clergy to a governmental agency or commission would not per se be violative of the Establishment Clause.

45. **(C)** With respect to abortions, the trimester test of *Roe* has been partially overruled by *Planned Parenthood of Southeastern Pennsylvania v. Casey*, 505 U.S. 833 (1992). As a result of *Casey*, the state may restrict abortion so long as they do not place **"undue burdens"** on the woman's right to choose. Here, the Islandia statute does place an "undue burden" on the right to abortion because **after the first trimester a woman can only have an abortion to protect her health and life**. Choice (A) is not the best answer because it utilizes the "fundamental" right to privacy language articulated in *Roe v. Wade*. However, the Court in *Casey* **appeared to reject the Roe view that abortion was a "fundamental" right and restrictions are no longer to be strictly scrutinized**. Choice (B) is wrong because the Court applies the undue burden test to abortions not an intermediate scrutiny standard as applied in gender discrimination.

46. **(B)** The Thirteenth Amendment is unique in two respects. First, it contains an absolute bar to the existence of slavery or involuntary servitude; there is no requirement of "state action". **Thus, it is applicable to individuals as well as states**. Secondly, like the Fourteenth and Fifteenth Amendments, it contains an enforcement clause, enabling Congress to pass all necessary legislation. In this regard, the Court has held that the enforcement provision of the Thirteenth Amendment has extended Section 1982 of the 1866 Civil Rights Act "to insure minorities the freedom to inherit, purchase, lease, sell, hold and convey real and personal property." Most importantly, the Thirteenth Amendment has been construed to prohibit both public and private racial discrimination in housing.

47. **(D)** Students should note that this question requires a two-step analysis to select the best alternative. First, students must determine the constitutional issue involved and then secondly, apply the appropriate constitutional principle to the question asked, i.e., the state's best rebuttal to a constitutional challenge to the pension forfeiture statute. Choice (D) is correct since the argument concerning a condition

of employment contract with a Senate staff member effects the Contract Clause of the Constitution. Belli, Caucus's attorney, could validly challenge the constitutionality of the statute alleging unconstitutional impairment of the obligation to contract. The pension forfeiture statute would be violative of the Contract Clause since under the circumstances Caucus has satisfied the conditions of retirement eligibility (he became fully qualified for his pension on retirement as stated in the facts). His retirement pay has ripened into a full contractual obligation and became a vested right. Therefore, the pension forfeiture statute would be an unconstitutional impairment of his vested right to receive retirement benefits (his pension). Choices (A) and (B) are irrelevant to the constitutional issues involved. Choice (C) is inapplicable since notice is not an issue here.

48. **(B)** The two **Ex Post Facto** Clauses in the United States Constitution prohibit Congress and the state legislatures from enacting laws that have a retrospective effect. The Public Employee Pension Forfeiture Act is an example of an *ex post facto* law which renders an act punishable in a manner in which it was not punishable when committed under the facts presented, (since Caucus qualified for pension benefits before the pension forfeiture statute was enacted). Thus the statute, which denied Caucus a pension because of the bribery conviction during his employment on the Senate staff, applied retroactively to Caucus. Hence, the pension forfeiture statute would be held violative of the *Ex Post Facto* Clauses of the U.S. Constitution. Students should be aware that although Choice (A) *is a correct statement of fact,* choice (B) is the preferred alternative, *because it is the correct statement of law.* When you are confronted with correct statements of fact and law, the latter is the preferred alternative.

49. **(B)** Students should note that of the four alternatives listed, only choice (B) provides a correct statement regarding the possibility of the reinstatement of Caucus's pension. Article II empowers the President to grant reprieves and pardons for offenses against the United States. The President may pardon absolutely or conditionally commute sentences, and remit fines, penalties and forfeitures. In this regard, note that the facts state that Caucus was convicted of bribery in **federal court.** In all likelihood, therefore he was being prosecuted for a federal criminal offense. Choice (A) is incorrect since Caucus does not have a constitutional right to discretionary review in the U.S. Supreme Court. Such right of appeal to the U.S. Supreme Court is not a constitutional right, but a **statutory** right; Congress has enacted legislation regarding the appellate review of the Supreme Court.

50. **(A)** The Supreme Court is the only federal court created directly by the Constitution. Article III, Section 1 mandates that judicial power be vested in "one Supreme Court." See Nowak, **Constitutional Law,** p. 24. Therefore, the Congressional statute to divide the Supreme Court into two panels is unconstitutional since *it contravenes Article III of the Constitution*. Choice (A) is therefore correct. Choice (B) is factually true, but the rationale is not as precise as choice (A). Students should be aware that Article III, Section 1 vests judicial power as to the *inferior courts—* including federal district courts and courts of appeal only "as the Congress may from time to time ordain and establish." This plenary power of Congress includes not only the establishment of such courts, but the authorization of their jurisdiction, the power to remove jurisdiction of certain classes of cases, and the power to terminate the courts' existence. Article III judges are appointed for life and their compensation may not be diminished during their term in office.

51. **(C)** Under Article II, Section 2, U.S. Constitution, the only constitutional limitation upon the President's power "to conduct foreign affairs" is with regard to treaties, which only become valid when ratified by two-thirds of the Senate.

52. **(D)** Under Article VI, paragraph 2, all treaties "which shall be made under the authority of the U.S." are the "Supreme law of the land" (along with the Constitution itself and laws of the U.S. made in pursuance thereof). As a consequence, it is clear that any state action in conflict with a treaty is invalid.

53. **(A)** or **(B)** According to Justice Berger, "the compatibility of a commitment to an uninhibited, robust, and wide-open discussion of public issues in a free press with a commitment to a criminal process in which the conclusions to be reached in a case will be induced only by evidence and argument in open court has been the subject of long standing debate." See *Nebraska Press Association v. Stuart*, 427 U.S. 539 (1976). In this area, the rights of the press often conflict with the rights of the accused. Accordingly, the Supreme Court offered a qualified response to this question when it invalidated a Nebraska District Court "gag order" which prohibited the press from the publication of certain implicative evidence pertaining to a murder suspect until the jury selection process was completed. Based on the *Nebraska* decision, choices (A) and (B) would both be arguably correct.

54. **(A)** *The Ex Post Facto Clause forbids both the states and the federal government from enacting retroactive criminal laws.* The most common sort of an ex post facto law is one which creates a new crime and applies it retroactively to conduct not criminal at the time committed. In addition, the Ex Post Facto Clause prohibits the retroactive application of an increase in the punishment for a crime which carried a lesser penalty when committed. Another aspect of the ex post facto prohibition is concerned with *retroactive changes in evidence and procedure which operate to the disadvantage of the criminal defendant by making conviction easier.* Thus, a statute which changes the burden of proof on the prosecution from the usual rule of beyond a reasonable doubt to one of the preponderance of the evidence is ex post facto if retroactive. By analogy, in this hypo we have a situation where the legislature changed the unanimity jury verdict requirement for capital offenses *after* the defendant was arrested and charged with murder. As such, choice (A) is correct.

55. **(B)** Although a city ordinance may prohibit the business practice of soliciting magazine subscriptions door-to-door without prior invitation of the homeowner, in *Beard v. Alexandria,* 341 U.S. 622 (1951) the Court specifically relied on the commercial nature of the transactions in question. On the other hand, in *Martin v. Struthers,* 319 U.S. 141 (1943) the Court held an ordinance invalid that forbade any person to knock on doors, ring doorbells, or otherwise summon any residents to the door as violative of the freedom of speech and press. In this regard, the substantive guarantee of due process requires that legislation have a rational relationship to the legitimate ends of government. If a law does not have such a relationship, it would be an unconstitutional deprivation of liberty as to those persons affected. Here, Adams' strongest argument is that the prosecution violates the intergovernmental immunity of a federal employee. Note that Adams's was performing essentially a governmental, not a proprietary, function (in the door-to-door canvassing). Thus, alternative (B) is the *best* answer.

56. **(D)** Quite often Multistate Constitutional Law questions are based upon case precedent. This question, for example, is based upon the ruling in *44 Liquormart v. Rhode Island,* 517 U.S. 484 (1996) in which a Rhode Island statute prohibited all advertising of liquor prices, except for price tags displayed with the merchandise. The Supreme Court invalidated the law because *regulations of commercial speech must be "narrowly tailored" and should be no more extensive than is necessary.* In both *44 Liquormart* and in this question, the state is attempting to entirely prohibit the dissemination of truthful, nonmisleading advertising. Choice (D) is correct because a state will not be permitted to *completely ban* commercial advertising but must use a means narrowly tailored to achieve the desired objective.

57. **(A)** Article I, Section 10, cl. 2, of the U.S. Constitution provides that "No State shall without the consent of Congress, lay any Imposts or Duties on Imports or Exports, except what may be absolutely necessary for executing its Inspection Laws." In *Michelin Tire Corp. v. W. L. Wages Tax Comm.,* 44 LW 4070, 423 U.S. 276, the U.S. Supreme Court held that while tubes in their corrugated shipping cartons were immune from *ad valorem* taxation, the tires lost their status as imports and became subject to taxation because they had been mingled with other tires imported in bulk, sorted and arranged for sale. Similarly, as this hypo, the bikes were immune from the tax since they remained "imports" in transit whereas the tires lost their "import status" once they became part of the tire inventory at the distribution warehouse.

58. **(B)** The state's power to enact such property taxes is derived from the Tenth Amendment's reserved powers. All other choices are incorrect since they reflect powers of the federal government.

59. **(B)** Under the Commerce Clause **Congress has the very broad power to regulate interstate commerce.** Generally speaking, Congress has the power to regulate any activity (whether carried on in one state or many) which has any appreciable effect—direct or indirect—upon interstate commerce. This is the so-called "affectation doctrine."

60. **(A)** It is important to point out that in the previous example Congress passed a law prohibiting the shipment and sale of FEEL-FREE *across state lines (or in interstate commerce).* This question states that the Vermont statute simply regulates the shipment and sale of FEEL-FREE within the state borders (or *intrastate*). As a result, where Congress has not acted, the states do have the *police power* to regulate any phase of local business (production, marketing, sales, etc.) provided that such regulations neither discriminate against nor burden interstate commerce. See Parker v. *Brown,* 317 U.S. 341 (1943).

61. **(D)** Article I, Section 8 provides: "The Congress shall have power to lay and collect taxes, duties, imposts and excises...." As a general rule, if Congress has no power to regulate the activity taxed, the validity of the tax ultimately depends on its validity as a *revenue-raising measure.* Choice (D) is correct because as long as **the dominant intent of the tax is revenue raising** it will be upheld even though the tax may have substantial regulatory effect.

Explanatory Answers

62. **(D)** As noted previously, Article I, Section 8 grants Congress (not the President) the power to regulate interstate commerce. Clearly, the President does not have any constitutionally delegated legislative power which is inherently law-making in nature. See *Youngstown Sheet & Tube v. Sawyer,* 343 U.S. 579 (1952) holding invalid a presidential order directing seizure of steel mills to prevent a threatened strike. Note that (D) "trumps" (C) because it is more narrowly correct because it addresses executive intrusion in the area of interstate commerce.

63. **(A)** The $200 per year excise tax on the commercial photographic studios operating in Passaic would be upheld as a valid license tax. Such license taxes (as well as privilege, franchise and occupation taxes) when applied to local activities, separate from the interstate commerce of which they are a part, are generally upheld if non-discriminatory, and not unreasonably burdensome in their impact on the interstate commerce involved.

64. **(B)** The $100 per year excise tax which is imposed upon the itinerant photographers would be upheld also. In *Dunbar-Stanley Studios v. Alabama* (1969), a similar fixed fee on transient photographers was upheld as constitutional when applied to an out-of-state firm taking photographs in the taxing state. The rationale being that the tax was levied not on the business as a whole but on a local activity of *taking photographs*, as opposed to their development and processing.

65. **(D)** Article IV, Section 2, so far as relevant reads as follows: "The Citizens of each State shall be entitled to all Privileges and Immunities of Citizens in the several States." It was designed to insure to a citizen of State A who ventures into State B the same privileges which the citizens of State B enjoy. In line with this underlying purpose, it was long ago decided that one of the ***privileges which the clause guarantees to citizens of State A is that of doing business in State B on terms of substantial equality with the citizens of that State.*** Like many other constitutional provisions, the Privileges and Immunities Clause is not an absolute. It does bar, nevertheless, discrimination against citizens of other States where there is no substantial reason for the discrimination beyond the mere fact that they are citizens of other States. Therefore, the New Jersey tax on nonresident photographers should properly be declared unconstitutional as violative of the Privileges and Immunities Clause.

66. **(B)** The Constitution contains no express provision that guarantees the right to be a candidate. The states are free, therefore, to create restrictions on the ability to become a candidate. Certainly, states have used several methods to qualify the right to become a candidate. Even though the Supreme Court has not directly ruled on candidacy age restrictions, interestingly enough this issue was tested on the Multistate exam last year. Choice (B) is correct because in dicta from previously decided cases, ***the Supreme Court apparently is applying minimal scrutiny to age restrictions***. See "Age and Durational Residency Requirements as Qualifications for Candidacy: A Violation of Equal Protection?", 1973, U.Ill. Law Review, 161.

    MBE Con Law Exam Update: This question needs to be distinguished from Question 67. In Question 67, the state enacted a party affiliation statute placing restrictions on independent candidates. States usually impose demonstrated support requirements on independent candidates or minor political parties. Typically, the demonstrated support statute requires independent candidates or minor parties

Constitutional Law

to submit petitions containing a certain number of signatures from qualified voters before they can receive access to the ballot. In such cases, the Supreme Court generally "has stated *that the state needs a compelling or overriding interest* to justify classifications and restrictions on political association." Nowak, pg. 891. On the contrary, this Multistate hypo deals with *age restrictions* on the right of candidacy. With respect to age classifications, the Supreme Court appears to apply the *rational basis test*. Although the Supreme Court has not directly ruled on this age candidacy issue, *all related cases involving age discrimination have been adjudged under the minimal scrutiny-rational basis test*. In *Trafelet v. Thompson*, 100 S.Ct. 219 (1979), the Supreme Court refused to review a state law imposing a mandatory retirement age for *elected state court judges* which was challenged as an age classification violative of equal protection.

Multistate Nuance Chart:

THE RIGHT TO BE A CANDIDATE

TYPE OF RESTRICTION	STANDARD OF REVIEW
Wealth Restriction	Strict Scrutiny
Residency Restriction	Strict Scrutiny
Property Ownership Requirements	No Articulated Standard
Party Affiliation	Strict Scrutiny
Racial Classification	Strict Scrutiny
Age Classification	Rational Basis
Prohibition On Officeholders From Being Candidates For Another Office	Rational Basis

67. **(B)** *The right to be a candidate is related to the fundamental right to vote.* In general, the state's interest in limiting ballot access is twofold: (1) to reduce voter confusion, and (2) to maximize the probability that the winning candidate will have received a majority of the popular vote. In *Storer v. Brown,* 415 U.S. 724, (19174), a California provision which prohibited independent candidates from running in the general election if the candidates either had voted in the immediately preceding party primary or had registered their party affiliation with a qualified party within one year of the primary was upheld. The Court determined that the "disaffiliation" statute furthered *the state's compelling interest* in the stability of the political system, and its interest in having "intraparty feuds" resolved in primaries rather than in the general election. Based on the Court's application of the *strict scrutiny standard of review,* choice (B) is the correct answer. The Court noted further in *Storer* that the state must adopt reasonable alternative means for independent candidates and minor political parties to get a ballot position, and the alternative means must not place too heavy a burden on the right to vote and the right to associate.

68. **(C)** In *Murphy v. Hunt,* 71 L Ed 2d 353, 102 S. Ct—(March 2, 1982), the United States Supreme Court held that a petitioner's claim against the state of Nebraska's prohibition of pre-trial bail to a person charged with sexual offenses had violated his constitutional rights under the Eighth Amendment was moot, since the petitioner-defendant had already been convicted of the offenses. As a general rule a case

becomes "moot" when the issues presented are no longer "live" or the parties lack a legally cognizable interest in the outcome of the case. In regard to test taking technique, students should note here that between a correct statement of law and a correct statement of fact, the best answer for MBE purposes is the statement of law. Among our answer choices, (A) and (B) are correct statements of fact and provide the underlying reasons for choice (C). However, (C) is a correct statement of law and therefore, the preferred answer.

69. **(A)** This is an extremely difficult Constitutional Law Multistate question. Choice (A) is correct because in *Bolger v. Young's Drug Products Corp.*, 463 U.S. 60 (1983), ***a law prohibiting the mailing of unsolicited advertisements for contraceptives was held invalid as violating First Amendment protection for commercial free speech.*** The Court held that the government's interest in protecting recipients from mail they find "offensive" is insubstantial. Note that choice (B) is wrong because this is not a state law that unduly burdens interstate commerce but rather a federal law. Choice (C) is wrong because the use of contraceptives is a fundamental right under the protected zone of "marital privacy." There is a subtle distinction because this question does not deal with a statute restricting use of contraceptives. On the contrary, the law restricts "unsolicited advertising" for contraceptives.

70. **(A)** Under its commerce power, Congress has plenary power to regulate interstate commerce and commerce with foreign nations. Obviously, the power of Congress to regulate commerce is very broad. It does, however, have limits so as not to obliterate the distinction between what is national and what is local. To be within Congress's power under the Commerce Clause, ***a federal law must either: (1) regulate the channels of interstate commerce; or (2) regulate the instrumentalities of interstate commerce; or (3) regulate activities that have a substantial effect on interstate commerce.*** Since the Tort Liability Reform Act does not affect interstate commerce, it will be invalidated as an impermissible intrusion on local affairs. Choice (A) is therefore correct.

71. **(B)** In accordance with 28 U.S.C. section 1257, ***when a state statute is declared unconstitutional by the highest state court, the route of appeal is by certiorari.*** The highest court in the state of Seneca held that Section 1123(b) of the Seneca Trade Statute was unconstitutional. Therefore, choice (B) is the best answer. Note that choice (A) is incorrect because in 1988 Congress practically eliminated obligatory Supreme Court review by appeal with a couple of minor exceptions. See PMBR Constitutional Law Outline, *supra*, pg. 2. Choice (D) is incorrect as the doctrine of adequate and independent state grounds is inapplicable because the state court decision was not based on state grounds. Under this doctrine, the Supreme Court may only review cases involving a "federal question."

72. **(B)** The case of *Miller v. California* 413 U.S. 15 (1973) states the present case for obscenity. The basic guidelines for the trier of fact must be (a) whether "the average person applying contemporary community standards" would find the work, taken as a whole, appeals to the prurient interest, (b) whether the work depicts or describes, in a patently offensive way, sexual conduct specifically defined by the applicable state law, and (c) whether the work, taken as a whole, lacks serious

literary, artistic, political, or scientific value. Applying this test, the best defense for Sleezy would be choice (B), which addresses the third element of *Miller*. If the materials the police purchased consisted of **serious scientific studies** of human sexual urges, then the materials, taken as a whole, would not be obscene. Choice (A) is incorrect since **normal** sexual conduct is irrelevant to the elements defined by the *Miller* standard.

73. **(A)** Under Article 1, Section 8, cl. 17 ***Congress has the power to exercise exclusive legislation over the District of Columbia*** and to govern places where the government has purchased and erected forts, arsenals, dockyards, and other needful buildings. Based on this enumerated power, Congress may properly legislate to make Pennsylvania Avenue a one-way street and the federal law will predominate over any conflicting ordinance passed by the District of Columbia City Council. Choice (A) is correct.

74. **(C)** In *Moore v. City of East Cleveland, Ohio,* 97 S.Ct. 1932 (1977), the United States Supreme Court held that a housing ordinance limiting occupancy of a dwelling unit to members of a single family and recognizing as a "family" only a few categories of related individuals, under which it was a crime for a grandmother to have certain grandchildren living with her, was violative of the Due Process Clause of the Fourteenth Amendment. The Court recognized that freedom of personal choice in matters of marriage and family life is one of the liberties protected by the Due Process Clause of the Fourteenth Amendment. Thus, a city may not regulate the occupancy of its housing by selecting certain categories of relatives who may live together and declaring that others may not. Students should note that this case is distinguished from *Village of Belle Terre v. Boraas,* 416 U.S. 1, where the housing ordinance affected only unrelated individuals.

75. **(D)** Once again, students should be advised that the best way to answer MBE (or any other multiple-choice) questions is by ***process of elimination.*** Here, choice (A) is wrong because a state does not have exclusive authority to regulate intrastate transactions. Rather, under the Commerce Clause, Congress has the power to regulate any activity that has a direct or immediate effect on interstate commerce, even though the activity takes place within a single state. Choice (B) is incorrect because the Supremacy Clause does not validate state laws. On the contrary, the effect of this clause is that to whatever extent Congress has exercised its powers, then any "inconsistent" state laws are prohibited. Similarly, alternative (C) is not the best answer because ***intergovernmental immunity, in general, places certain limitations on the state's power to regulate and tax the property and activities of the federal government.*** By process of elimination, choice (D) is therefore the *best* answer.

76. **(B)** In the area of Constitutional Law students will often be presented with a proposed state statute and will be required to determine the strongest argument IN SUPPORT of the legislation and the strongest argument AGAINST it. The strongest argument AGAINST an independent state postal service was held to be the negative implications that flow from the delegation to Congress of its postal power. This is so because the facts indicate that a state postal service will ***diminish the revenues of the U.S. Post Office***.

Explanatory Answers

77. **(C)** In *Jennessy v. Fortson,* 403 U.S. 431 (1971), the U.S. Supreme Court upheld a Georgia law requiring candidates for elective office who ran without winning a primary election to file petitions with signatures from qualified voters equaling five percent of the vote cast in the last general election for that office. The Court held that such state requirements (whereby a candidate or new political party demonstrate public support in order to get on the ballot) further a "compelling state interest," i.e., preserving the integrity of the electoral process by preventing the ballot from becoming unmanageable and confusing.

78. **(D)** Government action that discriminates against *a "fundamental right"* (i.e., a right explicitly or implicitly guaranteed by the Constitution) *is subject to the "strict scrutiny" test* and violates equal protection unless it is found necessary in furthering a "compelling state interest." In this situation, the state has the burden of proof to show that the authenticating requirement does, in fact, further a "compelling state interest." Refer to *San Antonio School District v. Rodriguez,* 411 U.S.1 (1973) for a discussion of the balancing test between fundamental rights/compelling state interest.

79. **(D)** In *U.S. v. Brown,* 381 U.S. 437, 1965, the United States Supreme Court found that a provision in the Landrum-Griffin Act making it a crime for a member of the Communist Party to act as an officer or employee of a labor union to be legislative punishment for Party membership, and hence a bill of attainder.

80. **(B)** Article I, Section 6 of the U.S. Constitution provides that "for any Speech or Debate in either House (members of Congress) shall not be questioned in any other place." Thus, the *Speech and Debate Clause would confer immunity upon Senator Cagey,* exempting him from liability for any remarks made by him during the Congressional hearing.

81. **(A)** In *Baldwin v. Montana Fish and Came Commission,* 436 U.S. 371 (1977) the United States Supreme Court held that the Montana elk-hunting licensing scheme as applied to nonresidents was not a fundamental right under the Privileges and Immunities Clause of Article IV, Section II. Furthermore, the Court majority found no discrimination in the distinctions drawn between residents and nonresidents under the Equal Protection Clause of the Fourteenth Amendment. The Supreme Court concluded that protection of the wildlife of a state is peculiarly within the police power of the state. The court also noted that the elk-hunting licensing scheme did not violate petitioners' "privileges and immunities," *because hunting (on the part of non-Montana residents) was primarily a recreational endeavor.*

82. **(C)** In *Austin v. New Hampshire,* 420 U.S. 656, the United States Supreme Court held that a similar *New Hampshire commuters' income tax on non-resident taxpayers to be violative of the Privileges and Immunities Clause* of Art. IV, Section 2 which provides that "The citizens of each State shall be entitled to all Privileges and Immunities of citizens in the several states."

83. **(A)** The power of eminent domain may be delegated directly or indirectly to a private person or enterprise subject to the requirements that the taking be (a) for a public use and (b) just compensation be given.

84. **(A)** In addition to the requirements that the taking of private property be for a public use and just compensation be given, the condemnee must be given adequate notice and a fair hearing as required by the Due Process Clause of the 14th Amendment.

85. **(D)** The amendment to the city charter constituted a valid exercise of power reserved by the people to themselves. Similarly, in *Eastlake v. Forest City Enterprises, Inc.,* 426 U.S. 668, the U.S. Supreme Court held that a city charter provision requiring proposed land use changes to be ratified by 55% of the votes cast did not violate the due process rights (14th Amendment) of a landowner who applied for a zoning change. Interestingly enough, the Supreme Court further noted that the amendment to the city charter did not involve a delegation of power by the legislature to a regulatory body. Although the Court did not enumerate the applicable constitutional amendment in reaching its decision, apparently the 10th Amendment acted as the basis for the Court's ruling.

86. **(A)** In like manner, the Court in Eastlake held that the referendum process does not, in itself, violate the Due Process Clause of the 14th Amendment when applied to a rezoning ordinance.

87. **(D)** In *Village of Belle Terre v. Boraas*, 416 U.S. 1 (1974), the United States Supreme Court **upheld a similar ordinance which prohibited unrelated, unmarried persons from residing in the same dwelling unit.** The Court held that a municipality can enact such an ordinance under its police powers, since the ordinance bears a substantial relationship to the health, safety, welfare and morals of the citizenry. Students should note, however, that a zoning or housing ordinance which limits occupancy of dwelling units to members of a single family and recognizing as a "family" only a few categories of related individuals is violative of the Due Process of Fourteenth Amendment. In *Moore v. City of East Cleveland*, 97 S.Ct. 1932 (1977) the United States Supreme Court declared such an (above-mentioned) ordinance unconstitutional, whereby a grandmother was charged with a crime for permitting her grandson to reside in her single family residence.

88. **(B)** Choice (B) is the correct answer. Students should be aware that although choice (C) is a correct statement (of fact), it is not the *best* answer because a correct statement of law is a more preferable choice than a correct statement of fact. Although a state may have a legitimate interest in creating a so-called support requirement on independent candidates, you must ask yourself the following question, "What is the state's standard interest in enacting such a statute?" According to the rule enunciated in *Williams v. Rhodes,* 393 U.S. 23 (1968), there are three state interests protected: (1) the statute promotes the two-party system; (2) the statute helps to prevent voter confusion; and (3) the law insures that the voters will elect a candidate with a majority vote. Note that choice (A) is incorrect because the Fifteenth Amendment provides that the right of citizens of the United States to vote shall not be denied or abridged by the United States or by any State on account of race, color, or previous condition of servitude.

89. **(D)** A permanent physical occupation of private property by the government or a government regulation which allows someone other than the property owner to have permanent physical occupation of a definable part of a piece of property should constitute a taking. Nowak, **Constitutional Law,** pg. 450. In *Loretto v. Teleprompter*

Explanatory Answers

Manhattan CATV Corp., 458 U.S. 419 (1982), a city ordinance requiring landlord building owner to allow installation of cable television receiver on apartment building and denying landlord the ability to demand payment in excess of $1 constituted a compensable taking because the ordinance allowed for "permanent physical occupation" of a small part of the building.

90. **(C)** The most clear case where a state can regulate to protect one's constitutional rights under the Fourteenth Amendment occurs when state action is involved. Thus, choices (A) and (B) are incorrect because private discrimination is involved. Choice (D) is likewise wrong because a federal official is doing the discriminating. Consequently, choice (C) is the *best* answer because a state is most able to regulate the actions of a state official when these actions violate one's constitutional rights.

91. **(A)** ***Such voluntary pupil prayer recitals during school hours in the school building have been invalidated as an establishment of religion,*** despite the fact that no religious sect was preferred or discriminated against, thus in violation of the Establishment Clause of the First Amendment and applicable to the States through the Due Process Clause of the Fourteenth Amendment.

92. **(B)** Applying the three-part requirement of *Lemon v. Kurtzman,* 403 U.S. 602, state aid such as this must have ***(1) a secular purpose, (2) a primary effect other than the advancement of religion and (3) no tendency to entangle the State excessively in church affairs.*** The New Haven statute should be upheld as non-violative of the Establishment Clause of the 1st Amendment. See *Roemer v. Board of Public Works of Maryland,* 426 U.S. 736. Moreover, it is important that the church affiliated institutions referred to in this problem must not be so "pervasively sectarian" under *Hunt v. McNair,* 413 U.S. 734, that (1) secular activities cannot be separated from sectarian ones and (2) that if secular activities can be separated out, they alone may be funded.

93. **(C)** Section 1 of the Doral City Ordinance 172 provided that demonstrations of fifty persons or more may not be conducted without first securing a permit from the chief of police. Since Bohan's demonstration attracted fewer than fifty demonstrators, there was no violation of the statute.

94. **(B)** Sections 1 and 2 of the ordinance should be upheld as constitutional as within the ambit of a state's police power to regulate the health, safety, and welfare of its citizens. Students should be cognizant of the fact that a state may control parades, processions and other gatherings in public places by narrowly drawn requirements pertaining to the time, place, size of the group and duration in the interest of public safety and convenience. See *Cox v. Louisiana* 379 U.S. 537. However, in this regard, no public official can constitutionally be given unbridled discretion to grant or withhold a permit or license for a parade or assembly as he sees fit. It is important to point out that Section 1 by itself, is a valid exercise of a state's police power. However, Section 3 would be struck down by allowing unfettered discretion in the chief of police to determine which expressions of view will be permitted and which will not.

95. **(C)** As noted above, Section 3 would be declared unconstitutional since no public official may exercise unbridled discretion in the issuance of parade or demonstration permits.

Constitutional Law

96. (A) Students should note that Congress has complete power to permit or forbid state taxation affecting interstate commerce. Where Congress is silent, the Court reviews nondiscriminatory state taxation by balancing the state revenue needs against the burden on interstate commerce. If, however, a state regulation of interstate commerce conflicts with a federal regulation, the state law is invalid under the preemption doctrine. To be sure, Congress in the exercise of its plenary commerce power may prohibit a specific form of state regulation.

97. (C) In *Terry v. Adams,* 345 U.S. 461, 73 S.Ct. 809 (1953), the State of Texas was held responsible for racial discrimination in the conduct of primary elections which it closely supervised and which were important in determining who was ultimately elected. Similarly, in the present hypo, the State of South Dakota would be held responsible for the American-Indian Party's expulsion of all non-Indians (from membership within the party). Clearly, in this regard, restricting membership to only Indians would be racial discrimination (e,g., by "suspect classification"), and therefore, violative of the Equal Protection Clause of the Fourteenth Amendment, as well as the Fifteenth Amendment.

98. (B) Following the holding in *Terry v. Adams,* the court would enjoin the American-Indian Party from conducting its mail ballot primary as a flagrant abuse of the Fifteenth Amendment. Under the Fifteenth Amendment, the right to vote cannot be denied by the evasive device of a party primary conducted as an activity of a "private club," if such primary is a "feeder" election into the election system.

99. (D) In *Jenness v. Fortson,* 403 U.S. 431, the United States Supreme Court upheld a similar Georgia statute requiring an independent candidate to file a nominating petition signed by 5% of the electorate as non-violative of the Equal Protection Clause of the 14th Amendment. The Court sustained the voting statute on the grounds that a candidate had alternative routes to getting his name on the ballot, namely, either entering the Primary of a Political party or circulating a nominating petition: therefore, no abridgement of constitutional rights of free speech and association under the 1st and 14th Amendments, nor violation of the Equal Protection Clause of the 14th Amendment.

100. (D) In *DeCanas v. Bica,* 424 U.S. 351, the U.S. Supreme Court held a California Labor Code statute which "prohibits an employer from knowingly employing an alien who is not entitled to lawful residence in the U.S. if such employment would have an adverse effect on lawful resident workers" not to be unconstitutional as a regulation of immigration or as being preempted under the Supremacy Clause by the Immigration Nationality Act (INA). The court further noted that it is clearly within a State's police power to regulate the employment relationship of illegal aliens.

101. (D) Choice (A) is incorrect because classifications based on sex have been held to violate equal protection. (B) is wrong because such discrimination has not yet been held "suspect," and therefore, need not be justified by a compelling interest. Alternative (C) is incorrect because the existence of similar facilities would not preclude a finding of "state action." As a consequence, (D) is the correct answer since discrimination based on sex is subject to a "quasi-suspect" standard of review.

Explanatory Answers

102. **(B)** Although Discrima-Boating, Inc. is a privately owned corporation, the state has affirmatively encouraged and facilitated its discriminating acts, thus (A) is incorrect because "state action" exists. Choice (C) is an incorrect statement and not applicable to the fact situation. (D) is wrong, since racial discrimination is "suspect" and therefore cannot be justified by some "rational basis." Thus, choice (B) is the best answer available.

103. **(B)** Choice (A) is clearly incorrect. Alternative (C) is too general a statement, because not all public rights are protected. Similarly, (D) is too broad a statement, because not all discrimination against the poor violates equal protection. As a result, choice (B) is the correct answer, since only important and basic deprivations have been held to violate the Equal Protection Clause of the 14th Amendment.

104. **(D)** In *Memorial Hospital v. Maricopa County,* 415 U.S. 250 (1974), the United States Supreme Court held that an Arizona statute requiring one year's residence in a county as a precondition to receiving non-emergency hospitalization or medical care at public expense was unconstitutional as "an invidious discrimination against the poor," thus violative of the Equal Protection Clause of the Fourteenth Amendment. The court found that this classification infringed upon interstate travel and in so doing, found that it was irrelevant that the classification also burdened travel by persons within their own state. Under the circumstances, the State of Arizona burdened the right to travel by denying benefits which were essential to the daily life of the new indigent in the state. The Court in reviewing the state's justification for this residency requirement, utilized the strict scrutiny test.

105. **(C)** This Constitutional law question presents some very close answer choices in the area of regulation of First Amendment freedom of speech. Regarding noncommunicative aspects of free speech, such as time, place, and manner regulations in public forums, courts will generally uphold **reasonable** restrictions. Choice (A) is persuasive on this issue. Where speech **content** is restricted, however, the courts apply a more rigid test whereby a compelling state interest must be justified before government regulation is permitted. Choice (B) addresses this issue since the restrictions of the "Fairgrounds Bill" are content-neutral. Choice (D) seeks to balance the rights of free speech against the patrons' right of privacy. Choice (C), however, presents the strongest argument to support the "Fairgrounds Bill." In the area of *solicitation,* the court uses a *balancing test* to determine, upon weighing the individual's rights of free speech against the state's police power interest in protecting the safety, welfare, and privacy interests of its citizens, that the challenged measure is reasonable and non-discriminatory, and that **there is no less drastic alternative means available.** See *Beard v. Alexandria,* 341 U.S. 622 (1951)—requirement of homeowner's consent held a valid restriction on *commercial* solicitation, whereas a ban on *all* door-to-door solicitation was found to be too restrictive.

106. **(B)** In accordance with *Foley v. Connellie, 98* S.Ct. 1067 (1978), the United States Supreme Court upheld the validity of a New York statute which limited the membership of the New York State Police Force to United States citizens. The Court stated that "in the enforcement and execution of the laws, the police function is one where citizenship bears a rational relationship to the special demands of the particular position." Thus, in applying the "rational basis" test, the Supreme Court

Constitutional Law

held that the performance of the police function is an important public responsibility which can be limited to a particular class, (here, United States citizens only). Students should note that **although aliens are extended the right to education and public welfare along with the ability to earn a livelihood and to engage in licensed professions, the right to govern and to carry on a governmental function is reserved to citizens only.** Therefore, the Evergreen Police Force statutory provision would not be violative of the Equal Protection Clause of the Fourteenth Amendment. Students should note that although choice (A) is also correct, choice (B) is the narrower, or more preferred alternative, as it specifies the underlying rationale for upholding the constitutionality of the statute.

107. **(C)** This Multistate question deals with the issue of *standing*. To satisfy the minimum constitutional requirements imposed by the "case and controversy" limitation of Article III, a plaintiff must demonstrate a definite and concrete personal stake in the outcome. First, the plaintiff must show *actual injury in fact.* Second, she must show causation (namely, that resolution of the grievance in her favor will eliminate the harm alleged). Under these facts, choice (C) is correct because the purchaser of marijuana cigarettes can demonstrate actual injury. Note that harm to other states (choice A) and the Vietnam veterans (choice B) is theoretical and thus too remote. Also, the association of doctors would lack standing since the general rule is against assertion of third party rights except in limited situations.

108. **(A)** Choice (A) is correct because Congress can tax an activity, even if such a tax has a regulatory effect, provided the *dominant intent of the tax is fiscal (i.e., revenue-raising).* Certainly, Congress has constitutionally taxed bookmakers, guns and narcotics despite its substantial regulatory effect. In addition, students should note that under its *spending power* Congress can spend money (it collects from taxes) to "provide for the common defense and general welfare of the United States." In this regard, a reasonable belief by Congress that payment of the tax fund proceeds to the Civil War Art Museum would benefit the cultural life of the nation as a whole would certainly fall within the proper scope of its federal taxing and spending power.

109. **(D)** Mork's best argument is the fact that the statute violated his rights under the Equal Protection Clause of the Fourteenth Amendment. Congress has plenary power over the admission of aliens, but once admitted most state discrimination against them is "suspect," and can only be upheld if necessary to protect a "state's special interest." Although there are earlier decisions upholding state statutes limiting or barring aliens from owning land (within the state), it is highly unlikely that such a statute would be upheld in light of recent decisions. Since Mork is not a citizen, choice (A) is wrong because the Privileges and Immunities Clause, is only applicable to citizens of the United States. Alternative (B) is wrong because the contract between Mork and Mindy did not take place prior to the enactment of the statute. Choice (C) is a poor argument because the limitation of land ownership is within the state and does not affect interstate commerce.

110. **(A)** Choice (A) is the only correct answer. Since the statute discriminates against a suspect class, in that Mork is an alien, the burden of proving compelling state interest shifts to the state. Furthermore, Mindy (as well as Mork) could establish standing based on the decision in the case of *Shelley v. Kraemer*, where it was held that one would have standing to assert the constitutional violation of an alien's rights in such a situation.

Explanatory Answers

111. **(A)** The U.S. Supreme Court has long recognized that almost all statutes and other forms of government regulation classify (or discriminate) people. As a result, the Court has established several different tests for determining their permissibility under the Equal Protection Clause. The two major tests are the "traditional" or rational basis test and the "strict scrutiny" or "compelling interest" test. For virtually all economic and social regulations, the Court employs the "traditional" equal protection test. This test is usually defined as follows: "The classification (or discrimination) is valid if it is rationally related to a proper (or constitutionally permissible) state interest." Under this "rational basis" test, a classification is presumed valid and will be upheld unless the person challenging it proves that it is "invidious" or "wholly arbitrary." Thus, the challenger has the burden to prove that ***no reasonable state of facts can be conceived to justify it***. See *McGowan v. Maryland,* 366 U.S. 420 (1961). Conversely, government action that intentionally discriminates against racial or ethnic minorities is "suspect" and thus subject to "strict scrutiny." Since this question deals with a matter of "economic and social welfare," it will be reviewed under the basic rationality test. Therefore, choice (A) is the best answer.

112. **(A)** Pursuant to the commerce clause, Congress has complete power to authorize or forbid state taxation that affects interstate commerce. Undoubtedly, the Grambling "Slot Tax" adversely affects interstate commerce because the facts indicate that all manufacturers of slot machines are out-of-state. As such, the commerce clause affords the strongest constitutional ground to attack the Grambling tax.

113. **(A)** With respect to standing, a person asserting the violation of a constitutional or statutory right must show a ***direct and immediate personal injury*** due to the challenged action. The facts clearly indicate that fewer slot machines are being purchased by casino owners on account of the tax. As a result, choice (A) is correct because a manufacturer of slot machines can show a "direct injury" from application of the tax. Note that associations of individuals may have standing to assert the rights of its members at least so long as the challenged infractions adversely affect its members' associational ties. However, choice (C) is wrong because the associational members have not suffered a "direct" and "immediate" harm since their tax liability is optional (namely, they are not required to play the slot machines).

114. **(D)** In *Arizona Board of Regents v. Harper,* 495 P2d 453, (1972), the Arizona Supreme Court held that a board of regents has the authority to adopt a rule requiring residence of one year before a student may be classified as a resident of a state to qualify for lesser charges. Thus, the one year residency requirement, in order for a student to qualify for lesser tuition charges, did not violate the Due Process, Equal Protection or Privileges and Immunities Clauses of the U.S. Constitution. In this regard, lower tuition rates at state universities are valid and do not trigger strict scrutiny. See *Starns v. Malkerson*, 326 F. Supp. 234 (1971).

115. **(A)** As a general rule, a government program will be valid under the Establishment Clause ***if it: (1) has a secular purpose; (2) has a primary effect that neither advances or inhibits religion; and (3) does not produce excessive government entanglement with religion.*** Many of the cases involving the Establishment Clause involve religious activities in public schools (e.g., prayer and Bible reading). This question

Constitutional Law

deals with an interesting "twist", namely, whether public school classes can be held in a church building. Under the circumstances, there does not appear to be an Establishment Clause violation because the city's action neither advances or inhibits religion. Therefore, choice (A) is correct.

116. **(D)** Choice (D) provides the best legal reasoning if Spector is successful in challenging the city of Wilton's sound amplification ordinance. In accordance with the First Amendment's guarantee of freedom of speech, a state or municipality may regulate the use of sound amplification equipment, depending on the interests involved. See *Kovacs v. Cooper,* 336 U.S. 77 (1949). The test applied by the courts in this First Amendment area (regarding the constitutionality of such an ordinance) is that "the government action must further an important governmental interest unrelated to the message being communicated." According to the facts presented here, the municipality would not have an overriding interest in prohibiting the use of any sound device, except clock chimes, by a property owner in the city of Wilton. Alternative (A) provides an incorrect rationale. Choice (B) is wrong as it contains an incorrect statement of law. Lastly, alternative (C) is also incorrect because a state may regulate the use of sound amplification devices (e.g., sound trucks) in the interests of privacy and public tranquility. See *Saia v. New York* (948).

117. **(D)** All four statements are valid arguments in support of Simpleton's position. Alternatives (A), (B) and (C) are less complete answers, since all four issues have merit.

118. **(B)** As a general rule, a case is "moot" when there is no case or controversy once the matter has been resolved. In our example, the township's WEAKEST defense is that Hobie's case is moot because the matter (whether Hobie is precluded from selling his surfboards in Malibu) has not been resolved.

119. **(C)** Under the circumstances, the police clearly violated Cuba Now's 1st Amendment right of peaceful assembly. It is well established that **assemblies or speeches that threaten imminent violence or serious disorder can be halted by the police to prevent physical injury,** but unless the risk of disruption is clearly demonstrated, the gathering is protected. In the case at bar, the police would not be justified to break up the rally merely because of the jeering of a few members of the crowd. Moreover, if the risk of disruption is caused by a hostile crowd, the first duty of the police is to protect the speaker from the crowd, not to stop the speech and arrest the speaker.

120. **(B)** In *Time Inc. v. Hill,* 385 U.S. 374 (1967), a case involving this particular invasion of privacy branch, the Supreme Court held that the First Amendment prohibited recovery for invasion of privacy in cases where the published matter was in the public interest, unless the plaintiff established that the defendant acted with malice. Malice here, as in *New York Times v. Sullivan,* goes to knowledge of falsity or reckless disregard for the truth. Moreover, choice (B) is the best answer because the First Amendment constitutional privileges likely encompass all pure *opinions*, whether false or not. As such, **only statements of fact can be actionable as defamatory.** In this example, the facts clearly state that Bud Mouthy, the TV commentator, said, "In my opinion.....these Castro sympathizers should be deported to Cuba." Since Mouthy was merely voicing his opinion, that would only substantiate why choice (B) is a better answer than (D).

Explanatory Answers

121. **(B)** Congress is granted broad powers of taxation by express constitutional provisions, namely, Article I, Section 8 (taxing and spending power) and the Sixteenth Amendment (federal income tax without apportionment). The taxing power is virtually plenary. The standard used to analyze the validity of a federal tax is whether or not the ***dominant intent is fiscal.*** In other words, even if a federal tax does have some incidental regulatory effect, it will nevertheless be upheld if it does in fact ***raise revenue.*** The stated purpose of the proposed Senate bill for a 15% gross receipts tax is to raise revenue and spur population growth. Applying the aforementioned standard, the proposed federal tax will be constitutional. Choice (B) is correct since it states the proper rationale. Choices (A), (C) and (D) are incorrect because validity of a federal tax is not analyzed under principles of equal protection, commerce clause, or right to privacy.

122. **(C)** The Mizzou statute providing that "any student ... who engages in disruptive campus activities will not be eligible for state aid" would be declared unconstitutional for vagueness and overbreadth. Clearly, the court will invalidate such a statute because "disruptive campus activities" is too general and overbroad and can be read as prohibiting constitutionally protected activity.

123. **(B)** Such laws explicitly distinguishing between males and females have been invalidated as violative of the Equal Protection Clause of the Fourteenth Amendment unless they serve the objective of offsetting unequal opportunities for women (or men as the case may be). In the present case, ***there is no important governmental interest*** available to support a tax exemption for only full-time female college students and not *male* students.

124. **(A)** Limited residency requirements (of one year or less) for obtaining divorces have been upheld as promoting a compelling state interest in the exercise of the state's police power to legislate to protect the health, safety, welfare and morals of its citizens. Choice (B) is incorrect since the concept of state action pertains to nullifying state legislation which impairs the privileges and immunities of citizens of the United States, or which injures them in life, liberty or property without due process of law, or which denies to any of them the equal protection of the laws.

125. **(C)** In accordance with *Hudgens v. NLRB*, 424 U.S. 507 (1971), the owner of a private shopping center may exclude persons who want to distribute pamphlets, since no "state action" is present. The Supreme Court held that so long as the state does not aid, command or encourage the suppression of free speech, the First Amendment would not be violated by the shopping center owners. The operation of the Christiana Mall was not part of a privately owned town and therefore did not involve the assumption of a public function by private persons. Since pamphleteering on private property is not a constitutionally protected activity, injunctive relief would not be granted to the black students. Furthermore, the owners of the shopping center had the right to permit pamphleteering by the white law students, while excluding the black students from such activities.

126. **(D)** Students should be aware that although choices (B) and (D) are correct, choice (D) is the more correct answer, since Section 1220 would be construed as ***overbroad*** and thus invalid under the First and Fourteenth Amendments. The Supreme Court, in *Lewis v. City of New Orleans,* 415 U.S. 130 (1974), applied the overbreadth

Constitutional Law

doctrine to a similar New Orleans ordinance which was invalidated under the First and Fourteenth Amendments. In that case, as well as in the factual situation here, the ordinance effectively punished all obscene and offensive speech, even though some of the speech may have been protected by the First Amendment. Since Section 1220 may have included constitutionally protected speech, the statute should have been more narrowly drawn to protect such First Amendment activities.

127. **(C) or (D)** In accordance with *Smith v. Gognen,* 415 U.S. 566 (1974), where the petitioner had been convicted of violating a similar flag-misuse statute for sewing a U.S. flag to the seat of his pants, the Supreme Court held that the ***statutory language was void for vagueness*** under the First and Fourteenth Amendments. The flag-misuse statute was declared vague because no clear distinction had been made between what type of treatment of the flag was or was not criminal. Furthermore, the statutory terminology, "treat the flag contemptuously" is lacking of any as certainable standards and is therefore, violative of the Due Process Clause of the Fourteenth Amendment. Students should note that the police and courts should not be given such broad discretion in determining what constitutes flag contempt as to be violative of the First and Fourteenth Amendment constitutional safeguards. Note that choice (B) is wrong because this question presents a due process violation, not an equal protection issue.

128. **(B)** The Fourteenth Amendment procedural due process operates as a limitation on state action by providing an individual the guarantees of both notice of the charges brought against him as well as an opportunity to be heard, whenever the deprivation of any life, liberty, or property interest has occurred. The individual whose interests are affected must be granted a fair procedure to determine the factual basis and legality for such action. If the government terminates an individual's ability to engage in a profession, a procedure must be afforded to determine the individual's fitness to engage in that profession. Specifically, in *Barry v. Barchi,* 443 U.S. 555 (1979) the court held that the New York licensing system for horse training created a "property" interest in licensed trainers protected by the Due Process Clause and ***a post-suspension hearing was required.*** In this question, the Delmarva statute affording a post-suspension hearing will be upheld. Choice (B) is thus correct.

129. **(D)** The Due Process Clause of the 14th Amendment would furnish Senator Turner's best grounds for challenging his exclusion from his party's caucus. Students should be aware that whenever a governmental instrumentality acts so as to deprive someone of any interest, the first question to ask is whether the interest qualifies as "life," "liberty," or "property." If so, the due process safeguards of notice and some form of hearing are required. In the present hypo Turner's exclusion from the caucus would be a deprivation of his "property" interest, i.e., stripping a duly elected public official of his right to participate in his party's meeting.

130. **(B)** Article I, Section 6, provides that "for any Speech or Debate in either house (members of Congress) shall not be questioned in any other place." It is important to note that virtually every State has adopted similar Speech and Debate Clauses in their respective State Constitutions.

131. **(D)** In *Griswold v. Connecticut*, 381 U.S. 479 (1965), the U.S. Supreme Court invalidated a similar statute restricting the **use of contraceptive devices by married couples as violating the right of privacy of married persons.** The Court held that the statute violated the due process clause because it deprived these married persons the liberty protected by the Fifth Amendment.

132. **(D)** In *Tileston v. Ullman*, 318 U.S. 44 (1943), the U.S. Supreme Court ruled that a medical doctor does not have third-party (*jus tertii*) standing to attack a state anti-contraceptive statute on the grounds that it prevents him giving his professional advice concerning the use of contraceptives to three patients whose condition of health might be endangered by child bearing. On the contrary, if the person is convicted of prescribing, selling, or giving away contraceptives, in the defense to that action he may then raise the third-party rights of the recipients. See *Eisenstadt v. Baird,* 405 U.S. 438 (1972).

133. **(D)** Students should be aware that there is no constitutional right of advertising under the First and Fourteenth Amendments. Certainly, a private newspaper is not required under the Constitution to accept and publish all forms of advertising.

134. **(D)** Stone's best constitutional argument will be based on the First Amendment's Free Exercise Clause which is applicable to the states vis-a-vis the Fourteenth Amendment. Even though it is not known whether Stone's belief is properly classified as a religion for First Amendment purposes, choice (D) still provides Stone's best argument. It is important for students to note here that although choice (A) seems correct, choice (D) is the better answer since state action is involved. When there are apparently two correct answers to a question, as a general rule you should select the narrower correct alternative. As illustrated in this question, in the area of Constitutional Law, when a particular question relates to one's rights under any of the first eight Amendments to the U.S. Constitution, such rights are only afforded vis-a-vis the Due Process Clause of the Fourteenth Amendment. Therefore, in our hypothetical, choice (D) is the preferred answer as it refers to both the First and Fourteenth Amendments.

135. **(A)** Under the so-called "affectation doctrine," the U.S. Supreme Court has recognized that Congress has **the power to regulate any activity, whether carried on in one state or many, which has any appreciable effect—directly or indirectly—upon interstate commerce.**

136. **(C)** It is important for students to remember that the Multistate examination not only tests your **knowledge of the substantive rules of law, but it also tests your reading comprehension ability.** In the present hypo, for example, the Ames statute prohibits the showing of any obscene film "in an area open to the public." Since the films were being shown in the privacy of the motel rooms (and occupancy was limited to consenting adults), Holmes's conviction would be overturned because the statute would be inapplicable. Also, for Multistate purposes students should be familiar with *Stanley v. Georgia,* 394 U.S. 557 (1969) in which the U.S. Supreme Court held that mere private possession of obscene matter is not a crime. Although the states retain broad power to regulate obscenity, that power simply does not extend to mere possession by the individual in the privacy of his home.

Constitutional Law

137. **(B)** In accordance with *Nyquist v. Mauclet,* 432 U.S., 97 S.Ct. 2120 (1977), the U.S. Supreme Court invalidated under the equal protection clause of the Fourteenth Amendment a state law which granted aid for higher education to citizens and resident aliens who were or would be applying for citizenship. The Court found no "compelling state interest" in encouraging citizenship or limiting general programs to those who determine its policy.

138. **(A)** As a general rule, state laws regulating roadways and highways are usually upheld as constitutional unless they unduly burden interstate commerce. Since the facts do not indicate that the Chippewa statute unduly burdens interstate commerce, choice (A) is preferred over (D). Note another variation how this rule can be tested involves the enactment of a state law prohibiting the use of metal studs or cleats on vehicular tires. Even though the facts may indicate that the cleats and studs give better traction in ice and snow, the statute may still be upheld as constitutional if it serves a legitimate state interest by reducing damage to state highways.

139. **(C)** Neither the privileges and immunities clause nor the comity clause apply to corporations because the term "citizen" does not include corporations. In addition, under the Fifth Amendment prohibition of compulsory self-incrimination, "person" falls to include corporation or other business entity. See *Bellis v. United States*, 409 U.S. 322 (1973).

140. **(C)** As a general rule, **the Commerce Clause prohibits a state from enacting regulations that discriminate or burden interstate commerce.** In accordance with *Dean Milk Co. v. City of Madison,* 340 U.S. 349 (1951), a state may not create economic barriers to out-of-state products, or impose on them costs which are more burdensome than those imposed on comparable local commerce, in order to protect local interests. However, the Commerce Clause does not prevent the state ' when acting itself as a purchaser or seller of goods, from buying only from or selling only to local business, or from giving subsidies only to its residents. See *Reeves v. Stake,* 447 U.S. 429 (1980), where discrimination merely affects a market created by a state's own purchases and the state is thus a market participant rather than a market regulator.

141. **(C)** In Constitutional Law students must be familiar with the area of **state regulation of interstate commerce.** As a general rule, where Congress has not acted and where no uniform national scheme of regulation exists, states are free to act in the regulation of interstate commerce, provided the purpose or the effect of such regulation does not discriminate against interstate commerce. In this regard, states may not favor local interests by protecting them against out-of-state competition. (See *Dean Milk Co. v. City of Madison,* 340 U.S. 349 (1951). In addition, the Court has struck down state laws regulating the *conservation of local natural resources.* Since state laws enacted to protect local, publicly-owned natural resources (e.g., minerals, wild animals) will generally be invalidated if they discriminate against interstate commerce, choice (C) is correct.

Explanatory Answers

Multistate Nuance Chart:
CONSTITUTIONAL LAW

STATE REGULATION OF INTERSTATE COMMERCE

Permissible	Not permissible
1. Where state is acting as a market participant (i.e., purchaser or seller of goods);	1. Supersession where state law *in conflict* with act of Congress;
2. Regulations for protection of public health or welfare;	2. When state regulation discriminates or unduly burdens interstate commerce;
3. Quarantine and inspection laws;	3. Regulations for conservation of local resources.
4. Regulations concerning the use of local highways;	
5. Regulations regarding the transportation or importation of intoxicating liquors as provided under the 21st Amendment.	

BASIC TEST

As a general rule, state regulation of interstate commerce is *permissible* if:

(1) the state regulation does not discriminate against interstate commerce;

(2) the subject matter is not one which the Court concludes inherently requires uniform, national regulation; and

(3) the state interest underlying the regulation is not outweighed by the burden on interstate commerce, i.e., the "balance of interests" favors state as opposed to national interests.

142. **(C)** Article I, Section 10 (Contract Clause) provides: "No State shall pass any Law impairing the Obligation of Contracts." In this example, the state of Brandywine was obligated under the terms of the bond agreement to apply at least $2 from each admission charge (to the racetrack) for the repayment of the bond debt. Consequently, it is ***an impairment of the Contract Clause*** for the state to pass a subsequent statute reducing the admission charge for senior citizens to 50 cents. By analogy, in *United States Trust Co. v. New Jersey*, 431 U.S. 1, 97 S.Ct. 1505 (1977), the U.S. Supreme Court declared a New Jersey statute unconstitutional because the law impaired the state's contractual obligation to the bondholders of The Port Authority of New York and New Jersey. Note that choice (D) is incorrect because the ***Ex Post Facto Clause applies to retroactive laws that are criminal in nature.***

143. **(A)** It is within the state's ***police power to enact legislation for the protection of the health, safety and welfare of its citizens.*** Clearly, most state regulations place some burden on interstate commerce. In such situations, the Court balances the nature and extent of the burden (which the state regulation would impose on interstate commerce) against the merits and purposes of the regulation. Choice (B) is

incorrect because the "clear and present danger" test applies to the abridgement or restraint of the freedom of speech where there is a substantial threat of violence. This doctrine is not applicable in our case because the question does not relate to freedom of speech.

144. **(B)** As noted in the previous question, under the so-called "balance of interests" test, the Court generally attempts to *balance the nature and extent of the burden* (which the state regulation imposes on interstate commerce) *against the merits and purposes of the regulation*. Accordingly, choice (B) is the preferred answer.

145. **(C)** Another *key* Multistate repetitive testing area deals with educational rights of students. In *Gross v. Lopez,* 419 U.S. 565 (1975), the U.S. Supreme Court held that fair procedures had to be established for determining the basis of the suspension of students from public school systems. As a general rule, a student is not entitled to a trial-type hearing when his dismissal or suspension is **with just cause**. Certainly, a rule prohibiting students from growing beards or mustaches would seem to be compatible with the orderly operation of the school. On the other hand, the Court in *Gross v. Lopez* did note that when the suspension or termination of a student's educational benefits may affect his/her employment or associational opportunities in the future, then there may be a due process violation involved. Note that choice (D) is incorrect because Herb was *not entitled to a hearing* under the circumstances.

146. **(C)** In *Hillman v. Elliott,* 436 F. Supp. 812, 1977, the U.S. Supreme Court held that due process with respect to a three day suspension of a student from public high school required that the student be given notice of charges, an explanation of evidence against him if he denied the charges, and an opportunity to present his version of the incident. In the instant case, David was afforded such due process safeguards.

147. **(D)** It is important to remember that in sex discrimination cases, **the plaintiff is required to show a discriminatory purpose, not merely a discriminatory effect**. There is no purposeful sex discrimination in keeping co-ed bathrooms, locker rooms and sleeping quarters sex-segregated. As a consequence, the statute will be adjudged under the mere rationality test and upheld since it furthers a legitimate state objective. Although the Supreme Court has not explicitly dealt with this sort of segregation, there is little reason to believe that maintaining separate co-ed living quarters would be violative of equal protection. Choice (D) is correct. Note that (A) is wrong because since Chuck and Jolene are *not married,* the privacy issue of related individuals living together is unripe.

148. **(C)** Another repetitively tested Constitutional Law area is to what extent does an executive agreement (or order) override an earlier enacted federal statute. According to Nowak, *an executive agreement does not supersede inconsistent provisions of earlier acts of Congress*. To be sure, the appropriations bill passed by Congress prohibiting funding for military operations in Chevnoski will be controlling. The President does not have the power to override this congressional act by issuing a subsequent executive order.

Explanatory Answers

149. **(B)** Juveniles are neither a suspect nor a quasi-suspect class of persons. Therefore, state laws dealing with juveniles will be scrutinized by the court under neither the compelling state interest nor the middle tier standard of review. ***The mere rationality test applies.*** Specifically, if the statute in question is rationally related to the furtherance of a legitimate state interest, the court will uphold it as constitutional. Choice (B) is correct because the sealing of court and police records of juveniles clearly serves the legitimate state interest in rehabilitation of juvenile offenders so as to be free from embarrassment in later life. Choice (C) is incorrect because by satisfying the requisite scrutiny of the rational basis test, the state law supersedes the right of the Committee of Bar Examiners to have access to otherwise public documents.

150. **(B)** The South Bend ordinance may be attacked as a violation of protected First Amendment freedom of expression since it prohibits **all** singing and chanting for **twelve** hours every day in areas which are traditionally viewed as ***public forums.*** Time, place, manner limitations on speech-related conduct are permitted when achieved by ***reasonable content-neutral*** regulations which further a significant governmental purpose. Such an ordinance must be narrowly drawn so as not to establish a total ban on protected rights of free speech. Since the South Bend ordinance does not appear to satisfy this standard, a First Amendment free speech attack by the students will be a strong challenge. Therefore, choice (A) is incorrect. Choice (C) is also incorrect because it presents a strong challenge in the form of the vagueness and overbreadth doctrines. By proscribing protected as well as prohibited speech for half of each day everywhere in the city the ordinance is clearly overbroad on its face. Similarly, due to the uncertainty-producing effect as to what conduct is restricted by the words "singing and chanting of songs" and "audible (to whom?) off the premises," a vagueness challenge should be successful. Choice (D), another strong argument, is incorrect since non-religious songs—which are certainly areas of protected speech—are being treated differently than religious songs, thereby raising an equal protection challenge to be reviewed using the strict scrutiny standard. By process of elimination, choice (B) is correct because the due process argument it presents is the weakest basis to attack the ordinance.

NOTES

Constitutional Law

MIG 1   FEDERAL JUDICIAL AUTHORITY

Organization of the Federal Court System

- **ARTICLE III** — vests the judicial power in the Supreme Court and such inferior courts as Congress may establish; jurisdiction limited to "cases and controversies" — cases arising under the Constitution, laws or treaties of the United States, and cases in which the United States is a party. Compare: Article I Courts (tax courts, courts in the District of Columbia) are vested with administrative, as well as judicial functions; no lifetime tenure for Article I judges. Role of Congress: plenary power both to establish lower federal courts and to confer and remove jurisdiction over Article III courts. Note that Article III courts may not give advisory opinions, although state courts may do so

- **POWER OF JUDICIAL REVIEW** — *Marbury v Madison* — held the Supreme Court may determine the constitutionality of acts of other branches of government; federal courts may also review state court decisions

- **JURISDICTION OF THE USCC** — Original (trial level) — extends to "all cases affecting Ambassadors, other public Ministers and Consuls, and those in which a State shall be a Party"; Congress may neither enlarge nor restrict, but may give concurrent jurisdiction to lower federal courts (except in cases between 2 or more states where the USSC has exclusive jurisdiction) Appellate — extends to all other Article III cases and controversies; Congress may broadly regulate, but may not preclude review of an entire class of cases

- **TWO STATUTORY MEANS** — Provided by Congress to Invoke USSC Appellate Jurisdiction: 1. Appeal (mandatory review) — applies to decisions of 3-judge federal district courts regarding injunctive relief
2. Certiorari (discretionary; 4 or more justices vote to hear a case) — applies to decisions of the highest state courts regarding the constitutionality or violation of federal law, and decisions of US Courts of Appeal

Judicial Review (doctrine empowering federal courts to refuse to hear a case, despite subject matter jurisdiction)

- **STANDING** — concrete personal stake in the outcome is required Constitutional Standard (required by Article III) — Injury in Fact — specific, not theoretical, injury must arise from the government conduct being complained of; usually economic injury, but need not be Redressibility (Causation) — the relief sought must eliminate the harm alleged; plaintiff's injury must be within the "zone of interests" Congress meant to protect Prudential Limitations — self-imposed by the Court; no "citizen" standing for abstract, generalized grievances; a corporation has standing to challenge a federal statute where the injury is to the organization itself. No third party standing, unless plaintiff herself has suffered injury which adversely affects her relationship with third parties, who have difficulty asserting their own rights No taxpayer standing because the interest is too remote, except a federal taxpayer has standing to make an establishment clause challenge to an expenditure which exceeds some specific limitation on the taxing and spending power (*Flast v Cohen*)

- **MOOTNESS** — a case brought too late; an actual controversy must exist at all stages of review, unless the issue is capable of repetition, yet evading review (pregnancy, elections)

- **RIPENESS** — a case brought too early; a genuine, immediate threat of harm must exist (no declaratory judgment allowed before a law is enforced)

- **POLITICAL QUESTIONS** — nonjusticable issues committed to other branches of government (i.e. foreign affairs, Guaranty Clause issues; congressional membership requirements; but not apportionment of legislative districts)

- **11TH AMENDMENT** — provides a state cannot be sued in federal court without consent; however, state officials may be sued for federal law violations; local governments can be sued; the United States or another state may sue a state; Congress can remove a state's immunity (i.e. for civil rights violations)

- **ABSTENTION** — Pullman doctrine applies where a federal claim is based on an unsettled issue of state law; procedurally, the federal court retains jurisdiction of the federal claim
Younger doctrine prohibits review/enjoining of pending state criminal proceedings, criminally related civil proceedings, and civil contempt proceedings; procedurally the party is sent back to state court for all purposes

- **ADEQUATE AND INDEPENDENT STATE GROUNDS** — The USSC will not review a final judgment from the highest state court that the case may reach where the state decision was based on a clear, adequate, independent and fully dispositive nonfederal ground

multistate issue graph

MIG 2　SEPARATION OF POWERS

Constitutional Law

Doctrine of Enumerated Powers

- **FEDERAL GOVERNMENT (FG)** — has only that authority which the Constitution confers on it, either express or implied
- **10th AMENDMENT** — powers not delegated to the FG are retained by the States under the 10th Amendment; under the police power, the States can legislate to protect any health, safety, welfare, morals, or aesthetics interest
- **NECESSARY AND PROPER CLAUSE** — grants Congress the authority to carry into execution any enumerated power; not an independent source of power

Federal Legislative Power (Article 1, §8 Enumerated Powers)

- **COMMERCE POWER** — plenary power which regulates both domestic and foreign commerce
  - Affectation Doctrine — regulates any activity which has a substantial economic effect on the stream of interstate commerce
  - Cumulative Impact Doctrine — even an entirely intrastate activity which has a cumulative impact on interstate commerce may be regulated
- **TAXING AND SPENDING POWER** — plenary power to tax and spend for the general welfare
  - Spending Power — Congress can attach strings to federal appropriations, thereby regulating indirectly where it cannot legislate directly
  - Taxing Power — a federal tax is valid if the dominant intent is fiscal; direct taxes (income tax) must be apportioned; indirect taxes (sales, use and excise taxes) must be geographically uniform; general welfare clause is not an independent source of power
- **WAR POWER** — to declare war, raise and support an army and navy, and make rules to regulate the armed forces; pervasive economic regulatory power during war; regulation may continue even after cessation of hostilities
- **OTHER ENUMERATED POWERS** — postal power; power over District of Columbia; power to coin money; to propose Constitutional amendments; immigration and naturalization; copyright, patent, bankruptcy powers; impeachment power
- **IMPLIED POWERS** — broad investigatory power enforceable by contempt sanction; plenary admiralty power

Delegation of Legislative Power

- **LEGISLATIVE VETO** — Congress can delegate its legislative power to executive and administrative agencies, but cannot subsequently retract it — such a "legislative veto" is unconstitutional (*INS v Chadha*)

Federal Executive Power (Article II)

- **DOMESTIC POLICY** — Power and obligation to faithfully execute the laws
  - Appointment Powers — President can appoint purely executive officers (Cabinet members), ambassadors, public ministers, consuls and USSC judges "with the advice and consent of the Senate"; Congress may not appoint members of bodies having administrative or enforcement powers, and may only appoint its legislative staff members; Congress can delegate appointment of "inferior officers" (special prosecutor) to either the President or the judiciary; the President may dismiss an independent counsel for good cause
  - Removal Powers — the Constitution is silent; the President may remove purely executive officers (Cabinet members) without cause, but good cause is required to remove federal judges and other fixed-term administrative officials; Congress has no power of summary removal
  - Veto Power — President has 10 days to exercise his veto, which may then be overridden by 2/3 vote of each house; President has no legislative power nor any power to impound funds
  - Pardon Power — extends only to federal crimes, not state crimes
  - Executive Privilege — to refuse to disclose information (military and diplomatic secrets); privilege must yield to important government interests
  - Absolute immunity in civil suits for damages based on actions taken while in office
- **FOREIGN POLICY** — Commander in Chief of the Armed Forces — may establish military governments in occupied territories; broad emergency powers
  - Treaty Power — requires consent of 2/3 of the Senate; where conflict between 2 laws exists apply the following hierarchy:
    1. Constitution
    2. Treaty/Act of Congress — equal footing; last in time prevails
    3. Executive Agreement
    4. State Law
  - Executive agreement — informal means by which the President can conduct day-to-day economic and business transactions between foreign countries without Senate consent
  - Foreign Affairs — President's power is not plenary, but is shared with Congress; sources of such power include: 1) Commander-in-chief; 2) Treaty Power; 3) Congressional Authorization (delegation by Congress of its commerce power to the President)

multistate issue graph

MIG 3 FEDERALISM (Federal limitations on state power)

Constitutional Law

Intergovernmental Immunities

- **STATE REGULATION OF THE FEDERAL GOVERNMENT** — FG and its agencies are immune from state taxation and regulation; however, nondiscriminatory state taxes on federal contractors are valid; a state may not require a state contractor's license to build on federal property located within the state

- **FEDERAL PROPERTY POWER (Art. IV, §3)** — Congress may dispose of and make all needful rules and regulations respecting the territory or other property of the United States; generally applies to wild animals, federal buildings and enclaves, military ships and planes, Indian reservations

- **FEDERAL GOVERNMENT REGULATION OF THE STATES** — states are not immune under 10th or 11th amendments (FG may sue a state; one state may sue another state); FG may tax proprietary state businesses

- **10TH AMENDMENT** — powers not delegated to the FG, nor constitutionally prohibited to the states, are reserved to the states; a weak limitation on the federal commerce power; FG may not compel states (rather than private entities) to enact a particular regulatory program [i.e. regulate radioactive waste or take title to it — *NY v U.S.*)]

Dormant Commerce Clause

- **NEGATIVE IMPLICATIONS DOCTRINE** — where Congress has not otherwise regulated, the states are free to regulate interstate commerce; regulation must be 1) non-discriminatory — may not favor or protect local interests, and 2) not unduly burdensome — state interest is balanced against the burden on interstate commerce such that no less restrictive alternative means is available

- **EXCEPTION** — Market Participant Doctrine — where the state uses its own taxpayer funds to create the market, it may favor its own residents with subsidies and hiring preferences

- **COMPARE:** Article IV Privileges and Immunities Clause — prevents discrimination by one state against citizens of another state regarding basic economic rights and liberties; N/A to corporations or aliens

State Taxation of Interstate Commerce

- **REQUIREMENTS:** state tax must be reasonable and nondiscriminatory to satisfy the Commerce Clause, and a substantial nexus (i.e. more than "minimum contacts") must exist between the state interest and the activity being taxed to satisfy the Due Process Clause

- **GENERAL PRINCIPLES** — goods or commodities "in the stream" of interstate commerce are exempt from state taxation, but may be taxed at the beginning and end of transit, as well as if there is a break in transit Instrumentalities (cars, planes, trains, etc.) may be taxed provided the tax is fairly apportioned to the extent of taxpayer use (taxable situs requirement)

Supremacy Clause Article VI, §2

- **PREEMPTION** — any state law in actual conflict with a federal law will be unconstitutional (i.e., FAA, NLRB)

- **SUPERSESSION** — any state law in an area where Congress intends to occupy the field is unconstitutional. Note: where federal law only establishes minimum standards, states may afford greater protection by enacting stricter laws than required by federal standards (i.e. health and safety regulations)

multistate issue graph

Constitutional Law

MIG 4 PROTECTION OF INDIVIDUAL RIGHTS

Bill of Rights (the 1st 10 Amendments restrict the FG)

- **SELECTIVE INCORPORATION** — under the 14th Amendment Due Process Clause, most Bill of Rights limitations are applicable to the states, except the following:
  - 2nd Amendment right to bear arms
  - 5th Amendment right to a grand jury in criminal cases
  - 7th Amendment right to jury trial for civil cases

Retroactive Legislation

- **CONTRACTS CLAUSE** — prevents the states (not the FG) from enacting legislation which retroactively impairs the obligation of both public or private contracts; traditionally, the state's police power "modification" argument prevails over the plaintiff's "impairment" argument

- **EX POST FACTO LAWS** — make criminal conduct that was not a crime when committed, or increase the punishment for a crime after its commission, or decrease the amount of evidence needed to convict; such legislation which retroactively alters the criminal law is unconstitutional as applied to both the state and federal governments

- **BILL OF ATTAINDER** — legislative punishment of a named group or individual without judicial trial; applies to both state and federal governments

State Action

- **DEFINITION:** a threshold requirement of government conduct which must be satisfied before private discrimination can be restricted under the 14th or 15th Amendments; 13th Amendment can punish purely private acts of discrimination without showing state action

EXAMPLES OF STATE ACTION

PUBLIC FUNCTION — where a private entity is performing activities traditionally and exclusively carried on by the state (e.g., a company town)

COMPARE: NO PUBLIC FUNCTION — a privately owned utility company under heavy state regulation; operation of a nursing home

SIGNIFICANT STATE INVOLVEMENT — public school system; use of state-owned textbooks by a private school; "symbiotic relationship" or situation where the state facilities, encourages, or authorizes discrimination in areas such as housing, employment, or providing essential services

COMPARE: NO STATE ACTION — granting of a liquor license; private school discharging teachers; private school licensed by the state

(continued below)

Constitutional Law

MIG 4 PROTECTION OF INDIVIDUAL RIGHTS *(continued)*

Procedural Due Process — the procedural safeguards of NOTICE and a HEARING are available whenever there is a serious deprivation of any life, liberty or property interest

- **PROCEDURE** — the court balances the severity of harm to the individual against the administrative costs of the government to determine what, if any, safeguards are required
- **PROTECTED LIBERTY INTERESTS** — commitment to a mental institution; right to contract; right to engage in gainful employment; right to refuse unwanted medical care; right of natural parents in the care and custody of their children; not injury to reputation
- **PROPERTY INTERESTS (entitlements)** — right to public education; welfare benefits; liability benefits; continued public employment where termination can only be "for cause"; revocation of a driver's license

Takings — private property may not be taken for public use without just compensation; property may be taken by eminent domain, inverse condemnation, or by a state police power "regulation"

- a taking consists of either a confiscation (public easement granted across owner's beachfront property) or a physical occupation (cable TV wire installed in all the hallways of city rental units) or a regulation which denies the owner all reasonable economically viable use (post-purchase zoning ordinance which prohibits the owner from erecting any permanent structures on his land)

Substantive Due Process

ECONOMIC REGULATION — regulation must meet rational basis scrutiny

FUNDAMENTAL RIGHTS — regulation must meet strict scrutiny standard

- **RIGHT TO VOTE** — other than for minimum age or residency requirements or payment of reasonable filing fees, regulation must meet the strict scrutiny standard. Generally voting districts for federal, state, and local elections are required to adhere very closely to the one person-one vote principle *(Reynolds v. Sims)*; exception for special limited-purpose districts (water storage district). Apportionment and districting schemes which distort voting districts for racial or political purposes is unconstitutional gerrymandering
- **RIGHT TO TRAVEL** — durational residency requirements are invalid for receiving state medical care or welfare benefits, but valid for reduced tuition at state universities, obtaining a divorce, or registering to vote in a state primary election; foreign travel is subject only to rational basis scrutiny
- **RIGHT TO PRIVACY (mnemonic CAMPER)** — Contraception — applies to the sale and use of contraceptives by both married and unmarried persons
  - Abortion — states may not prohibit abortions, but may regulate as long as they create no "undue burden" on the right to obtain an abortion *(Planned Parenthood v. Casey)*; there is no right to abortion funding, even for indigents; consent of one or both parents or a judge, may be required for a minor to obtain an abortion
  - Marriage — any restriction on the right to marry (interracial marriage) is prohibited
  - Procreation — closely related to contraception
  - Education — right of parents to educate their children outside of public schools
  - Relations — Right of related (not unrelated, not homosexual) persons to live together; "anti-group" ordinances generally prohibited

multistate issue graph

Constitutional Law

MIG 5   EQUAL PROTECTION

an equal protection challenge arises where persons similarly situated are treated differently

3 Standards of Review

- **STRICT SCRUTINY** — burden on the state to show the law is necessary (i.e. no less restrictive alternative means exists) to a compelling interest; applies to 3 areas:

  (regulation unlikely to succeed)

  1. Protected 1st Amendment **R**ights
  2. Suspect Classes (mnemonic **RAN**)
     - **R**ace — purposeful discrimination required; race-based affirmative action plans are subject to strict scrutiny whether passed by the state *(Richmond v Croson)* or by the federal government *(Adarand Construction v Pena)*
     - **A**lienage — federal regulation is subject only to rational basis scrutiny, whereas state regulation is subject to strict scrutiny, except where participation in government (policemen, teachers, serving on a jury list) is involved; illegal aliens are not suspect
     - **N**ational Origin
  3. Fundamental Rights — Right to Vote
                          — Right to Travel
                          — Right to Privacy

- **Middle-tier (Intermediate) Scrutiny** — burden on the state to show the law is substantially related to an important interest, applies to 2 areas:

  1. Gender — purposeful discrimination required; affirmative action permitted subject to middle-tier test
  2. Illegitimacy —

- **Rational Basis Scrutiny** — burden is on plaintiff to show the law is not rationally related to any legitimate interest; applies to all other classifications including 1. Poverty 2. Age 3. Mental Retardation 4. Necessities of life (food, shelter, clothing, medical care) 5. Economic and social welfare measures

  (regulation likely to succeed)

multistate issue graph

Constitutional Law

MIG 6 — FIRST AMENDMENT GUARANTEES

Freedom of Religion

FREE EXERCISE CHANGE — an individual's religious beliefs are absolutely protected (it would be unlikely that a government interest would be "compelling" enough to punish a religious belief); conduct in furtherance of those beliefs may be regulated; e.g. use of peyote during religious ceremonies is conduct which may be prohibited despite the individual's religious beliefs which required this practice (*Oregon v Smith*); a Jewish soldier may be compelled to wear his yarmulke as part of his military uniform (*Goldman v Weinberger*); to regulate conduct the Court balances the severity of the burden on the individual's free exercise of religion against the government interest in regulation

ESTABLISHMENT CLAUSE — Main Principle: the government may not aid or prefer one religion or sect over another, subject to strict scrutiny review; — Test: to be constitutional, a sect-neutral government aid/program must satisfy 3 requirements under the *Lemon* test — the law must 1) have a secular purpose; 2) have a primary effect that neither advances nor inhibits religion, and 3) not foster excessive government entanglement with religion

— General Principles: government sponsored religious activities in public schools are unconstitutional (daily Bible readings; a moment of silent, voluntary prayer; prohibition of the teaching of evolution); government aid to parochial schools may not be used for religious purposes (use of textbooks, busing, health tests), but such aid is constitutional if made available to all students at public and private schools

— Tax Deduction — reimbursing parents for tuition paid only to *religious* schools is invalid; similarly, tax exemptions available only for religious organizations (no sales tax for religious publications) is an invalid endorsement of religion, but property tax exemptions for religious property have been upheld; religious displays (nativity scenes; menorahs) are permissible in public places provided no one religion is being favored over another

Freedom of Speech Approach

4 TYPES OF FACIAL ATTACKS — Overbreadth — statute punishes both protected as well as unprotected speech

Vagueness — statute is so unclearly defined that persons of ordinary intelligence must guess at its meaning

Prior Restraint — government action restricting free speech in advance of publication is generally invalid (licensing permits, injunctions; 'gag' order barring the media from pretrial publicity); valid where national security interests are compelling, or the regulation of obscene books and films where procedural safeguards are afforded

Unfettered Discretion — where a licensing official has unfettered discretion as to whether to confer or deny a permit

ESSAY APPROACH

Ask: Is the Speech the Statute is Regulating **Content Specific** (regulates the message)

If content specific, then ask: Is the speech being regulated

Protected	or	Unprotected
If "protected" then apply strict scrutiny i.e. — the statute is unconstitutional unless the government can show the law is necessary to a compelling interest		Unprotected includes clear and present danger; defamation; obscenity; child pornography; fighting words; fraudulent commercial speech

Track One — or — **Track Two**

Content Neutral — Time, Place, Manner Regulation (statute exists regardless of the message)

If content neutral regulation of time, place, manner, then apply a 3-part test: the regulation must
1) further a significant government interest (noise, crowd, or litter control; traffic safety)
2) be narrowly tailored (no more restrictive than necessary), and
3) leave open alternative channels of communication (commercial door-to-door solicitation without invitation of the homeowner may be restricted because other avenues of communication exist such as the mail, newspaper advertisements, radio and television)

Freedom of Association

unmentioned First Amendment right encompassing activities such as accepting government benefits, public employment or seeking membership in various organizations

Public Employment and Bar Membership — may not be denied based upon an individual's group affiliation unless the government can show the person 1) is a knowing (scienter) and active (dues-paying) member of a subversive group and 2) has the specific intent to further the group's unlawful objectives (*Keyishian v Bd. of Rights*)

Loyalty Oaths — generally *invalid* as a condition to public employment, however, an oath to support the Constitution and oppose overthrow of the government has been upheld (*Cole v Richardson*)

Disclosure Requirements — to avoid a chilling effect on First Amendment activities disclosure is generally not required, unless the government could make such membership illegal

Freedom of the Press

read together with the "free speech" clause as a single guarantee; generally the press has no greater privilege than the ordinary citizen

Right of Access — both the public and the press have a right to attend a criminal trial, which may be outweighed by an overriding government interest

Newsperson's Privilege — no privilege exists to refuse to disclose confidential sources to a grand jury (*Branzburg v Hayes*), but states may enact "shield" laws to afford such protection

Broadcasting — may be regulated more closely than the press due to the limited number of frequencies available (*Red Lion*), yet on the other hand a newspaper need not provide "equal time" broadcasts may be required (*Red Lion*), yet on the other hand a newspaper need not provide equal space for political rebuttal (*Miami Herald*)

(continued below)

Constitutional Law

MIG 6 FIRST AMENDMENT GUARANTEES *(continued)*

Freedom of Speech Content — most forms of speech are protected subject to the strict scrutiny standard; 6 forms of unprotected speech may be regulated

- **CLEAR AND PRESENT DANGER** — speech 1) directed at producing imminent unlawful action and 2) likely to produce such action *(Brandenburg v Ohio)*

- **DEFAMATION** — public officials, public figures, and limited public figures (those who voluntarily inject themselves in the limelight) must prove malice: knowing falsity or reckless disregard for the truth *(Times v Sullivan)* — private person plaintiffs — constitutional limitations apply only where the defamatory statement involves a matter of public concern, in which case negligence must be proven (no liability without fault); punitive damages are not awarded absent proof of malice *(Gertz v Welch)*

- **OBSCENITY** — to be obscene, the speech must 1) appeal to the prurient interest in sex applying contemporary community standards, 2) depict sexual conduct in a patently offensive way, and 3) lack serious literary, artistic, political, or scientific value *(Miller v California)*
  - merely offensive language is not obscene; however, profane language on the airways may be restricted *(Pacifica Foundation)*; private possession of obscene materials in one's home is protected (except for child pornography), although viewing, sale and distribution of such obscene material may be vigorously regulated (movie ratings, zoning ordinances)

- **CHILD PORNOGRAPHY** — outside the protection of the First Amendment; visual depictions of sexual conduct including children may be punished even if not "obscene" under *Miller (N.Y. v Ferber)*

- **FIGHTING WORDS** — restricted speech includes personally abrasive language likely to invite the average person to commit acts of physical violence *(Chaplinsky v N.H.)*; however, statutes designed to punish only particular viewpoints are invalid — e.g. fighting words that provoke violence on the basis of race, religion, or gender *(R.A.V. v St. Paul)*

- **FRAUDULENT COMMERCIAL SPEECH** — generally commercial speech is protected but may be restricted as to false or deceptive advertising or illegal products; a lawful, narrowly tailored regulation will be valid if it directly advances a substantial government interest and there is a reasonable "fit" between the means used and the legislation's end *(Central Hudson; SUNY v Fox)*; attorneys may advertise, provided it is not misleading; in-person solicitation for profit is not protected.

- **OTHER AREAS** — symbolic speech (where the medium itself is the message) may be restricted where the regulation furthers an important government interest unrelated to the suppression of speech and the incidental burden on speech is no greater than necessary; e.g. unconstitutional to ban flag burning *(U.S. v Eichman)*
  - freedom not to speak — allows children not to be compelled to salute or pledge allegiance to the American flag, and allows a motorist to cover the motto ("Live Free or Die") portion of her license plate

Time, Place, Manner Restrictions — reasonable restriction of speech conduct is permitted by means of content-neutral time, place, manner regulations

- **PUBLIC FORUMS** — (streets, parks, sidewalks) — regulations must satisfy 3-part test (See Track Two test)
- **NONPUBLIC FORUMS** — (jails, military bases, mailboxes, billboards, public buses, government buildings, airport terminals)
  - to be valid the regulations must be 1) viewpoint neutral (i.e. content may be regulated, but limiting the presentation to only one view is impermissible) and 2) reasonably related to a legitimate government interest

Licensing Statutes

- **REQUIREMENTS** — to be valid, a licensing scheme must relate to an important government objective, be clearly written, narrowly drawn, and reasonably regulate time, place and manner of speech
- **IF STATUTE IS VALID ON ITS FACE** — the speaker may not ignore the statute and must seek a permit. If the request is denied, even wrongfully, the speaker must nonetheless seek prompt judicial relief before speaking; otherwise a subsequent claim of violation of 1st Amendment rights will fail
- **IF STATUTE IS VOID ON ITS FACE** — due to overbreadth, vagueness, prior restraint, or unfettered discretion) — the speaker may ignore the statute and speak, as well as successfully defend against any subsequent prosecution *(Shuttlesworth v Birmingham)*
- **IF AN INJUNCTION IS ISSUED** — where the speaker is enjoined from speaking, she must obey the injunction (even if it is facially invalid) or appeal from it. Invalidity of the injunction must be established on appeal and is no defense to a subsequent charge of contempt *(Walker v Birmingham)*

multistate issue graph

KAPLAN) pmbr

NOTES

NOTES

NOTES

NOTES

NOTES

NOTES

NOTES

NOTES

NOTES

NOTES

NOTES

NOTES

NOTES

With products serving children, adults, schools and businesses, Kaplan has an educational solution for every phase of learning.

KIDS AND SCHOOLS

SCORE! Educational Centers offer individualized tutoring programs in reading, math, writing and other subjects for students ages 4-14 at more than 160 locations across the country. We help students achieve their academic potential while developing self-confidence and a love of learning.
www.escore.com

We also partner with schools and school districts through Kaplan K12 Learning Services to provide instructional programs that improve results and help all students achieve. We support educators with professional development, innovative technologies, and core and supplemental curriculum to meet state standards.
www.kaplank12.com

TEST PREP AND ADMISSIONS

Kaplan Test Prep and Admissions prepares students for more than 80 standardized tests, including entrance exams for secondary school, college and graduate school, as well as English language and professional licensing exams. We also offer private tutoring and one-on-one admissions guidance.
www.kaptest.com

HIGHER EDUCATION

Kaplan Higher Education offers postsecondary programs in fields such as business, criminal justice, health care, education, and information technology through more than 70 campuses in the U.S. and abroad, as well as online programs through Kaplan University and Concord Law School.
www.khec.com • *www.kaplan.edu* • *www.concordlawschool.edu*

PROFESSIONAL

If you are looking to start a new career or advance in your field, Kaplan Professional offers training to obtain and maintain professional licenses and designations in the accounting, financial services, real estate and technology industries. We also work with businesses to develop solutions to satisfy regulatory mandates for tracking and compliance.
www.kaplanprofessional.com

Kaplan helps individuals achieve their educational and career goals. We build futures one success story at a time.